LIBRARIES WITHOUT WALLS 4
the delivery of library services to distant users

LIBRARIES WITHOUT WALLS 4

the delivery of library services
to distant users

Proceedings of an international conference held on 14–18 September 2001,
organized by the Centre for Research in Library and Information Management
(CERLIM), Manchester Metropolitan University

EDITED BY
**Peter Brophy
Shelagh Fisher
Zoë Clarke**

facet publishing

© Peter Brophy, Shelagh Fisher, Zoë Clarke 2002

Published by
Facet Publishing
7 Ridgmount Street
London WC1E 7AE

Facet Publishing (formerly Library Association Publishing) is wholly owned by
CILIP: the Chartered Institute of Library and Information Professionals.

First published 2002

British Library Cataloguing in Publication Data
A catalogue record for this book is available from the British Library.

ISBN 1-85604-436-X

Typeset in 10/13 Caslon 540 and Zapf Humanist from authors' disk by Facet
Publishing.
Printed and made in Great Britain by MPG Books Ltd, Bodmin, Cornwall.

CONTENTS

CONTRIBUTORS

Ann Apps, Researcher, MIMAS, Manchester Computing, University of Manchester, UK

Tracy Bentley, Research Officer, The British Library Copyright Office, UK

Julie Brett, Deputy Head, Central Management Team, Information Services Management, The British Council, Manchester, UK

Peter Brophy, Professor and Director, Centre for Research in Library and Information Management (CERLIM), Manchester Metropolitan University, UK

Elizabeth J. Burge, Professor, Adult Education, University of New Brunswick, Atlantic Canada

Sally Chambers, Electronic Library Project Officer, University of London Library, UK

Zoë Clarke, Senior Research Fellow, CERLIM, Manchester Metropolitan University, UK

Antony Corfield, Software Developer, JAFER Project, Libraries Automation Service, Oxford University, UK

Jenny Craven, Research Fellow, CERLIM, Manchester Metropolitan University, UK

Sarah Currier, Research Fellow, Centre for Digital Library Research, Andersonian Library, University of Strathclyde, Glasgow, UK

John Davey, Learning Technology Designer, Edge Hill College of Higher Education, Ormskirk, UK

Rob Davies, Project Manager, MDR Partners, London, UK

Heather Dawson, Subject Librarian, London School of Economics, UK

Matthew Dovey, Research and Development Manager, Libraries Automation Service, Oxford University, UK

Juliet Eve, Lecturer, School of Information Management, University of Brighton, UK

Shelagh Fisher, Reader, Department of Information and Communications, Manchester Metropolitan University, UK

Anna Fragkou, Director, University of Macedonia Library, Greece

Jillian Griffiths, Research Fellow, CERLIM, Manchester Metropolitan University, UK

Catherine Grout, Assistant Director, DNER Programme, JISC, London, UK

Kirsi Heino, Helsinki University of Technology Library, Finland

Kees Hopstaken, Utrecht University Library, Delft University of Technology, The Netherlands

Caroline Ingram, Programme Manager, DNER Learning and Teaching Programme, JISC, London, UK

Jo Kibbee, Head of Reference, University of Illinois at Urbana–Champaign Library, USA

Jan Kooistra, Utrecht University Library, Delft University of Technology, The Netherlands

Marina Korfiati, Reference and User Support Librarian, University of Patras, Greece

Ross MacIntyre, Senior Project Manager, Manchester Computing, University of Manchester, UK

Richard Mawby, Administrator, JAFER Project, Libraries Automation Service, Oxford University, UK

Linda McCann, Project Director, Los Angeles Comprehensive Bibliographic Database (LACBD), University of Southern California, USA

Lou McGill, Distance Learning Services Librarian, University of Leicester, UK

Paul McLaughlin, Senior Sub-Librarian (User Services), University of London Library, UK

Clare Nankivell, Director, Centre for Information Research, University of Central England, Birmingham, UK

Gill Needham, Learner Support Manager, Open University Library, Milton Keynes, UK

Bo Öhrström, Deputy National Librarian, Danish National Library Authority, Copenhagen, Denmark

Virpi Palmgren, Information Specialist, Helsinki University of Technology Library, Finland

Emma Place, Project Manager, RDN Virtual Training Suite, Institute for Learning and Research Technology, University of Bristol, UK

Sue Roberts, Acting Head of Library and Information Services, Edge Hill College of Higher Education, Ormskirk, UK

Debbie Rogenmoser, Reference Librarian, California State University, Sacramento, USA

Betty Ronayne, Distance Education Librarian, California State University, Sacramento, USA

Evelyn Simpson, Senior Librarian, Open University, Milton Keynes, UK

Colin Tatham, Software Developer, Libraries Automation Service, Oxford University, UK

Katerina Toraki, Head of the Documentation and Information Unit, The Technical Chamber of Greece, Athens, Greece

Sassa Tzedaki, Serials Librarian, University of Crete, Greece

Judy Watkins, Copyright Office, the British Library, UK

Lynn Wiley, Head of Information Resource and Retrieval Center, University of Illinois at Urbana–Champaign, USA

Claudine Xenidou-Dervou, Site Librarian, Physics and Informatics, Aristotle University, Thessaloniki, Macedonia, Greece

1

INTRODUCTION

Peter Brophy, Shelagh Fisher and Zoë Clarke

The fourth *Libraries Without Walls* conference, held in Molivos on the Greek island of Lesvos in September 2001, has confirmed the importance and popularity of the series, building on the achievements of the earlier conferences (Brophy et al., 1996; Brophy, Fisher and Clarke, 1998; Brophy, Fisher and Clarke, 2000) while exhibiting a strong progression in thinking and practice. It is clear that, while the topic of library services to remote users was novel and specialized when the first conference was held in 1995, it has now become a matter of widespread interest and concern. The almost universal adoption of information and communications technologies (ICTs) among libraries, coupled with the use of the world wide web as a delivery vehicle, means that more and more users are accessing services remotely. The implications of this 'disintermediation' of library service are profound, and have been discussed elsewhere (e.g. Brophy, 2001). The reality is that most libraries in developed countries – and many elsewhere – now operate as 'hybrid' services (Brophy and Fisher, 1998), relying on a managed mix of electronic and traditional 'information objects' to deliver appropriate services to their clientele.

The introduction to the proceedings of the previous *Libraries Without Walls* conference had ended with the following words:

> The conference as a whole demonstrated that the concept of the library without walls is no longer a theoretical perspective, nor the preserve of a small group, but is being implemented across the world in many different ways to meet the needs of many different users. Each of the examples presented at the conference and published in the proceedings demonstrates the continuing relevance of the library in our networked global society and provides pointers to innovative thinking and exemplary practice which should aid others as they too develop their services. (Brophy, Fisher and Clarke, 2000, 5)

Those conclusions could equally have described the fourth conference – but with one important difference. Whereas in 1999 we could claim that 'libraries without walls' was a concept that had entered the mainstream, by 2001 it was clear that much of the development being reported was itself driving the mainstream of library service forward. Remote access is now the norm for many supposedly 'on-campus' students and for citizens requiring information from home, office or while on the move. From its beginnings as a niche interest, the topic has moved to take centre stage.

At this fourth conference, we were privileged that Liz Burge, a renowned expert in distance learning who has a background in librarianship, accepted an invitation to present our keynote address. Echoing the theme of disintermediation, she challenged delegates, in a novel form of address which demanded considerable participation, to think 'sideways', to think creatively, to think critically and to think 'transformatively'. This last challenge demands that librarians develop new visions of the library which will enable it not just to survive but to contribute positively to learning at a distance.

A paper by Sue Roberts and John Davey provided a springboard for discussion of the relationships between libraries and virtual learning environments (VLEs). As more and more institutions deploy technology-based delivery systems, sometimes containing pre-packaged content, there is a clear danger that libraries could be by-passed. However, this presentation described the opposite effect, drawing on a case study of close integration between the library and the VLE and demonstrating how integration can be achieved, providing enriched student learning experiences through seamless access to resources and support.

Sarah Currier continued the theme with a report on a project which was investigating the relationship between digital libraries and online learning environments. The paper emphasized the importance of taking a learner-centred perspective and asked questions about what learners themselves expect and need from digital library services within virtual environments. Integration was again a key issue.

From the perspective of the University of London Library, Sally Chambers and Paul McLaughlin described the development of a new model of service targeted at students engaged on the University's extensive external programmes. The Virtual Library Service was designed to play a full part in the Virtual Campus, and the authors described a case study demonstrating the delivery of legal information resources to remote learners engaged on the University's Laws Programme.

Turning to an even more distributed perspective, Julie Brett gave a fascinating account of a project designed to support learners in multiple locations worldwide. The Distance Learning Zones concept, developed by the British Council, had been described at the previous *Libraries Without Walls* conference by Richard Weyers (Weyers, 2000). Here, conference delegates were updated with information on the pilot service which had been rolled out at a number of locations, and provided with details of the evaluation being carried out.

The University of Leicester, UK, with over 7000 postgraduate distance learning students based around the world, has had to develop new services to ensure that the library could be accessed remotely and, in particular, to provide an online enquiry service. The innovative and interesting feature of this service is the use of 'chat' facilities to enable students and librarians to engage in an online conversation. This enables librarians to conduct the kind of reference interview which is familiar in physical libraries – expanding the query, drawing out the key points and offering alternative avenues to explore in seeking a solution. Lou McGill included sample chat sessions in her paper, bringing this novel form of service delivery to life for delegates.

The UK Open University has of course been a leader in distance learning for many years, but its library has not always been in the forefront of learner support. All that has changed, however, and Gill Needham and Evelyn Simpson were able to demonstrate the pioneering work of the OU Library by describing OPAL – the Online Personal Academic Librarian. In contrast to the online chat approach being pioneered at Leicester, the OU Library is introducing a fully automated enquiry service capable of handling natural language questions and available 24 hours a day, seven days a week, 52 weeks a year.

Following these initial papers, each describing how different institutions – some with worldwide roles – are using their ingenuity to deliver services in new ways, the conference turned to examine examples of nationally planned services. First was a paper from Caroline Ingram and Catherine Grout describing the UK's Distributed National Electronic Resource (DNER), a national information environment designed to support learning and teaching in all of the UK's higher education institutions. The range of services being developed – from national schemes to make quality-assured online content available at the desktop to subject-based portals drawing together resources to meet individuals' specific needs – is immense. So too is the challenge of planning at national level when institutions are themselves autonomous. Again, integration was a watchword, and so too was interoperability – ensuring that each service could mesh seamlessly with the rest to provide a truly unified service to the user.

Bo Öhrström also spoke of a national initiative, this time in Denmark. Delegates were updated on developments since the previous conference, when the Danish Electronic Research Library concept had been described (Kvaerndrup, 2000). He emphasized that co-operation between libraries is essential if national-level services are to succeed, but equally all libraries – and their users – stand to benefit where this collaboration can be secured.

A further example of national planning and delivery was presented by Claudine Xenidou-Dervou, Sassa Tzedaki, Anna Fragkou and Marina Korfiati, who described the experience of Greek academic libraries in establishing the HEAL-Link service, which has used a consortium approach to secure access to electronic resources previously unavailable to members.

The discussion of national developments was completed with a paper by Shelagh Fisher, who returned to the UK's DNER but spoke of the independent, formative evaluation which she is co-ordinating. The idea of running an independent evaluation alongside a major development programme, so as to encourage it to learn lessons from implementation, is relatively new. The paper described the evaluation methods being used and presented some early findings.

The conference never lost sight of the fact that, in all the discussion of new and innovative services, it is the needs of the users which must be pre-eminent. Emma Place and Heather Dawson, at the start of a group of papers devoted to users' specific needs, described the development of the Virtual Training Suite which is designed to teach internet information skills via the web, and provides a highly subject-focused approach. Jenny Craven and Jillian Griffiths presented research findings which demonstrated the heterogeneity of user communities and the need to be aware of the very different approaches which users, including those with disabilities, take to information seeking and information use.

Betty Ronayne and Debbie Rogenmoser of the California State University in Sacramento explored the use of interactive television to teach library research skills to distance learners. Again, the emphasis was on interactivity: librarians – working in teams – using new technologies and interacting with students to help them learn new skills despite the disadvantages of distance. Virpi Palmgren and Kirsi Heino from Helsinki described the Finnish approach to developing students' information skills, emphasizing the need for librarians to be aware of, and to use, insights from modern pedagogical theory and to act as supporters of learners.

Katerina Toraki of the Documentation and Information Unit of the Technical Chamber of Greece described how a professional organization is taking seriously the need to deliver library services to its members – in this case engineers. A careful analysis of requests received by fax and e-mail, and of website traffic, was used as the basis for developing a survey of engineers to discover what would be expected of a virtual library, leading to detailed planning and delivery of services.

Clare Nankivell and Juliet Eve shifted the focus from academic and professional users to the clients of the public library. Each of the *Libraries Without Walls* conferences has featured consideration of public library issues, and in this paper the authors explored how the role of librarians in this sector is changing as they become more heavily involved in supporting education, including the development of services for users engaged in informal learning. Rob Davies then presented a description of the EC's PULMAN (Public Libraries Mobilizing Advanced Networks) initiative – a major 'network of excellence' involving all EC states and many of those which are candidates for future EC membership.

Jan Kooistra and Kees Hopstaken described Ommat, a program which enables students to explore electronic scientific material and to learn through a structured approach which identifies the different steps in acquiring, analysing, evaluating and using information sources in a virtual learning community. The theoretical basis of Ommat blends together understanding of the nature of knowledge with understanding of its social construct, and encourages students to learn collaboratively within a co-operative discourse.

Of course, libraries and their users do not operate in isolation, and the conference was reminded of the importance of the legislative framework of the information society in a paper by Judy Watkins and Tracy Bentley which had the challenging title 'Copyright made interesting'. They succeeded in doing just that! New copyright legislation, designed to harmonize practice across Europe and to cater for electronic resources, could have profound effects on the services which libraries are able to offer.

In the concluding papers, Ross MacIntyre and Ann Apps described the British Library's '*zetoc*' service, which provides Z39.50 access to the Library's Table of Contents database, including end-user alerting services, while Antony Corfield, Matthew Dovey, Richard Mawby and Colin Tatham described the development of new, 'lightweight' Z39.50 tools which will enable new services to be delivered without huge investment of development effort or the need for a high level of technical skill.

It will be apparent to readers of the Proceedings that the fourth *Libraries Without Walls* conference covered a huge range of issues. While the pace of change seems to accelerate inexorably, librarians are proving themselves innovative players on the world information stage. Once again the conference provided a meeting-point at which to share ideas, test established thinking and plan the future of libraries. From the evidence of the papers presented, that future will be both challenging and exciting.

References

Brophy, P. (2001) *The library in the twenty-first century*, London, Library Association Publishing.

Brophy, P. et al. (1996) *Access to campus library and information services by distant users: final report*, Preston, University of Central Lancashire.

Brophy, P. and Fisher, S. (1998) The hybrid library, *New Review of Information & Library Research*, **4**, 3–15.

Brophy, P., Fisher, S. and Clarke, Z. (1998) *Libraries without walls 2: the delivery of library services to distant users*, London, Library Association Publishing.

Brophy, P., Fisher, S. and Clarke, Z. (2000) *Libraries without walls 3: the delivery of library services to distant users*, London, Library Association Publishing.

Kvaerndrup, H. M. (2000) Denmark's Electronic Research Library (DEF): a project changing concepts, values and priorities. In Brophy, P., Fisher, S. and Clarke, Z. *Libraries without walls 3: the delivery of library services to distant users*, London, Library Association Publishing, 121–32.

Weyers, R. (2000) Distance Learning Zones: providing global information support to distance learners. In Brophy, P., Fisher, S. and Clarke, Z. *Libraries without walls 3: the delivery of library services to distant users*, London, Library Association Publishing, 238–49.

2

KEYNOTE PAPER – BEHIND-THE-SCREEN THINKING: KEY FACTORS FOR LIBRARIANSHIP IN DISTANCE EDUCATION

Elizabeth J. Burge

Introduction

Groucho Marx (1890–1977), that wonderfully incisive humorist, once quipped, 'Outside of a dog, a book is a [person's] best friend. Inside of a dog, it's too dark to read.' Undeterred, he also observed, 'I must say that I find television very educational. The minute somebody turns it on, I go to the library and read a book.' S. R. Ranganathan also valued the book, but he had to be more serious; he developed the now-famous Five Laws of Library Science for the context of his time.

Today, a layperson might amend Groucho's first quip thus: 'Outside of a library, the internet is a person's best friend. Inside of a library, it's the internet too!' Crawford and Gorman valued technology – in its place, of course; they proposed 'five new laws of librarianship' for their professional contexts (Crawford and Gorman, 1995, 7–12). Six changeful years on, do we need even newer laws or maxims?

Teachers and librarians, as educators in distance education, know too well the obvious impacts of changing distance educational times. Aren't we sometimes at the bleeding edge? We confront change at a cracking pace, adjust to changing student demographics and work in resource-constrained and technology-dominated environments. We analyse some of the changes within the biases and habits of our critical and reflective thinking capacities, but we can derail such work too easily as immediate tasks command our energies. It's often a matter of 'adopt, adapt and keep the job' (if one is not being squeezed out of the middle of library work hierarchies) (Harris, 2000) or hired as a 'gypsy' teacher existing on part-time contracts in several institutions. Sexty's case study (2001) is a good example of librarians working successfully, and against some odds, in a challenging, innovative slice of online life; while Harris's work reveals some of the less visible, insidious issues in librarianship's adoption of technology. At this conference we will hear many examples of excellence in library and learner-focused activity. But we should also use our time together to step back and reflect about broader, long-term factors that operate behind our computer screens.

I often recall a *bon mot* left in a 1946 'idea notebook' by the famous Canadian communications philosopher (and mentor of Marshall McLuhan), Harold Innis: 'Most forward-looking people have their heads turned sideways.' Join me now to look sideways and see what an educator sees. We shall look at eight factors that appear to be most relevant to libraries in distance education. Let us also engage in some metaphorical and reflective thinking, with the classic chair design exercise being just one example. [Editor's note: the 'classic chair exercise was a practical exercise carried out at the conference and designed to identify participants' thinking styles.]

What is my 'street credibility'? For 14 years I practised professional librarianship in South Australia, including being on the front line at night listening to anxious distance-mode adult learners who just needed a sympathetic ear and reassurances that, while their anxieties were typical, they'd survive now and thrive later. Then followed collaborative work in Canada (post-1980) with Judith Snow of OISE (Ontario Institute for Studies in Education)/University of Toronto's Educational Commons (**www.oise.utoronto.ca/library**) to help our Ontario-based distance learners, spread over one million sq km. We survived funded research into the perceived and actual links between librarians and distance education learners and teachers (Burge, Snow and Howard, 1989). Now, as a distance-mode teacher, writer, researcher and staff developer, I actively promote librarians' work in distance and open education and push for their involvement in course planning. I am very concerned about what I see as the decreasing presence of librarians-as-professionals (as distinct from 'library services') in the distance education field (Burge and Snow, 2000). Might librarians be replaced in users' minds by the very technology they helped to install? Or might the technology imperative be replaced by a human imperative?

Eight factors relevant to libraries in distance education

1 Significant advances in the development and use of online library and information literacy (IL) services. The papers of this conference exemplify the advances.
2 Changes in learner profiles. Many adult learners, of all ages and taking distance-mode courses on or off the campus, manage multiple life roles, stay job/career-focused, learn part-time, chase credentials, and prefer time and effort efficiencies more than being given the traditional 'campus experience' (Powell, McGuire and Crawford, 1999). Their loyalty to, and use of, institutions is based more often on perceived service satisfaction than on geographical proximity. Criteria for that satisfaction include academic advice and support that is just in

time (not just in case), task-relevant, respectful and accurate.

3 Greater attention to learner advisory services. Virtually and actually, adults can get help for realistically assessing their life role time demands and make informed decisions about how, why and where to complete courses (e.g. **www.uni4me.co.uk**). The work accomplished by The Open University (UK) over 30 years (e.g. **www.open.ac.uk/learners-guide**) is a leading example (Philips and Kelly, 2001), and other institutions now produce online diagnostics and helpfully frank stories from learners. Part of such advisory work entails accepting that many learners (or teachers for that matter) are not *au fait* with contemporary library services; indeed to some of them a modern library is nothing short of a major innovation to be dealt with, with all the attendant adoption dynamics (more on this later).

4 Academic tutoring and any other support deemed relevant for course work – for example, information literacy (e.g. library database use) and learning skill development (e.g. how to run discussions). The recent mini-explosion in 'supporting the learner' literature (e.g. Simpson, 2000) commands attention but it may not command your respect because of the very shadowy presence (or even non-presence) of modern library services. It appears that librarians, as sophisticated professionals, are less visible than their technologies.

5 The expansion of 'virtual' distance and flexible learning course offerings. Online technologies are still attractive to fiscally challenged administrators and the 'early adopters' of technology. But, as the field matures, increasing numbers of educators with extensive experience in using various learning technologies move their focus to the deeper factors such as accessibility ethics, infrastructure maintenance, staff development, adoption of learning models, and disaggregated institutional operations (see, for example, Farrell, 2001; Jakupec and Garrick, 2000).

6 The explosion in publishing online and in paper modes. One refereed journal, *Journal of Distance Education*, published by the Canadian Association for Distance Education (**www.cade-aced.ca**), now has full texts of articles since 1986 online (**http://cade.icaap.org**). A first-level response would be to say that we cannot keep up with all this literature, cognitively or financially. A second, more reflective response is to question how much literature may be derivative or repetitive, and which writers have the best 'street credibility'. Assessments and choices have to be made in consultation with other experts in the field.

7 Increasing numbers of 'gypsy' or part-time teachers/tutors. The point here is the extent to which these academic folk are brought fully into institutional operations. How many of you know how many such teachers are on the staff and how often do any of them engage consistently with the library or with you?

8 Disintermediation – the removal or apparent irrelevance of brokerage or the

'middle person'. In some situations, such as getting money via the instant cash machine, disintermediation is a real advantage: the task can be done quickly with minimum effort and cost (assuming mobility), with no one asking difficult questions, and one can usually get enough to get by (the formal term is 'satisficing'). But when complex information topics are flung at relative novices, or when the enquiry terms remain unclear, then disintermediation has to give way to proactive, 'intelligent agent' intermediation. It would seem that actual 'face time' for intellectual engagement, advice and affective encouragement (or 'professional care work', Harris, 2000) is being displaced by virtual interfacing with e-materials and 'technological self-service in public' (Harris, 2000). Local, teacher-prepared learning materials are also slowly being displaced by external banks of packages for mixing and matching (e.g., Feemster, 2001).

Here is some language of the future:

> Content can be harvested from the vast array of information resources such as personal homepages, commercial, governmental, and educational websites, and discipline-specific learning object repositories. (Metros, 2001, 91)

Note those last three words. Librarians in the field of education are, generally, not asked to participate in course teamwork or to behave as consistently proactive educational partners. This is in marked contrast to the way in which highly proactive special librarians are regarded by, and work with, staff in commercial companies (Nardi and O'Day, 1999, chapter 7). I still meet faculty members who have not yet had time to use the repertoire of e-library databases and e-based services. Disintermediation occurs too when learners, teachers and advisors seek off-the-printer, rather than off-the-shelf, items. Disintermediation can have emotional overtones: when some learners experience software problems, their first reaction may be to feel stupid or inadequate, so they will ask a 'safe' helper such as a classmate before going to that super-smart librarian behind the desk/computer screen. Disintermediation may develop insidiously as learners realize that, when they have the time to study (e.g. at night or on weekends), usually only the new, less experienced librarians or student assistants are on duty. Time and intellectual energies are then saved by taking what the internet can deliver via a fast search-print-and-leave sequence. In general, disintermediation does not announce itself but, having arrived, is difficult to dismiss. No point in assigning blame here: librarians and educators have yet to figure out the practical and educational benefits of a truly symbiotic relationship.

Given the implications of these eight factors, what might we do next? When in doubt, think.

Thinking tasks

Thinking 'sideways', beyond our habitual frameworks, takes work. It may even cause frissons of discomfort. Reading the titles of our conference papers gives some sense of our selected key clients and where we should invest conceptual and logistical energies. Allow me then to suggest that we move 'sideways' and consider four thinking tasks.

Think analytically about what you notice in your work contexts

Which issues and tasks most often attract your attention, and why? If we take technology adoption as a focus for such an analysis, how do you interrogate its processes? How might you reflect on the placement of technologies – for example, as the centre of attention or as just one part of an integrated partnership strategy? It is said that the railway system in the USA got into trouble many years ago because its staff thought their business was to install and manage the technology of railways – the rolling stock, the railway lines and the signals. It took years of gradual passenger desertion from the rail system and its underlying assumptions before the rail bosses realized that they had missed something rather important: their ultimate business was to move humans comfortably and efficiently, to provide all the attendant 'people services'. Once that kind of transformative shift in perspective showed up in the day-to-day operations, and travel became outright enjoyable, the passengers began to return. A comment from my Toronto colleague, Judy Snow, is relevant: 'Librarians need to move past just the demonstration of downloading/how to access the web, etc., to thinking about how all this supports the learning process' (personal communication, 24 August 2001).

How much workplace time are you given, or can you command, for thoughtful discussions that get past matters technological, for examining how professional values match and conflict with institutional politics, for creating realistic (even wry) maxims of practice, and for balancing innovation adoption and tradition maintenance? Which actors and their world views are not consistently present in your thinking? Where can you safely save your energies on matters that are ultimately insoluble or irrelevant in users' minds?

Think about library services in terms of change

Two paths at least are open. If we focus on the technologies in librarianship path, we might use four questions from the 'Laws of Media' to help analyse the long-term impact of any new technology:

What does it enhance or intensify?
What does it render obsolete or displace?
What does it retrieve that was previously [made obsolete]?
What does it produce or become when [pushed] to an extreme?'
(McLuhan and McLuhan, 1988, 7)

Take any technology and see how its forms may change – for example, with print-on-paper: how writing by hand on 'smart paper' sheets can be instantly transmitted as e-mail; or with correspondence: how e-mail has influenced today's features of 'messaging' and the return of handwritten notes for special occasions; or with paper-bound books: how e-books that look like a book and feel like a book have spines that are pre-loaded with various digitized materials for on-demand, on-time transfer to the pages.

Actually, we could replace 'technology' – the 'it' in the excerpt above – with 'ourselves' in those four questions. If librarians are not shut out of course team development work or excluded by default as active information research helpers in online classes, what as professionals do they actually enhance or intensify in distance education? What current work of yours now renders which of your earlier tasks 'obsolete', and to what extent is that rendering a good thing? We appear to be coming close to losing the librarian-as-human, the librarian as a personable and highly skilled 'intelligent agent' who knows my informational idiosyncrasies (Nardi and O'Day, 1996).

The second change path takes us into the thickets of innovation adoption and the five key attributes that influence the rate by which any change or innovation will be adopted. Judith Snow and I recently considered Rogers' well-known attributes (given in brackets below), but they retain relevance even now:

> If librarians are to [avoid disintermediation] their presence and their behaviours will have to be perceived as (i) just as significant as all the great websites but for very different reasons (Relative Advantage attribute); (ii) relevant to and reflective of how learners [and teachers and others] idiosyncratically think, feel, act, and juggle learning against other life demands (Compatibility). [Library staff] will have to be consistently easy and convenient to talk with, as human as anyone else, i.e., not always cool, competent, error-free professionals but learners too (low Complexity); and (iii) their work and their products developed in experimental stages with early and continuing advice from intended users (Trialability). Finally, their everyday activities have to be visible – but visibility matters most on the users' territory, not the librarians' territory (Observability). (Burge and Snow, 2000, 31)

Try first with the teachers – introduce yourselves as an innovation to make their lives easier and their academic reputations bigger. Think symbiotic relationships and reduce the barriers against them. Teachers act as role models for learners, and if you can win teachers en bloc, you can do almost anything!

Think creatively

Our classic chair exercise is fun but it is also a metaphorical thinking exercise to help you check some assumptions. Another strategy is to design statements that are pithy and go beyond the idea that libraries and librarians should be valued because they are 'a good thing'. Here's a draft set that came as I worked on this paper: 'We focus on brains more than books, response more than restriction, partnership more than power, and performance more than promise.' It's startling sometimes how memorably succinct messages, even word plays, may provoke lateral thinking. Judy Snow and I recently explored the implications of librarians 'strengthening leadership behaviours instead of receivership behaviours . . .' (Burge and Snow, 2000, 30).

Think critically and transformatively about just about everything

We shall take two areas – terminology and roles in the academic institution. You have discussed name changes to reflect new job occupations. Do you deserve a job title ('librarian') that harks back to earlier days when people were custodians and cataloguers for print materials and needed buildings called libraries? So much information now is in virtual form, and then often on licence from an external supplier. A fixed and visible location is no longer the major issue. For many users today, cognitive engagement, time efficiency and task completion are the issues. Might you benefit from a job title that focuses more on users' preoccupations? 'Reference interview' is a classic term, but as Nardi and O'Day (1999, 85) point out, it's 'a modest name for an impressive deployment of tact, diplomacy and persistence, as well as a skillful interviewing technique.' What term might arise from a user-centred view? 'Bibliographic instruction' betrays a librarian-centred view, but for the learner a relevant title is 'getting the best information fast'. A final example: liberation from edifice-centric thinking would mean deleting the word 'remote' and 'distance learners' from the vocabulary. Who is perceived as remote depends on location, and that is no longer very relevant.

Regarding roles in the whole institution, I long have wished that, since e-technology has (apparently) taken over much of the old work of 'readers' services' staff, many librarians could be transformed out of the 'library' into a more diffuse public profile associated more with learning and teaching skill development, allied visibly with educators' on-the-ground work. When you are seen in our corridors, on our web screen classes, in our study centres, in our audio-conferenced classes, in our coffee spaces, or working on joint projects with us (e.g. course development), we are far more likely to assume that you are partners-in-practice rather than in theory. I think here about some disaggregation and innovation of function and location, with the library's importance not based on square metres or loan statistics.

One contrasting view from Stanley Katz, a respected and experienced USA academic and administrator, calls for a critical re-visioning of the library building and its services:

> Do we know what we want the virtual library to be and do? Is enough money, and appropriate personnel, being allocated to libraries to perform their potentially expanded role in both teaching and scholarship? Do library directors have sufficient independence and training to lead libraries into the new era? Who should train faculty members and students to use the library's information technology? Does, for example, a teaching and learning center belong in the library? In essence, these questions come down to the need to clarify the goal of the library in the electronic era, and to consider how the library should be restructured to attain that goal. (Katz, 2001, B8)

Five maxims for librarianship in distance education

I end with a request for creative thinking. Have some fun and design your own quip to rival the wit of Maestro Marx. Or create your own new maxims for today's librarianship. Here are mine:

- clarify and conduct work in users' terms (defined broadly)
- build relationships (political, educational, informational, logistical)
- value your intermediation as essential
- reach past the technology tools to the human conditions
- grow tall from the soil of a fine tradition, but avoid being root-bound.

References

Burge, E. J. and Snow, J. E. (2000) Candles, corks and contracts: essential relationships between learners and librarians, *The New Review of Libraries and Lifelong Learning*, **1** (1), 19–34.

Burge, E. J., Snow, J. E. and Howard, J. (1989) Distance education: concept and practice, *Canadian Library Journal*, **46** (5), 329–35.

Crawford, W. and Gorman, M. (1995) *Future libraries: dreams, madness, and reality*, American Library Association.

Farrell, G. (2001) Issues and choices. In Farrell, G. (ed.) *The changing faces of virtual education*, The Commonwealth of Learning, available at **www.col.org/virtualed/index2.htm**

Feemster, R. (2001) Ready or not, here come the digital libraries, *University Business*, available at **www.universitybusiness.com/0107/feature.html**

Harris, R. (2000) Squeezing librarians out of the middle: gender and technology in a threatened profession. In Balka, E. and Smith, R. (eds) *Women, work and computerization*, Kluwer.

Jakupec, V. and Garrick, J. (2000) *Flexible learning, human resource and organizational development: putting theory to work*, Routledge.

Katz, S. N. (2001) In information technology, don't mistake a tool for a goal. *The Chronicle of Higher Education*, **47** (40), (15 June), in *The Chronicle Review*, B7–B9.

McLuhan, M. and McLuhan, E. (1988) *Laws of media: the new science*, University of Toronto Press.

Metros, S. (2001) Engaging online learners, *Lifelong Learning in Europe*, **6** (2), 85–95.

Nardi, B.A. and O'Day, V. (1996) Intelligent agents: what we learned at the library, *Libri*, **46** (3), 59–88.

Nardi, B. and O'Day, V. (1999) *Information ecologies: using information with heart*, The MIT Press.

Philips, M. and Kelly, P. (2001) Learning technologies for learner services. In Burge, E. J. (ed.) *The strategic use of learning technologies*, New Directions in Adult and Continuing Education, vol. 88, Jossey-Bass.

Powell, R., McGuire, S. and Crawford (1999) Convergence of student types: issues for distance education. In Tait, A. and Mills, R. (eds), *The convergence of distance and conventional education: patterns of flexibility for the individual learner*, Routledge.

Sexty, S. (2001) Web-based research assistance. In Burge, E. J. and Haughey, M. (eds) *Using learning technologies: international perspectives on practice*, Routledge Falmer.

Simpson, O. (2000) *Supporting students in open and distance learning*, Kogan Page.

THEME 1
LIBRARIES AND VIRTUAL LEARNING ENVIRONMENTS

CHAPTER 1

3

DISTANCE LEARNING ZONES: A PILOT PROJECT

Julie Brett

Introduction

This paper looks at the role of the British Council in supporting trans-national distance learners enrolled on UK postgraduate courses. It describes a British Council pilot project to provide information support to distance learners through its global network of libraries and information centres. The Distance Learning Zones are the result of partnership with four UK universities and support 150 learners in six locations. Six core information services are provided and the evaluation of the project will form the basis of a master's dissertation (due May 2002) and will be the first published research into the information needs of trans-national distance learners.

Background and context

Many learners are attracted to UK qualifications because of the assured quality of courses and the whole learning experience. There are no exact data for the number of overseas learners studying for a UK higher education qualification, but estimates range from 30,000 to 120,000 (Healey, 2000). Around 70 institutions offer distance learning courses to learners in over 30 countries. It is clear that UK higher education institutions understand the importance of the international market and are keen to offer courses internationally, but it is important to consider the responsibility for supporting trans-national learners. (The term 'trans-national' is used to denote a learner enrolled on a course offered by an institution in another country.) Even where institutions state that courses are delivered 'in a box', learners, especially at postgraduate level, are keen to undertake further reading. Learners and academics both agree that supplementary reading is an integral aspect of study:

> It is universally acknowledged that the research material required by undergraduate and postgraduate students cannot be provided from course packs or remote book depositories alone. Some form of value-added service is required to boost the current level of information available to students. (Vassie and Woodhead, 1998)

The quality of UK distance learning courses is monitored by the Quality Assurance Agency for Higher Education (QAA), which includes an assessment of student support provision as an integral quality measure. Most higher education providers offer specific library and information services for distance learners but the range and quality of support is varied. Specific library services for distance learners are usually the same whether a learner is in the UK or overseas, even though needs are likely to be different. In addition to physical distance and time differences, transnational distance learners can experience certain constraints to effective learning, such as linguistic and cultural barriers, which can potentially further alienate them. Distance learners, often paying high fees by local standards, have the right to expect a certain level and quality of support.

The British Council works closely with the UK education sector to promote UK education overseas. Traditionally this involved individual learners coming to study in the UK, but with the development of, and improved access to, information communications technology and growth of UK courses offered 'off-campus', distance learning is now the preferred option for many learners.

The British Council is uniquely placed to offer on-the-ground library and information support to distance learners. It has a network of 220 libraries and information centres managed by local information professionals who have developed strong links with local information communities and institutions.

Many learners will already have developed a relationship with the British Council through its education counselling service, and to many the organization represents the public face of the UK. Thus it is able to provide a human interface between the learner and the UK institution in a way that UK-based institutions cannot.

Richard Weyers, a colleague in the British Council, delivered a paper at *Libraries Without Walls 3* (Weyers, 2000) on the provision of global information support to distance learners, proposing the concept of 'Distance Learning Zones'. As a result of this, consultation with UK institutions, a review of the literature and discussions with learners overseas, the concept of 'distance learning zones' was transformed into a pilot project to provide support for distance learners through British Council libraries and information centres.

Distance Learning Zones
Introduction

The Distance Learning Zone forms a link between the local learner and UK university, by providing value-added information services to enhance the individual's learning experience. The scenario given in Figure 3.1 outlines how a learner can benefit from a Distance Learning Zone.

Learner scenario

Mrs Chan is a teacher at a school in Singapore. She has been teaching for four years and is keen to continue her professional development by taking a postgraduate qualilication. She recently enrolled on a distance learning MEd course with Sheffield University. Although she would have preferred to study lull-time in the UK, this is not practical for both personal and professional reasons.

Before Mrs Chan begins her course she receives an email from the British Council office in Singapore inviting her to attend a Distance Learning Zone welcome session. She discovers that the British Council and her university have an agreement which will provide her and other distance learners with support during her study. At the welcome session she and other people on her course have the opportunity to meet each other and are told about the assistance available to them through the British Council. This includes computer training, work space, access to computers, help in using Sheffield University databases and assistance with obtaining articles from the British Library.

Over the next few months Mrs Chan attends an internet group training session and receives personal help from British Council staff on searching specialist education databases. She discovers that, as a member of the Distance Learning Zone, she can access the education library of a local university for a small fee. She attends a social event at the British Council office which includes a display of books and resources on special needs education.

Throughout her course Mrs Chan uses the Distance Learning Zone for weekend work on computers. She does not have access to a computer at home and finds it quieter to study at the British Council. She also uses a meeting room at the British Council to get together in the evenings with other learners on her course to discuss project work.

At the end of her course Mrs Chan goes to the farewell session which includes a video-conference with the course leader in Sheffield who praises the group on their work and congratulates them on completing the course. She joins the British Council alumni association and receives regular updates and invitations to events.

Fig. 3.1 *Learner scenario*

The pilot project

The aim of the one-year Distance Learning Zone pilot project, which ran from November 2000 to November 2001, was for the British Council, working in partnership with UK higher education institutions, to provide customized inform-ation services for distance learners studying on UK postgraduate programmes in six overseas markets. Table 3.1 (see page 24), outlines the locations, the provider institutions and the courses.

The services

The services provided by the Distance Learning Zone are:

- access to an 'information broker'
- information on local library access

- study space with assisted use of ICT
- ICT and information handling courses
- interlibrary loans and document supply
- social and networking opportunities.

Access to an information broker

Each Distance Learning Zone is managed by a trained British Council 'information broker'. Each information broker is a local, qualified library/information specialist who has developed strong links with academic and library communities and has attended an extensive seven-day training course in the UK. This training event included two days spent with library staff at the partner university to obtain first-hand experience of using proprietary databases and institution-specific resources.

The information brokers provide personal assistance to students in understanding and exploiting their information environment, using a variety of resources. They also provide help and assistance in setting up ATHENS authentication and the dissemination of passwords.

Information brokers lessen the alienation felt by some distance learners by using their detailed knowledge of the local environment and course materials to deliver face-to-face support.

Information on local library access

Each Distance Learning Zone collates information on access to local significant libraries overseas on behalf of institutions and learners. Information brokers use their considerable local knowledge and strong links with library professionals to seek opportunities for Distance Learning Zone members to access specialist collections. Data on local access is forwarded to the partner institution and learners and will eventually form the basis of a global database accessible via the internet.

Study space with assisted use of ICT

Distance Learning Zones provide quiet space to study and access ICT. Training on the use of equipment and resources is provided by experienced staff, who are always on hand to troubleshoot problems and provide assistance. Many British Council libraries and information centres open in the evenings and at weekends. All are connected to the internet and provide access to a collection of online and printed resources.

ICT and information handling skills courses

Each learner is offered a training session in information handling skills and assistance with authentication procedures necessary to access proprietary products through the internet. This varies in length according to the numbers of students involved, their overall levels of ICT awareness, and the expressed needs of the UK institution. Each information broker is provided with access to protected databases for training and troubleshooting purposes. Once initial training of students has been undertaken, information brokers are available to provide ongoing help and assistance in developing learners' information handling strategies on a one-to-one basis as required.

Interlibrary loans and document supply

Learners receive assistance in dealing with interlibrary loans and document supply, including use of the British Library Document Supply Centre (BLDSC). If they cannot obtain documents locally, learners are encouraged to obtain these through their course provider, where this service is offered. The British Council acts as a delivery point for documents and books.

Social and networking opportunities

The Distance Learning Zone acts as a link between the course provider and the individual. It offers a social meeting point for learners to interact with each other. Many learners can feel isolated and 'distant' from their university, so membership of a Distance Learning Zone provides them with a sense of belonging to a community of learners and enables them to identify with the UK through a recognized UK institution – the British Council. Learners are also invited to other British Council events and activities, giving them the opportunity to meet a wider community of contacts.

Courses and locations

Table 3.1 (see over) show the provider institutions, the courses provided, and where they are located.

Table 3.1   *UK institutions participating in the pilot project*

Provider	Location	Course
Open University	Zimbabwe	Masters in Development Management
Sheffield Hallam University	Bahrain	MBA
	Dubai	MBA
	Hong Kong	MBA
University of Sheffield	Singapore	Masters in Education
University of Sunderland	Malaysia	MBA

Approximately 150 learners are participating in the pilot.

Each information broker has attended a training course in the UK which explored delivery of core services and included a visit to the partner institution to gain a detailed understanding of the resources available to distance learners.

Funding

For the purposes of the pilot project, the British Council is sharing costs with partner institutions. The British Council funded the training event for information brokers, which brought eight members of staff to the UK for a seven-day course. British Council offices in the pilot locations are meeting the local costs of delivering services. Each participating institution has contributed an initial joining fee and per capita fee for each student enrolled. For pilot purposes the rate of contribution for the universities is the same regardless of location, but it is likely that under the next phase of the project a formula will be agreed to set fees which reflect local costs.

Evaluation

The evaluation data will indicate the success of the pilot and how the Distance Learning Zone concept should be taken forward. It is important that the research undertaken includes data from each group involved in the pilot project: learners, university staff and information brokers. The success of the pilot will be assessed by:

- reaction from learners on the impact of the Distance Learning Zone on their learning experience
- feedback from university staff on the impact the pilot has had on their work
- willingness of partners to continue the project.

These indicators will be assessed using a range of methodologies, and the project evaluation will form the basis of the author's MSc Information Management dissertation. This research will be the first study to examine library and information support for trans-national distance learners.

Learners were surveyed before they joined the Distance Learning Zone to record their perceived needs and constraints on their study. They will be surveyed at the end of the pilot to discover their actual information needs, any actual constraints on their ability to study effectively and their experience of using the services. Unwin et al. (1998) discovered that there was a mismatch between the information needs of distance learners as perceived by the university and the learners' own perceived needs. It could be argued that, in this case, the perceived information needs of a trans-national distance learner are greater than his or her actual needs due to physical distance and, in some cases, a contrasting cultural context. Learners may think they need access to a wide range of resources, local libraries, training etc. before they embark on their study, but the take-up of such services may not match expectations.

Focus groups will be held in each location to gather qualitative data from the learners on the information support they have received. This will give learners an opportunity to discuss the pilot project with each other and stimulate discussion, comment and suggestions for the delivery of future services. All information brokers and staff from each university will be interviewed to provide data on the pilot from their respective viewpoints.

The results of the initial questionnaires have provided data on the learners participating in the project (see Table 3.2). Unsurprisingly the majority (95%) are in full-time employment and this was the main reason most decided to study 'at a distance' (94%).

Table 3.2   *Why did you choose to study by distance?*
(learners could select more than one reason)

work/employment	94%
domestic responsibilities	20%
cost	8%

Learners believed that there would be some specific constraints that would adversely affect their ability to study, with the biggest concern being employment (see Table 3.3).

Table 3.3   *Which of the following do you think may adversely affect your ability to study?*
(learners could select more than one option)

work/employment	67%
acess to resources	53%
domestic responsibilities	37%

Of those who had already been studying for a year or more, 33% felt that access to resources adversely affected their ability to study, as opposed to 53% of new learners (i.e. learners at the beginning of their courses). The actual constraints on study could be quite different from the perceived constraints and this will be illustrated when the results of the second questionnaire (given to learners at the end of the pilot project) are collated. Generally most learners (67%) know that their university provides specific library services for distance learners but this varied between institutions from 100% down to 20%. Communication with university library staff was anticipated by most respondents (76%) but by contrast none of the existing learners (i.e. learners who have been studying by distance for one year or more), all on the same course, reported contacting library staff. It will be interesting to see whether the university library staff report a change in the number of learners contacting them. All existing learners expressed an overwhelming need to access more resources than those provided by their university, along with 91% of new learners, even when their course material states they do not need access to a library. Access to academic libraries or other specialized collections is important to the learners surveyed.

Learners were asked to identify the services they think they will use (see Table 3.4). Results so far indicate that they anticipate the most useful services will be access to an information broker and information on local library access, both identified by 72% of participants:

Table 3.4   *Which of the following services provided by the Distance Learning Zone do you think you will use?*
(learners could select more than one option)

Access to a British Council 'information broker'	72%
Information on local library access	72%
Training on IT and using information	53%
Interlibrary loans and document supply	52%
Study space with assistance using IT	39%
Social/networking events	26%

The actual take-up and use of services is likely to differ between locations, and learners will have differing needs according to their local situation. Additional services suggested by learners at this stage focused on personal contact (mentoring/counselling and opportunities for interaction with tutors), help with book purchasing and suggestions for specific resources.

At this stage it is difficult to assess the impact of the Distance Learning Zone, as the data collected so far concentrate on the perceived information needs of learners and their anticipated use of pilot services. After they have received their course material and begin producing their coursework, learners' needs may differ from what they anticipated. Although anecdotal evidence (informal comments from British Council information brokers) has shown that take-up of some services has been better than that of others, the second questionnaire and focus groups will provide useful information on the delivery, value and impact of the six pilot services.

The future

Without pre-empting the results of the evaluation, those of us closely associated with the project feel that the Distance Learning Zone concept is worthwhile, and that its services will be offered to a wider number of markets, establishing partnerships with UK institutions who are keen to offer a value-added information service to trans-national learners.

The British Council is currently developing Knowledge and Learning Centres. These centres will create a global network of enhanced conferencing, learning and knowledge opportunities through a combination of physical and virtual services. Each Knowledge and Learning Centre will include a Distance Learning Zone. In addition to the services currently provided, distance learners will have access to subject specific portals, an electronic library of journals and e-resources, and will be able to attend tutorials and hold discussions with learners globally using video-conferencing facilities.

Within the next five years, there may be 30 or more Distance Learning Zones around the world, providing a wide range of enhanced support services to thousands of trans-national distance learners in partnership with the UK education community.

The next stages of the evaluation and progress on the project will be reported on the British Council website at **www.britishcouncil.org/infoexch/dlz/index.htm**.

References

Healey, P. (2000) *Report on the project on distance learning and in-country delivery*, The British Council.

Unwin, L. et al. (1998) *The role of the library in distance learning: a study of postgraduate students, course providers and librarians in the UK*, Bowker Saur, 45–55.

Vassie, R. and Woodhead, M. (1998) *Access to libraries: a blindspot in state-of-the-art distance learning?*, seminar report (ILL for Distance Learning), 20 November.

Weyers, R. (2000) *Distance Learning Zones: providing global information support to distance learners*. In Brophy, P. et al. (eds) *Libraries without walls 3: the delivery of library services to distant users*, London, Library Association Publishing, 238–49.

4

University of London – Virtual Campus Project. Information Resources for Distance Learners: the Implementation of a Model

Sally Chambers and Paul McLaughlin

Introduction

This paper illustrates the University of London Library's (ULL, **www.ull.ac.uk**) model for providing a dedicated Virtual Library Service (VLS) to support the information needs of students registered with the University of London's External Programme. The Virtual Library will offer access to a range of information and learning resources and related services as one of the principal elements in the External Programme's Virtual Campus Project.

The University of London External Programme

The University of London (**www.lon.ac.uk/**), established by Royal Charter in 1836, is one of the oldest universities in the United Kingdom. It is now a federation of 17 self-governing colleges, all of which are members of the University by choice and are empowered to award the University of London degree. The University of London External Programme was established in 1858 to make University of London degrees accessible to students who were unable to come to the University to study. The degrees awarded to students on the External Programme are of the same academic standard as those awarded internally to students studying at one of the University's colleges in London. Currently the programme offers over 100 qualifications at undergraduate and postgraduate level to over 28,000 students in more than 180 countries. At undergraduate level over 65% of students are currently studying in the Asia Pacific region, whereas at postgraduate level the students are more widely distributed, with 30% in the Asia Pacific, 30% in Western Europe and almost 30% from Africa and America combined. The University of London External Programme is a distinctly global programme, with the majority of students studying at a considerable distance from London. Each qualification is led by a Lead College within the University, co-ordinated by the Lead Colleges Committee. Funded wholly from student fees, surpluses are re-invested in the

Programme through new course developments and through major initiatives such as the Virtual Campus Project.

The Virtual Campus Project

In October 2000, the External Programme (**www.londonexternal.ac.uk**) embarked on a period of significant investment to develop new and redevelop existing qualifications, the majority of which will be delivered wholly or partially online. In parallel with these academic developments, the External Programme is currently developing an online environment, the Virtual Campus. Anyone visiting the Virtual Campus from a computer anywhere in the world will be able to access a range of information, advisory, resource and support services that would be expected on a physical campus mirrored into a virtual context. The Virtual Campus Project is a collaborative initiative bringing together three central academic services of the University of London: the External Programme, The University of London Library and the University of London Computer Centre (ULCC, **www.ulcc.ac.uk/**). Running from October 2000 to July 2003, the aim of the project is to provide a common infrastructure to support the development, delivery and management of internet-based courses and services for the External Programme.

The Virtual Library Service

One of the central services within the Virtual Campus Project is the Virtual Library Service (VLS, **www.external.ull.ac.uk**), which is being co-ordinated by the ULL. Founded in 1837, the ULL is the central research repository of the University of London with particular research strengths across the arts, humanities and social sciences. Any student registered with the External Programme is entitled to membership of the ULL on payment of a subscription. However, because of the global distribution of students, use of the library in this way is not usually possible. With the development of the VLS all External Programme students who have a computer with an internet connection will be able to have access to library support at whatever time, and from whatever geographical location they have chosen to study.

The VLS is a web-based portal (see Figure 4.1) providing access to a variety of online learning and research resources to support a range of the qualifications offered by the External Programme. As within a physical university library there will also be a reference collection containing dictionaries, encyclopaedias, newspapers and other relevant reference resources enabling students to find rapid reference facts to support their studies.

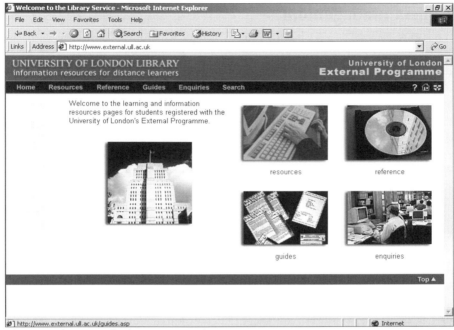

Fig. 4.1 *The Virtual Library Service home page*

To complement resource provision, the VLS will offer an enquiry service which will allow students to ask library-related questions at a time convenient to them. Initially, the queries will only be answered within core library opening hours, 09.00 to 17.00, Monday to Friday (UK Time), but this provision will be monitored to ensure that the needs of the students are being met, given that most of them will be working across the entire spectrum of time zones.

To contribute to the development of the students' information literacy skills, the Virtual Library will provide access to a selection of externally developed guides and tutorials to help students improve the quality, efficiency and effectiveness of searching for academic level information on the internet. Such tutorials will include: *The Resource Discovery Network's Virtual Training Suite* (**www.vts.rdn.ac.uk**), which offers internet skills training in a wide range of academic subjects covered by the External Programme's qualifications. In addition, there will be a range of quick start guides to introduce students to the Virtual Library resources. As the project progresses, the ULL hopes to develop a range of tutorials tailored to suit the specific needs of the External Programme, including a generic information skills training module delivered via a Virtual Learning Environment.

Project management

The VLS Project is a 33-month project, which will run concurrently with the Virtual Campus Project between October 2000 and July 2003. Within the ULL, a dedicated full-time Project Officer has been recruited to co-ordinate the day-to-day running of the project. The work of the Project Officer will be overseen by the VLS Project Manager (a senior member of the ULL Senior Management Team) and the VLS Project Director (the Librarian of the ULL). During the summer of 2001, an Electronic Library Projects Assistant was recruited with key responsibilities for front-line support of the enquiry service and maintenance of the VLS website. In addition, the ULL Electronic Libraries Project Team, drawn from amongst existing staff with relevant skills and expertise, will provide substantial input. The development work is expected to provide considerable benefit for all user constituencies served by the Library in the longer term.

Implementation

The first 11 months of the project saw the recruitment of the Electronic Library Project Officer in December 2000, who took up her post in mid-February 2001. One of the primary tasks of the Project Officer was to undertake an academic audit to establish which resources are needed for each of the External Programme's qualifications which will take part in the VCP. These qualifications range across a wide variety of subjects including law, social sciences, international primary healthcare, clinical dentistry and distance education. Currently there are requirements for a wide range of resources, including subject-specific databases, e-journals, copyright-cleared journal articles and book chapters, as well as websites and subject gateways.

Resource integration and Virtual Learning Environments

From September 2001, the preliminary version of the Virtual Campus became available to students studying with the Laws Programme and across a variety of qualifications co-ordinated by the London School of Economics and Political Science. At this stage, the resources are accessed through the student area of the External Programme website. These pages provide a seamless link to the relevant resource pages within the VLS. Each resource page contains a standard navigation bar, which enables the student to move around the entire VLS from within their student area (see Figure 4.2).

A significant element of the VCP is the development of new qualifications and the redevelopment of existing ones. The majority of these qualifications will be delivered either wholly or partially online via a Virtual Learning Environment.

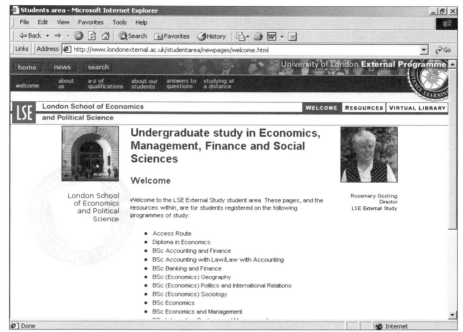

Fig. 4.2 *The London School of Economics student area*
Reproduced with permission of the London School of Economics and the University of London External Programme.

Although many of these qualifications will not be available to students until 2003, the Electronic Library Project Officer is being involved in their development from the initial stages. Within the Virtual Learning Environment, the provision of resources will be closely integrated with the study materials. Initially these resources will be copyright-cleared journal articles and book chapters in either HTML or PDF (portable document format).

Case study: online resources for law

The Laws Programme will be the first set of qualifications with resources in the VLS. The law resources page will initially provide access to generic law resources across all of the law qualifications; however, as the programme redevelops its courses, these resources will be further integrated with the study materials. Currently the law resources page contains a range of resources, including gateways to academic law resources from around the world, organized by both jurisdiction and topic; links to organizations connected with the legal profession, such as the Law Society and the Bar Council in the UK; a selection of legal e-journals; and even an internet tutorial for lawyers (see Figure 4.3).

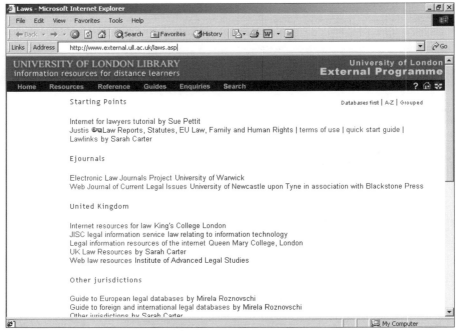

Fig. 4.3 *The Laws Programme resources page*

Remote access to legal information

The main resource for the Laws Programme, which has been available to students from September 2001, is the legal research database *Justis.com*. *Justis.com* contains full-text documentation in the areas of case, statute, European and human rights law. As External Programme students are not based on campus, it is necessary to provide remote access authentication for *Justis.com*. This type of authentication will also be necessary as other resources are acquired for the VLS.

Access and authentication are essential elements of the Virtual Campus Project. The aim of the project is to provide seamless access to distributed learning and information resources and services from the External Programme's website. Some of the information on the website will be freely available to all. However, there will be areas limited to registered students and staff, which will require a username and password to access. The objective is to develop a solution where the staff or students will only log in to the Virtual Campus once. Any further authentication required, such as for library resources like *Justis.com*, will be done behind the scenes by data exported from the External Programme's student registry, without the students or staff having to re-enter their username and password.

Authentication is also an integral part of the VLS. In line with the Virtual Campus, it is intended that students and staff will not have to re-enter their username or password once they have logged into the VLS. In order to ensure this, ULL is currently investigating a variety of authentication solutions including the use of a proxy server. Attention is also being paid to the development of a second-generation access management system for UK higher and further education, building on the current system, *ATHENS* (**www.athens.ac.uk**). While this investigation is in progress, resources such as *Justis.com* will be authenticated via *ATHENS*, which allows remote access to licensed resources with the input of a username and password.

Communicating with the students

Although the Virtual Campus will be an online environment for External Programme students, currently the main method of communication with students is by post. As the Laws Programme will be the first to have qualifications with resources in the VLS, it was necessary to send students a printed leaflet to inform them about the Virtual Campus and VLS developments including their usernames and passwords for *Justis.com*. Along with the more general information, the leaflet contained a quick start guide to introduce students to logging in and basic searching and other functions within *Justis.com*. A web version of this guide is also available on the VLS website (see Figure 4.4 overleaf). In order to encourage students to use the VLS, a follow-up letter will be sent to students after six months to remind them of the new online resources that are available. As the VLS develops they will be able to sign up to an e-mail discussion list that will alert them to new developments in the VLS as they happen.

In addition to paper-based communication, each year the Laws Programme offers a one-day induction course for new and potential undergraduate law students. This year the Electronic Library Project Officer will give a presentation on this course, introducing the VLS for law students. Throughout the year, intensive weekend courses for existing undergraduate law students are also offered, which may also offer opportunities to introduce students to the VLS. It is hoped that these face-to-face presentations will also encourage students to use the service.

Website design

As VLS is the library for the External Programme, it is important that as many students as possible are able to access it. One of the most important issues to consider when designing the website is that the majority of students will be

Fig. 4.4 *The* Justis.com *quick start guide*
Reproduced with permission of Context Ltd and the University of London.

accessing the internet via slow dial-up connections. We therefore need to ensure that students can access the material that they need as quickly and simply as possible, and that the pages are not overloaded with large graphics. Once the preliminary version is in place, which has taken into account these particular issues, an accessibility policy, which is currently in its draft stages, will be implemented throughout the website. A statement of this policy will also be available on the website, with opportunity for students to give feedback to the Electronic Library Project Officer if they have difficulty accessing the service.

Ease of use is another crucial element of the VLS. In order to aid functionality, ease of use and maintenance, the website is partially database driven. Constructed in Access 2000, the database contains links to all the resources in the VLS. The majority of the pages are constructed dynamically from the database using SQL (Structured Query Language) queries within the HTML of each web page. In this way, resources can appear on several of the VLS web pages but only need to be maintained once in the database. The database design of the website also allows resources to be sorted in alphabetical order, by subject classification or even by resource type by the student, thus increasing the flexibility of the pages.

The enquiry service

As part of the preliminary version of the VLS, a fully operational academic enquiry service was launched in September 2001 (see Figure 4.5). In a physical library the enquiry desk is one of the busiest sections in the library. For remote users it is important that such a facility is also made available. For the VLS an experienced team of information and subject staff are on hand to answer questions from External Programme students, within two working days of receipt. Although this is a 'virtual' library service, it is important that students can choose how they prefer to communicate with the library, whether by e-mail, telephone, fax, letter or perhaps even face to face if possible. Questions received via the VLS will be recorded and analysed to determine such information as the subject matter of questions; what times the service is used; and which methods of communication are preferred. Such information can then feed into the future development of the enquiry service. It is anticipated that such developments will include an electronic help desk supplying answers to frequently asked questions (FAQs). It is intended that this will encourage confidence amongst students as they answer their own questions. As with many enquiry services, a significant number of enquiries will

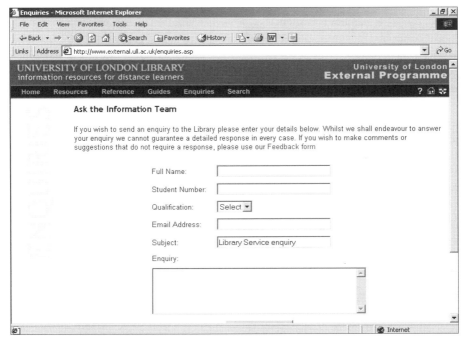

Fig. 4.5 The VLS enquiry form

need to be referred on to other parts of the university and beyond. To anticipate this, the Electronic Library Project Officer has developed a quick reference guide for information and subject staff so that they can efficiently refer queries.

Once appointed, the Electronic Library Projects Assistant will be the first point of contact for External Programme Library users. Having a main contact person for the VLS will help to reduce the isolation experienced by students who are studying at a distance from the main university campus. Staff contact details and areas of responsibility, usually including photographs, will be added to the VLS website to increase the personal tone of the service. Furthermore, in order to provide a dedicated service, a separate telephone number has been set up for enquiries from External Programme students. In the first instance queries will only be answered between 09.00 and 17.00 (Monday to Friday) London time. However, because of the range of time zones in which External Programme students are studying, a voice mailbox has been set up so that the library can receive telephone enquiries, as with e-mail, 24 hours a day, seven days a week. An assessment will then be carried out as to the best way of handling these.

Feedback and evaluation

Once the VLS has been launched, the user evaluation phase of the project can begin. A feedback form is already available on the VLS website (see Figure 4.5), which will be received directly by the Electronic Library Project Officer. Such feedback will be recorded and wherever appropriate used as a basis for service development. It is anticipated that more proactive methods of evaluation such as online and postal user surveys will be carried out once use of the VLS has reached a critical mass, in addition to carrying out regular analysis of website usage statistics. A VLS user group for staff of the university has already been set up to assist in targeting service developments. Initially this group, convened by the Electronic Library Project Officer, will interact via an electronic discussion list. However, face-to-face meetings will take place as appropriate. The agenda for these meetings could include debates about the integration of library resources into a Virtual Learning Environment or the validity of using e-books for academic study. The issues raised at such debates can again contribute to the development of the service.

Issues for the future

The model that has been described so far is for the prototype version of the VLS that has been available from September 2001. During the second year of the project an emphasis will be placed on establishing and acquiring resources for the remaining qualifications, including further developing the reference collection to reflect the needs of the international student community. The analysis and testing of various proxy servers for authenticating users will also be of high priority to ensure a seamless experience within the Virtual Campus. Furthermore, by assessing the information skills needs of the student community, and analysing the questions received via the enquiry service, we can continue to develop the Virtual Library, focusing on the needs of the users. One of the aims of the VLS project is to test the robustness and sustainability of such a model. Appropriate definitions of service will be created, including recommendations of how sustainability may be achieved. With the research-focused University of London, the ULL has anticipated the needs of postgraduate students and is leading a separately funded Virtual Research Environment Project on behalf of the University Libraries Committee to address these issues and feed into the overall virtual developments.

5

DEVELOPING A WORLDWIDE DISTRIBUTED RESOURCE TO FOSTER REGIONAL STUDIES

Linda McCann

Introduction

The new environments for the delivery of library services to remote users created by developments in information and communications technologies (ICTs) permit, and indeed call for, innovations in the content librarians provide. One way the University of Southern California (USC) in the USA supports the delivery of library and information resources, both to users in the library and to those who remotely access library resources, is through the creation of unique online distributed resources presented through the university website. An example of such a distributed resource is the *Los Angeles Comprehensive Bibliographic Database* (LACBD).

LACBD is a bibliographic database based on two print bibliographies that together constitute the most comprehensive and useful bibliographies for the study of the Los Angeles area to date. These bibliographies are consulted by researchers and students in many disciplines, particularly in humanities and social sciences, including history, American studies and ethnicity, urban and regional studies, geography, political science, and environmental studies. The new electronic edition of LACBD, distributed through the USC network via the world wide web, will be generally available to the USC community and internationally to anyone who has access to the web. This resource will be accessible 24 hours a day, seven days a week, to researchers, educators and students interested in the topic of Los Angeles and surrounding cities.

The first part of this paper discusses the university environment at the University of Southern California for distance and distributed learning and other university programmes building on resources related to the study of Los Angeles and Southern California. This part of the paper answers the question most frequently asked in the last two years: why was USC doing this? The second section provides a description of the design and development of the LACBD. The paper concludes with a discussion of general issues related to the design and development of this type of worldwide distributed resource and the lessons learned in the process.

USC environment for distance and distributed learning

USC is involved in a number of distance and distributed learning programmes. Distance education is described as:

> use of ICTs, ranging from mail to the internet, that enable students to complete courses or degree programs remotely, without necessarily being physically present at a particular time and place, such as in a classroom or on a college campus

and distributed learning as:

> use of ICTs in ways that enhance learning within the classroom, such as by permitting students to interact with an author at a distant location, or to use a simulation, or to extend the classroom, such as by allowing students to communicate with their instructor or fellow students outside class hours, such as by e-mail from their dormitory residence. (USC Academic Senate, 2000)

A distinction is made between distance education, which uses information and communication technologies to enhance the education of students participating away from the campus, and distributed learning, which is a programme augmenting traditional courses for locally resident students through ICTs using online media.

While each uses similar ICTs for different audiences, both require online resources to support educational goals. The LACBD supports both distance and distributed learning through the development of a new resource which is distributed over the web to support the teaching and research needs of university faculty and the learning needs of USC students regardless of geographic location. It also supports the research needs of the general scholarly community for the interdisciplinary study of Los Angeles and its environs.

USC programmes building on resources of Southern California and Los Angeles

In addition to supporting distance and distributed education programmes, the LACBD project specifically supports all four major educational initiatives outlined in the USC's 1994 Strategic Plan (USC, 1998):

- undergraduate education
- interdisciplinary research and education

- programmes building on the resources of Southern California and Los Angeles
- internationalization.

It ties in with the third initiative particularly, as well as accompanying strategic pathways in the fields of communications, the arts and the urban paradigm.

The initiative to develop new research and education programmes encourages university partnerships for teaching and research at local and regional levels and promotes opportunities for professional development for people in industries and professions. Southern California, especially the Los Angeles area, is viewed as a paradigm for the study of urbanism in the new century. This initiative is based on the conceptualization of Southern California and Los Angeles as a 'center of urban issues, multiculturalism, arts, entertainment, communications, and business' (USC, 1998, 7).

The LACBD project also supports another programme: the Provost's Urban Initiative on Information Technology, Society and Space (**www.usc.edu/schools/ sppd/research/urban_initiative/itGrant.htm**). The purpose of this is to promote interdisciplinary research on the indirect impacts of information and communications technology with the idea that Los Angeles is a region which 'is a prototype for the post-industrial city'. One of the ways this initiative encourages interdisciplinary research is by providing seed grants to support pilot studies, preliminary research and proposal development.

In addition, the LACBD supports a new graduate programme in American studies and ethnicity (**www.usc.edu/dept/LAS/pase/FRAMES/NONFRAMES/ nonframes.htm**). The programme is based in the humanities and the social sciences, as well as in several professional schools, such as cinema/TV, communication and law. One component of this programme focuses on California and the West.

The LACBD project is thus vitally involved in a number of the most important current institutional initiatives and emphases identified and supported by the Provost, the President and the Board of Trustees of USC.

LACBD project design
Goal and justification

The particular goal of the LACBD project is to bring together the two print bibliography volumes into one comprehensive electronic edition and expand the scope of the new electronic edition and companion thesaurus over a period of the next several years. The source documents are Nunis (1973) *Los Angeles and its environs in the twentieth century: a bibliography of a metropolis* and Rudd (1996) *Los Angeles and its environs in the twentieth century: a bibliography of a metropolis: 1970–1990.*

Collectively, these volumes contain approximately 15,000 citations of works on Los Angeles over a period of almost 100 years. Nunis is out of print and Rudd does not have a wide distribution in print. One benefit of the LACBD project is to bring these two volumes together in one electronic edition which will be easily and immediately available to anyone with access to the world wide web. It will also provide for easy and frequent updating as new material appears, as well as filling some gaps in subject coverage in the original editions. Another benefit is that the database for the expanded electronic edition will incorporate new subject and date coverage and new formats of materials.

Support

The project has been supported by Jerry Campbell, Chief Information Officer, USC Information Services Division, and by the Los Angeles City Historical Society. The first phase of the project received funding in the form of a grant from the USC Southern California Studies Center and the James Irvine Foundation (**www.usc.edu/dept/LAS/SC2/**). The Phase I test database deliverable was presented in May 2000. The second phase received funding from the Urban Initiative of the USC Office of the Provost through Lynn O'Leary-Archer, Associate Dean of Research and Resource Services, Information Services Division.

Programmatic conceptualization

The LACBD began as an innovative collaborative project in September 1999. Jerry Campbell asked the author to work on this as project director under Lynn Sipe, Director of Collection Resources in the Information Services Division, in collaboration with Philip J. Ethington, Associate Professor, Department of History at USC. Hynda L. Rudd, Division Chief, Los Angeles City Clerk Records Management Division also collaborated in the project.

Project staff met with representatives of the Los Angeles City Historical Society to develop a licensing agreement to allow USC to publish an electronic edition of the Rudd (1996). USC and the Los Angeles City Historical Society agreed a partnership to create an electronic version integrating this volume with Nunis (1973) and to create for the first time one document to be accessible through the world wide web.

Thesaurus conceptualization

Early in the conceptualization of the project, a need was recognized for a thesaurus and a way to fit this into the project as a whole. The problems of concatenating two print bibliographies (which included citations from journals, books and dissertations covering a period of 90 years) involved more than standardizing elements and devising a structure for the database design. The print bibliographies cover different periods of time, are organized differently, and have variations in citation formats. In addition, the index to each follows a different organizational scheme, and the use of terms has varied considerably over time.

Given how little text there was to search in each citation, it was important to include the index terms to facilitate searching. From an information retrieval perspective, however, the problem of inconsistencies in terminology would limit precision and comprehension in a database search. The creation of a controlled vocabulary for synonym control was therefore of particular interest. A research study by Raya Fidel demonstrated that synonym control using a Boolean 'or' is theoretically possible but not always practical during online searching (Fidel, 1992, 8). A thesaurus which could provide consistent points of access, with references to related terms and between different forms of terms to provide different points of access, appeared to be worth funding as part of the project.

Linda Rudell-Betts, an experienced professional lexicographer, was engaged to address this text retrieval problem, by formally conceptualizing and developing a new thesaurus, *The Comprehensive Bibliographic Database Thesaurus*, for USC. Funding was obtained to develop a three-part work as a companion resource for the LACBD compiled from index headings in the print bibliographies. Some terms were added from other vocabularies to collocate legacy terms. Because the thesaurus is specifically developed from these two bibliographies, not all terms and names relating to Los Angeles are present, though the current structure allows for future growth. The thesaurus was developed for versatility so that it could be used for browsing or as part of a subject search builder for a search interface. It is also a useful tool for the creation of metadata for digital resources relating to Los Angeles. User aids explaining the structure and format of the thesaurus, and lists of resources providing online standard sources consulted in its construction, are part of the documentation on the web (**www.usc.edu/isd/archives/arc/lacbd/about/ index.html**).

The thesaurus provides search and index terms for LACBD which can also be used for multi-database searching of additional Los Angeles-related digital collections at USC as these become available. The thesaurus now consists of the following:

• LACBD Subject Thesaurus, Version I
• LACBD Personal Names Authority List, Version I
• Geographic Names Thesaurus, Version I.

The thesaurus is published and accessible on the university website through the Archival Research Center at (**www.usc.edu/isd/archives/arc/lacbd/subject/index. html**).

USC owns the intellectual property rights to the LACBD thesaurus through registration of this as an original work with the United States Copyright Office.

Project development

Coverage

The coverage of the print bibliographies is from 1900 to 1990. The citations are primarily to books, academic theses and journal articles, but exclude newspaper reports. The LACBD intends to incorporate recent publications for primary and secondary source materials. The database in its current form is searchable by author, title, format and keyword.

Scope

The current scope is limited to the 20th century, and Los Angeles and surrounding cities. Dependent on available funds, plans are in place to expand geographical coverage to include the five-county Southern California area and date coverage to include the 19th century and earlier, as well as the 21st century. Additional contributions from editorial consultants will be solicited.

Timeline

The first task was that of converting both bibliographies into electronic format. The 1973 print bibliography was scanned and converted to a text-readable format by an outside vendor using OmniPage software for optical character recognition. The second task was to determine a methodology which would bring together the organizational schemes of the two bibliographies and merge the texts into one compatible scheme.

The third task was to work with USC programmers to design database fields and a web interface for the bibliographic database based on the new organizational scheme. The fourth task involved developing with programmers a method for tagging the electronic text of the print bibliographies for entry of records into the LACBD test database. Two graduate students in the USC History Department and one librarian worked on this task for the first phase, and the project director continued this work during the second phase. Throughout this period she also performed the editorial tasks of review and error correction of files. The thesaurus for LACBD based on the indexes of the two print bibliographies was developed at the same time as the database.

Future plans

The editorial board has responsibility for determining new directions and priorities. These currently include adding new material formats, including electronic publications and materials which may not be catalogued or appear in other bibliographic resources. It would also be desirable to create linkages to electronic versions of primary documents and images and other relevant materials. Another goal is to provide links to holdings information. At this time there are few references to materials in languages other than English. This is another dimension where the scope of the LACBD could be expanded.

The LACBD resource could also be linked to course web pages on the study of the Los Angeles region, include links to online reference research assistance, and provide for user feedback.

Ultimately the current model of collaboration between ISD and USC faculty and the Los Angeles City Historical Society could be expanded to include collaboration with external contributing researchers as consulting editors. This would enhance the building of a dynamic distributed interdisciplinary bibliographic database representing all research on Los Angeles and its environs as the urban paradigm of the 21st century.

The thesaurus is also projected to develop as a richer data set through the addition of controlled terms to correspond with database growth, and the augmentation of the thesaurus with new subject areas. Of particular interest would be the possibility of a new conceptual hierarchy that is place-oriented as well as classified to set place terms in a new geo-spatial context which could facilitate integration of all USC Archival Research Center projects. If funding is available, LACBD could explore as a possible direction for the future the co-ordination of LACBD geographic place names with Geographic Information System (GIS) elements carrying geo-coding information which could be used with a GIS searching system.

The thesaurus now represents a new knowledge domain and can eventually be expanded to include related knowledge domains resulting from linkages to other Los Angeles-related digital projects.

Discussion

The following are general issues identified and lessons learned from the LACBD project relevant to the collaborative development of distributed resources.

Design

Design of an online database, elements and structure, as well as a user interface, can benefit from the different perspectives presented by teams including librarians, programmers, interface designers, library system designers, faculty and other consultants involved in the creation of the final product, integrating databases to facilitate seamless searching for the user. Distributed resources are not created by one person working alone.

Project direction

The role of project director for this type of project includes working closely with general editors to conceptualize the project design and direction, as well as the more narrow role of managing project implementation. Project direction also means serving as a primary resource during all phases of the project. This can include a range of responsibilities, including participating in discussions on licensing and consulting with legal counsel on copyright issues, determining realistic project goals and timelines, general management responsibilities, and answering questions related to the project, as well as broader subject-oriented reference questions on research strategies.

Librarians would seem to be ideally suited for such roles in the development of library resources to support distance and distributed learning as well as traditional educational environments. Most valuable for me over the past two years were courses in database design, online searching and principles of information, which I completed at UCLA for my Masters in Library Science. Professional involvement in associations such as the American Society for Information Science and Technology kept me current on issues related to information studies and related topics. Professional experience as an information consultant in public and private organizations working on information and records management projects, and as a reference librarian at USC, also helped me gain a broad perspective on the issues that were important for this project. The most important role for me as a project director has been understanding the many perspectives and points of view that are presented when working with a team of experts, whose expertise lie in quite different areas, to design a resource like LACBD, which is expected to be used by many types of users.

Communication

Communication is high priority for the development of an authoritative and unique resource such as LACBD. A collaborative bibliographic database project such as this, particularly one involving parties within and outside the organization, needs editorial review for consistency and authority. Communication is also required for ongoing development once the project is publicly available. Communication can provide unique opportunities for ongoing contributions by end-users, who may be remote from USC. The task of providing new content can be distributed to subject experts, but then close and constant editorial review becomes even more important.

Intellectual property

Considerations of intellectual property must be worked out before a new resource becomes publicly available. USC and the Los Angeles Historical Society entered into a licensing agreement to publish electronically the one print bibliography which was not in the public domain. Licensing conditions may have implications for database design. In addition, when developing a completely new resource such as the LACBD thesaurus – one which represents a new domain of knowledge – consideration must be given to the rights of the author and the owner of the work. It is especially important, given the ease with which digital resources can be copied, that copyright issues are worked out *before* the resource is published. When creating an original resource, copyright issues involve more than just acquiring the right to use published works, and may involve considerations of protection of materials created during the course of the project.

Information retrieval and standards

Information retrieval issues, and standards for content and distribution of content, need to be considered. It is particularly important to remember that text retrieval in a networked environment presents a particular set of problems, especially in an international multilingual context. New developments in information and communication technologies include graphical displays of full-text and image content. Search engines can build on metadata and controlled vocabulary to improve the retrieval of content, both text and multimedia, for online distributed resources. Issues such as multiple languages, name authority, consistent linking to related resources, and standards for metadata and citation format are all-important considerations for future development of distributed resources.

Remote users

In doing this project I myself was engaged in a form of distance learning. This past year, I worked remotely as project director from Cambridge, Massachusetts, more than 3000 miles (or 4800 km) away from USC in Los Angeles, California. My most valuable lessons as a virtual project director were those I learned as a remote user. Heuristics of knowledge management in organizations stress the importance of being present to keep up with changing organizational structures and overall political climate. However important this may be at the present time, if institutions are going to aspire to build true virtual learning environments, this will have to change. Technology issues relating to ICTs in a networked environment, and content issues relating to distributed library resources and services to support distance and distributed learning, are undeniably important in the creation of virtual learning environments. However, my recent experience in the virtual world indicates that issues of communication are equally important. Real collaborative efforts require open and effective communication. We are all learners in virtual learning environments.

Acknowledgements

While the project depends on the collaborative efforts of all involved, the contributions of Lynn Sipe, Philip J. Ethington and Linda Rudell-Betts have been especially crucial to development of the LACBD and the LACBD thesaurus. Other contributors to the development of the first two phases of this project have been Eileen Flick, April Lundsten, Dennis Smith, Nava Herman and Chris Sterback. Of special importance to me was the mentoring provided by Lynn Sipe.

References

Fidel, R. (1992) Who needs controlled vocabulary?, *Special Libraries*, (winter), 8.

Nunis, D. B., Jr (ed.) (1973) *Los Angeles and its environs in the twentieth century: a bibliography of a metropolis*, Ward Ritchie Press.

Rudd, H. L. (ed.) (1996) *Los Angeles and its environs in the twentieth century: a bibliography of a metropolis: 1970–1990* (with a directory of resources in Los Angeles County), Los Angeles City Historical Society.

USC (1998) *Four-year report on the 1994 Strategic Plan*, available at **www.usc.edu/admin/provost/strategicplan/98plan.html**

USC Academic Senate (2000) Resolution: 00/01-01, 9/20/2000, Notes 1, 3–4, available at **www.usc.edu/academe/acsen/about_senate/resolutions/res000101.html**

6

INSPIRAL. DIGITAL LIBRARY SERVICES AND ONLINE LEARNING ENVIRONMENTS: ISSUES FOR INTEGRATION

Sarah Currier

Introduction

INSPIRAL (INveStigating Portals for Information Resources And Learning, **http://inspiral.cdlr.strath.ac.uk/**) is a six-month study funded by the UK's Joint Information Systems Committee (JISC) of the Higher Education Funding Councils. INSPIRAL's remit is to discover and analyse the non-technical challenges involved in linking virtual and managed learning environments (VLEs and MLEs) with digital and hybrid libraries. The needs of the UK learner in higher education (HE) are the focus, with an eye to UK further education (FE) and international developments. The aim of INSPIRAL is to inform JISC's future strategy and funding of initiatives in this area. It is intended that the research process itself will benefit stakeholders by facilitating networking, discussion and co-operation. The project was funded from 1 May to 31 October 2001, based at the University of Strathclyde's Centre for Digital Library Research (CDLR, **http://cdlr.strath.ac.uk/**) and Centre for Educational Systems (CES, **www.strath.ac.uk/ces/**).

JISC is also currently funding the ANGEL (Authenticated Networked Guided Environment for Learning) project to develop software to enable the integration of learning environments and digital library resources (**www.angel.ac.uk/**). ANGEL is a two-year project finishing on 31 March 2003.

At the time of writing, INSPIRAL has just passed the four-month mark. The initial stakeholder consultation phase, designed to capture the relevant issues, has largely been completed. This paper presents the issues raised and discussed in this process, and outlines the succeeding phase of the project, involving analysis and prioritization of the issues, recommendations to JISC, and reporting back to the stakeholder communities.

Background to INSPIRAL: a convergence of evolution

VLEs/MLEs and digital/hybrid libraries represent two of the most important recent developments in e-learning. Their evolution in the UK has thus far proceeded along largely separate paths. Librarians have concentrated on meeting the information needs of their users in the new electronic environment, while educators have been finding innovative ways of using technology to enhance learning in response to new understandings of how and why people learn, and to the expectations of an increasingly busy and information-saturated society. Educational bodies are now beginning to look at ways to integrate these learning tools for the benefit of the learners. A fully integrated online learning experience is the dream – what are the barriers, and are there solutions?

Research methodology

INSPIRAL is a qualitative study, designed to advise JISC on the next phase of planning and funding online learning initiatives. The methodology involves:

- an initial issue-capture phase, including:
  — consulting key stakeholders
  — conducting a literature review
  — identifying appropriate case studies
  — researching issues outside the UK
- followed by an analysis phase, involving:
  — analysing results of stakeholder consultation and literature review
  — undertaking case studies
  — holding further stakeholder consultation, with an emphasis on analysing and prioritizing issues
  — identifying exemplars of best practice.

The results of the INSPIRAL study will be ultimately disseminated via the INSPIRAL final report.

Stakeholders

Learners

The most important stakeholder is the learner. For the purposes of INSPIRAL, only learners who have participated in (but not necessarily completed) online modules or courses are being consulted, on account of the time and resource restrictions on INSPIRAL. However, the issue of non-uptake of online learning resources, by both learners and teachers, has been flagged as an area requiring further study.

Educational staff

Those who work directly with learners in providing their education are also important, both for their own experiences and perspectives, and for their 'coal-face' experience of learners' needs. INSPIRAL is focusing mainly on those who work in HE, but is also, where possible, welcoming input from FE, given that many important developments in learning environments are taking place in FE. The stakeholder groups within education may be divided into distinct 'tribes' as follows:

- library and information resource provision staff
- academics and other teachers
- research staff
- administrative staff
- systems support staff
- staff developers and educational developers
- institutional managers
- educational funding body managers
- staff of e-learning projects and services.

In addition, there is a newer grouping which includes people with backgrounds in any or several of the aforementioned, who may be termed 'learning technology specialists'.

Commercial organizations

A more peripheral stakeholder group to INSPIRAL's immediate remit is the commercial providers of online content and systems. Representatives of three content providers, one MLE system developer/vendor and one library management system vendor, have taken an active part in the stakeholder consultation so far.

Stakeholder consultation
Interviews

The initial issue capture phase of INSPIRAL's research took the form of stakeholder interviews. Semi-structured interview plans were developed for each of the three main stakeholder groups listed above. The plans all followed the same basic format, covering six main areas:

- the interviewee's present occupation, project or course
- any relevant prior posts or courses undertaken

- current or planned involvement in any linkage between digital libraries and VLEs/MLEs
- what they saw as potential benefits and drawbacks to VLE/digital library linkage
- what their vision for the future was with regard to digital library/VLE linkage
- what they believed the barriers were to achieving that vision.

Nineteen individuals were interviewed. Eight interviews were conducted face-to-face; five were conducted over the telephone; and the remaining four were carried out by sending the interviewee the relevant interview plan to fill out as a questionnaire. In view of the emphasis on institutional problems, the interviews were confidential, which encouraged some very candid responses. For the most part, the interviews were not transcribed verbatim, although certain pithy quotes were noted word for word.

All those interviewed had experience with a number of roles utilizing learning technologies, including library technologies. Most interviewees fell into more than one occupational category, exemplifying the evolution and complex inter-relationships of e-learning roles in education today. This made a simple analysis based on respondent occupation very difficult. The interview summary report (Currier, 2001) was therefore a general overview of stakeholder opinions and experience, which drew no definitive conclusions about types of stakeholders.

Only two learners were interviewed. After the first interview, it was clear that the use of individual interviews would not be the most efficacious method of establishing learner needs. As there are few learners in the UK who have actually used a VLE with integrated library resources or services, it was difficult for the respondent to imagine potential scenarios, so it was left to the interviewer to give examples of what might be offered via a VLE. In the end, this amounted to 'leading the witness'. It was decided, therefore, that learner focus groups, where participants could be introduced to the relevant ideas in a more structured way, would be a better way to gain an understanding of learners' needs. Because of the timing of INSPIRAL in relation to student availability, these focus groups are to be held late in the project.

Community forums

Two half-day stakeholder forums were held in Glasgow and London. Both involved mainly HE-based participants. They included predominantly librarians and information scientists, with a smattering of IT and learning technology specialists, academics and commercial representatives.

The first forum was designed to elicit similar information to the interviews, while the second forum built somewhat on the outcome of the first.

First forum

The Forum (Brown, 2001) began with an introduction to INSPIRAL and a brief summary of issues raised in the stakeholder consultation so far. Participants discussed relevant experiences from their own institutions. A breakout session followed, where participants were asked to come back with a wider vision for the integration of learning environments and digital libraries. This led to a general discussion of potential problems and barriers. To close, in order to begin eliciting priorities, participants were asked: 'If you had a magic wand which could solve one of the problems discussed, which would it be?'

Second forum

Participants at the second forum (Currier and Brown, 2001a) were asked to read the report from the first forum in preparation, in order that the discussion could be moved along another stage. A brief presentation of interim findings was made, incorporating results of the first forum, interviews to date, and online discussion from the INSPIRAL discussion list (**www.jiscmail.ac.uk/lists/inspiral.html**). Breakout groups were asked to take these issues and prioritize them from the perspective of their own work. This was followed by a general discussion aiming to prioritize the issues for JISC's future strategy.

Workshops

At the time of writing, a one-day INSPIRAL workshop (Currier and Brown, 2001b) has been held in Leicester. This event was the first part of the analysis phase of INSPIRAL. Participants were asked to read the forum reports, the stakeholder interview report, and the interim findings document in preparation. An up-to-date presentation on INSPIRAL's findings so far was supplemented by the following presentations:

1 A formative evaluation of ANGEL by Nicole Harris (2001b). This presentation offered results from a similar stakeholder consultation carried out at the beginning of the ANGEL project (Harris, 2001a).
2 *Management and implementation of virtual learning environments within universities and colleges: a UCISA funded study* by Martin Jenkins (2001). The results of this study showed recent trends in the implementation of VLEs, with an organizational slant.
3 *Virtuous learning environments: how to make library systems and VLEs interoperate* by John MacColl (2001). A vision for the future of linked VLEs and digital libraries was given by an expert with wide experience and knowledge in the field.

Present problems were highlighted, with examples. More information about the ANGEL project was included.

Two breakout sessions were held. At the first, groups were asked to decide on the two most important issues, with an eye to future JISC strategy and funding. In preparation for the second breakout session, the 'magic wand' question from the first INSPIRAL forum was repeated. The results were collated and divided into three groups of three issues each. The breakout groups were then assigned three issues to discuss, and asked to come back with two practical solutions for each. A final general discussion followed, drawing out the priority areas for JISC.

Consultation results
The vision

The following key points include some of the concepts and caveats expressed, usually by the more experienced e-learning experts (although no one seriously disagreed with any of these ideas).

Seamless, one-stop access

This includes seamlessness between the learning environment and the library environment at any point in the VLE/MLE, and seamlessness within one user's portal across different courses, departments or even institutions.

Some warning notes were sounded, including the problems of interoperability of search vocabularies across subject areas, and the fact that experienced users may sometimes not mind coming out and going into several databases if they know how to search on them.

All library functions online

These should include a reference enquiry service; interlibrary loans; checking user records; paying fines; accessing all the catalogues and databases available through the library; online versions of required reading packs such as those offered by the HERON project (**www.heron.ac.uk/**).

Concerns about this included the potential diminishment of the serendipitous browsing function of physical libraries, and their social function as a place to meet fellow students and discuss sources of information, etc.

Individualized for the students

This included ideas such as: the student portal, which could cross institutions and be available throughout a learner's life; the Amazon idea of tailoring resources and notifying the user about relevant resources; settings for 'level' such as undergraduate, third-year, etc., with options to adjust upwards if the user wishes.

Some stakeholders felt this could be taken too far, that not all students want or need this much hand-holding, and that some, particularly the technically proficient or information literate, might even find it restrictive.

Flexible for the teachers

Teachers would like to be able to adapt or update courses easily, and the information resources available for the courses, from anywhere. Flexibility in terms of being able to embed their own pedagogical approach, rather than having it dictated by the system, was seen as extremely important, and vital for bringing academics on board with VLEs and MLEs.

Some teachers may find this too time-consuming, and prefer the kind of VLE system that is an easy-to-use but difficult-to-tinker-with template.

Universally accessible

The Holy Grail: accessible to all those with different physical abilities; adaptable to differing learning styles; available on and off-campus (an issue with regard to certain subscription library materials); useable on any platform or hardware.

The barriers

A vocal minority of stakeholders expressed the view that 'technical issues are not the most significant barriers', making the point that, if we could solve the organizational problems which exist at every level, we could easily train our ingenuity on the technology and move forward. The barriers which were identified throughout the INSPIRAL stakeholder consultation fall into the following areas, each of which leads into the next:

Resource issues

There is a need for coherent vision and adequate resources from a high level, responsive to the demands and needs of the learners and the coal-face expertise of educational staff. This is a common problem in HE, but it is exacerbated in this area because these e-learning developments demand the collaboration of disparate groups, with different priorities and viewpoints.

Top management needs to understand that developments in e-learning are *not* cost-savers, and may require additional resources to be implemented effectively. However, there was wide agreement that the considerable benefits, if properly presented, should make this palatable.

The question of who controls the resources is also significant. Once again, the overlap of interests within and between institutions (e.g. between library services and academics) requires strong, responsive leadership from above.

There was considerable feeling that too many projects are funded, and not enough services, particularly amongst enterprises which should be services, incorporating long-term strategic thinking and stability of staffing and other resources.

Institutional infrastructure and politics

The nature of the proposed integration requires collaboration, co-operation, mutual understanding and sharing of resources. The traditional culture within HE was seen by many to be inimical to this, constituting a serious barrier to efficacious implementation in many institutions. The same barriers exist at the level of HE and FE funding bodies, professional associations and government. This ties into the previous issue of resourcing, but some other points include:

- competition and territorialism
- resistance to change in general
- resistance to new technologies
- fear of changing and evolving professional roles
- inter-professional difficulties, particularly between libraries, academia and systems (there are cultural barriers, mutual misperceptions, and differences in priorities and visions)
- incentives: a research culture where teaching skills and developments are not rewarded, and support staff such as librarians are not accorded equal status with their academic colleagues, even when they teach.

Staff development issues

Staff development could be seen to come under either of the first two headings, but has its own important issues. It was raised as an absolutely necessary part of the success of any new venture in education. Points raised included:

1 Support and training for staff needs to be ongoing, and means more than just teaching them to use the technology.
2 Pedagogical issues need to be incorporated, to ensure the academic validity of teaching and using information online.
3 Staff development must be applied to all staff, not just the teachers.
4 Some kind of incentive must be offered, such as accreditation.

Teaching and learning issues

Time and again, concerns over the potential for spoon-feeding students information versus overwhelming them with information overload were raised. The traditional role of the library and librarian in teaching information literacy skills must not be lost in the rush to a complete online experience. In fact, many stakeholders said that online learning must be an enrichment tool, not a replacement for campus-based learning. However, as others pointed out, distance learners must be supported in equivalent ways to students in classrooms. If universities want to increase their student numbers through distance learning, avoiding the need for more physical space, they have a duty to ensure that those learners are not disadvantaged.

The issues of differing learning styles and preferred modes of learning were also raised.

Content issues

The development and availability of high-quality content was of concern to some teachers, who felt that what is presently available is off-putting to teachers. There was also some discussion around how much time and effort teachers should spend developing their own content, versus commercial production of content and the attendant access and quality issues. 'Who judges content to be worthy?' is an important question, particularly in an environment where it is very easy for anyone to post anything on a web page.

The sharing of content was put forward as an ideal, with its own problems.

Access issues

Authentication, IPR and copyright, privacy, and plagiarism were all common concerns. These are being investigated in various JISC projects and studies.

Ways forward for JISC

Many of the issues raised with INSPIRAL are probably out of the realm of JISC's influence, being either institutional responsibilities or wider cultural problems. However, many stakeholders took the opportunity of this pre-funding consultation to suggest ways in which JISC may be able to influence both institutions and the culture. A number of the themes arose at this stage in INSPIRAL's study:

Provision of information and guidance

Suggestions for potential roles for JISC in providing information and guidelines included:

- national standards for VLE/library integration
- price guides and real cost surveys for implementation (including the cost implications of training, hardware resources, etc.)
- guides to specific VLE/MLE and library systems (so that users are not reliant on company information)
- advice, case studies and best-practice guidelines on such issues as staff development and training, raising awareness of IPR/copyright issues, user support and training, use of particular software and packages
- collaboration within and between institutions
- information on changing roles and what skills are needed
- collation and presentation of prior research.

Facilitating collaboration and forming consortia

JISC's roles in encouraging collaboration, in the forming of consortia for bargaining with commercial organizations, and in promoting general cultural change within education, were also raised and discussed at INSPIRAL events. The benefits of FE/HE sharing and collaboration were seen as very important. FE participants also raised issues of social inclusion and working with public libraries.

Further research

Questions for further study by JISC which were raised included:

1 Who is using VLEs/MLEs, what VLEs/MLEs are they using, and why?
2 What do the learners themselves want and need in terms of VLE-library integration?

3 What are the visions that librarians have for VLEs/MLEs? Collating this type of research may encourage institutions to work more closely with librarians.

Final report

At the time of writing, INSPIRAL's major deliverable, the final report, is due to be presented to JISC in late October 2001. The significant content of the report will include:

- an analysis of the needs of the learner with respect to VLEs/MLEs and digital libraries
- a summary of critical issues, detailing related problems, methods and solutions practised elsewhere
- a prioritization of key issues from the point of view of the UK HE learner
- recommendations of priority areas for future study and strategic investment.

References

Brown, S. (2001) *Report from the first INSPIRAL forum, held at the University of Strathclyde, Glasgow, June 12, 2001*, available at
http://inspiral.cdlr.strath.ac.uk/documents/forumrep1.html

Currier, S. (2001) *INSPIRAL stakeholder consultation: stakeholder interviews summary report*, available at
http://inspiral.cdlr.strath.ac.uk/documents/interviewsumm.pdf

Currier, S. and Brown, S. (2001a) *Report from the 2nd INSPIRAL forum, held at Parsifal College, Open University, London, July 10, 2001*, available at
http://inspiral.cdlr.strath.ac.uk/documents/forumrep2.html

Currier, S. and Brown, S. (2001b) *Report from the 1st INSPIRAL workshop, held at the Kimberlin Library, De Montfort University, Leicester, August 21, 2001*, available at
http://inspiral.cdlr.strath.ac.uk/documents/workshopleicester.pdf

Harris, N. (2001a) ANGEL: *Authenticated Networked Guided Environment for Learning: workpackage 2: final report: initial formative evaluation*, available at
www.angel.ac.uk/public-files/WP2_final.pdf

Harris, N. (2001b) *The ANGEL project initial formative evaluation INSPIRAL workshop presentation, 21 August 2001*, available at
www.angel.ac.uk/public-files/inspiral 210801.ppb

Jenkins, M. (2001) *Management and implementation of virtual learning environments within universities and colleges: a UCISA funded survey*, available at
www.ucisa.ac.uk/SG/events-papers/mle-vle/jenkins.ppt

MacColl, J. (2001) *Virtuous learning environments: how to make library systems and VLEs interoperate*, available at
www.sellic.ac.uk/publicat/staffpub/inspiral.ppt

7

TAKE US WITH YOU!: DELIVERING LIBRARY RESOURCES AND SERVICES TO USERS IN THE FIELD

Jo Kibbee and Lynn Wiley

Introduction

Libraries Without Walls is a clever catchphrase for the idea that libraries are no longer bound to their buildings. But, since walls likewise represent barriers, the phrase can also refer to a library free of obstacles that impede its use. This paper addresses both meanings: providing resources and services beyond the library's physical walls, and ensuring that off-campus users can readily take advantage of them. The focus is on users who are currently affiliated with the university but who study or conduct research away from the physical campus. Unlike readers in established distance learning programmes, they do not necessarily have formal ties to library support services. And although they may have significant library needs, they may be unaware of available resources or unable to access them easily. To address this dilemma, we propose an outreach initiative that we are calling *Take us with you!* This project, currently in development at the University of Illinois at Urbana–Champaign (UIUC), strives to ensure that our users can take the library with them whether they are working across town or across the ocean.

This paper describes the issues surrounding effective remote access, and details our efforts at putting together a program which replicates the services provided through formal distance learning programs. We believe the resulting initiative will reduce existing barriers – walls, if you will – to the use of the 'library without walls'.

Statement of the problem

Seamless access is increasingly available to students enrolled in open or distance learning programmes. The Open University (**www.open.ac.uk/**), for example, provides a well-organized suite of resources and services for its readers. Students in these programmes know what services are available, how to begin, and where to go for help. Our own university provides library services for students and faculty in distance education courses offered through the Division of Academic

Outreach (**www.outreach.uiuc.edu/aolibrary/**). A significant portion of off-campus users in academic libraries, however, are not part of a formal distance education programme. Fieldwork, doctoral research, study abroad, exchange programmes, internships, sabbatical leaves and other endeavours take many of our clientele off-campus. These users rarely benefit from the type of umbrella services provided to formal distance education readers. Although these distance users typically can gain access to their home library's network from an internet provider, a host of problems can impede their use of the library. Lack of awareness of available resources and services, technical concerns such as database authentication, and a host of other problems often mean that faculty and students leave the library behind when they leave the campus.

To get an idea of remote users' library needs, the barriers they face, and potential solutions, we met with a focus group from the University's International Programs and Studies (IPS) Office (**www.ips.uiuc.edu/**). IPS study-abroad programmes, postgraduate research fellowships, and international collaborations (e.g. partnerships with the Centre National de Recherche Scientifique), among others, represent potential stakeholders for distance services. At our meeting it became clear that many of the constituents are not aware of the range of digital resources and services currently available to them. It also became clear that knowing about resources and actually being able to use them are separate issues. Availability of properly configured computer equipment, network connections, authentication and a host of other challenges must be met in order for the library without walls to become a reality for many of our distance users.

Though the solution to some of these problems (e.g. robust telecommunications infrastructure) lies outside the library's scope, nonetheless the library bears responsibility for maximizing the use of existing resources and minimizing technical barriers. To this end, we applied for an internal grant to develop an outreach programme called *Take us with you!* Through this effort, we hope to not only raise awareness of distance resources and services but also to facilitate their use. Before we detail the specifics of the programme, however, let us take a closer look at these twin challenges of informing readers about available resources and services, and ensuring that they are accessible.

Awareness of resources and services

Though UIUC's Library Gateway (**www.library.uiuc.edu**) serves as a portal to a wide variety of digital resources and services, like other libraries we struggle to clearly present all that we have to offer. The library invests heavily in digital resources, but on-site and distance readers alike are not always aware of what is available. The lack of integration between the various online products (e.g. the library catalogue and commercial bibliographic databases) presents the biggest challenge to resource discovery. At the time of writing, only a fraction of the e-resources to which we subscribe are linked from our online catalogue (e.g. individual titles from *Early English Books* online are not represented), and we construct independent portals to link to useful websites such as *The Electronic Reference Collection* (**www.library.uiuc.edu/rex/erefs/**). Article indexes do not necessarily link to the full text of e-journals to which we subscribe, nor are individual journal titles in serial aggregator packages represented in the online catalogue. The result is that whether on- or off-campus, users are not aware of the wealth of digital resources available at their desktop. Without a print collection to fall back on, the lack of integration works particularly to the disadvantage of distance users. The problem is not unique to our library, as evidenced by the growing attention in the profession to the future of the online catalogue, web portals, and issues in the cataloguing of e-resources. The Library of Congress recently held a Bicentennial Conference on Bibliographic Control for the New Millennium (**www.loc.gov/catdir/bibcontrol/**), in which these concerns were raised. Until a solution evolves, however, libraries must organize these resources and target them to users as best they can. Typically this means developing library websites to provide visibility to otherwise hidden digital resources.

As our meeting with International Programs and Studies illustrated, our users are likewise unaware of the variety of remote services the UIUC Library already offers. Some of these are described below.

Electronic document delivery of scanned items (excluding books) from UIUC's print collection

In an effort to extend use of our substantial print collection, our library developed a service called *UIUCDocExpress* (**www.library.uiuc.edu/irrc/feephoto.htm**), through which articles, chapters, reports and other documents in the collection are scanned, converted to PDF, and posted to a website for retrieval by a user. A state-ment about copyright restrictions accompanies the image file. Thus, if an electronic version of an article or document does not exist, we can make one available. In this way, distance users can continue to make use of materials (with the exception of whole books) from our print collection. The service is currently fee-based: the equivalent of £1.35 sterling for faculty and £2.25 sterling for students.

Electronic document delivery of articles requested through interlibrary loan

Users can request articles from journals not held in our collection by filling out a form on our interlibrary loan website (**www.library.uiuc.edu/irrc/borrow.htm**). There is no charge to the user for this service. As with the *UIUCDocExpress* service, articles received are converted to PDF and posted to the ILL central server for the user to view.

Electronic reserves

Scanning technology is also used to mount reserve readings for classes. Since our library already owns most of this material, it is not subject to copyright fees. Materials not owned are scanned under fair use guidelines and the library pays any appropriate permission fees. Students can then access these materials through our online catalogue. Study-abroad programmes, in which students live in another country but take classes with a University of Illinois professor, are a potential market for this service.

Digital reference service

We strive to extend information services to users who are not in the library building. As in many libraries, we provide the option of asking reference questions via e-mail (usually with 24-hour turnaround) or through a real-time reference service, whereby they can 'ask a librarian' directly via their computer, during the hours the library is open (see **www.library.uiuc.edu/ugl/vr/**).

Conclusion

Though these services are all available from our Library Gateway, our meeting with the focus group revealed that potential constituents are largely unaware that they exist. We speculate that this is a result of poor web design and insufficient promotion and marketing, which we need to address. The other side of the coin, however, is being able to access them from off-campus.

Technical considerations

It is one thing to come into a library and use its resources on site: staff members are on hand to guide users through their research process and are using standard equipment and familiar network configurations for electronic resources and services. It is quite another thing to access these remotely, particularly from a foreign country. Remote users, of which UIUC has many, must not only know to enquire about library resources, they must be equipped – literally – in order to connect to and obtain the required material. All the digitized resources available at our library are inaccessible to users unable to connect to the campus network. We must be able to facilitate access for these users and must therefore be prepared to troubleshoot technological issues. These issues include:

- how the user is connecting
- capabilities of the computer being used
- software utilized for web browsing or document downloading (including the specific version)
- output desired by the user
- authentication processes: required to access restricted services or to enforce publishers' licensing agreements, but which can shut out valid users.

Trying to understand the users' technical problems and give instruction in their resolution can be frustrating because library staff do not necessarily have the requisite tools, training or information. We also recognize that our programme will heighten awareness, and therefore use, of the UIUC collections and services for the travelling researcher. More users will be encouraged to try to access from remote areas, but they will possess a wide range of computer skills, from those who have never dialled into the campus network to the researcher who never leaves home without a loaded laptop. We knew to plan for a larger volume of users with a wider range of problems, due not only to inexperience but also to changes in the users' environments as equipment and connection varies from country to country, and from provider to provider. Our *Take us with you!* programme will attempt to anticipate as many problems as possible, arm users with the information they need before they depart, and then lay a framework to resolve situations as they occur. To do this effectively requires help from the experts.

At UIUC, the Computing and Communications Services Office (CCSO) is the unit that supports the computer use of the faculty, staff, and students on- and off-campus. We met with CCSO staff to develop a partnership designed to address the needs of the off-campus library users. We outlined our programme goals, in particular our need to maximize successful electronic access. We reviewed the ideal situation, in which every user leaves campus fully prepared for any problem in the field. But we recognized that we could not reach all users who need remote access nor will those we do reach be able to anticipate their research needs. So we also planned for options to help the users at the point of need. CCSO staff offered assistance in reviewing the technological help offered in our web pages and our guides dealing with equipment setup. CCSO staff also talked about concerns we had not been aware of, such as commercial internet providers which are not recognized by our campus network. Overseas users contracting with those services could be denied access.

We settled on a two-pronged approach: tips for preplanning and an FAQ list to help troubleshoot problems as they occur. We set up and advertised an e-mail address to be used to communicate problems encountered when users attempt to use the library resources. The e-mail address is **offcampus@library.uiuc.edu**, and is prominently displayed on the *Take us with you!* website and literature. Staff are assigned to monitor the messages, resolve problems and communicate solutions to the users, and to utilize CCSO staff when advisable.

The tips for planning ahead were kept fairly concise since users may consult with CCSO prior to their departure on anything they are not sure of. These user tips are provided below and are grouped by general category:

Equipment – computers and printers

- minimum speed: 100MHz with at least 32Kb of internal memory – older computers should be checked
- printer (optional) must be laser or inkjet, capable of printing at 300dpi
- modem if dialling up to a local network should be capable of transmitting at 56K
- when travelling with a laptop, carry (or make sure that there is access to) the electrical adapters and network cables that will work at the host site.

Software that must be installed and their download sites

- an internet browser, either Netscape version 4.0+ or Microsoft Internet Explorer version 4.0+
- Adobe Acrobat version 4.06+ in order to obtain full-text documents online
- telecommunications software may be required to dial into a network.

Internet connectivity

Faculty and students travelling overseas will have different experiences when making a connection through the internet, depending on their country, host or temporary internet provider. Sometimes the host site will provide all the necessary connections and instructions. Our experience, however, indicates that a majority are on their own when it comes to the network provider.

They may connect via:

- a host network such as a university or research institute
- a commercial provider such as aol.com
- a cybercafe, where users buy temporary access.

The types of access may include:

- a DSL (Digital Subscriber Line) service
- a broadband service such as one of those offered by commercial telecommunications services like AT&T
- a dial-up service (should be used at 56K in order to download documents effectively and requires telecommunications software).

There are many internet providers worldwide. They use a variety of networks and have unfamiliar interfaces with unpredictable results for the users. Campus computing at UIUC is exploring devices to make this more consistent with software such as the VPN or Virtual Private Networks. Virtual Private Networks can be set up so as to emulate the home network environment, giving the users familiar applications and trouble-free secure access to home. This could be an ideal solution combined with referrals to valid network providers worldwide.

Authentication

1 Memorize the NetID and associated password.
2 Know how to reach CCSO for help when unsure of the NetID *before* leaving campus!
3 Once authentication has been completed, there may still be problems connecting to specific electronic resources. Be aware of these and contact help at **offcampus@library.uiuc.edu** to determine the availability of the resource required. The problem is often easily remedied and worth the communication.

UIUC affiliates are authenticated with the centrally managed network-based Kerberos system. Kerberos is a protocol used at UIUC to provide secure access to client–server applications with the use of an encrypted password – at UIUC a unique identifier called the NetID and supplied by CCSO. Students must use this unique identifier frequently to sign to their account where they can accomplish such tasks as class registration. Faculty or staff may not need it as often – they can forget its significance and file it away until confronted by the need to input it. Long-time faculty members may never have known they had a NetID. User NetID help is offered at the CCSO office or via a fax form designed to offer more remote help but which requires a long-distance phone call. Our programme emphasizes the importance of testing the identifier before leaving campus.

Vendors for electronic resources require the libraries to enforce restrictions for access in many ways. Problems may be minimized when setting up resource access by making the vendor requirements transparent to the users. For example, passwords are scripted in or an approved range of IP addresses is set up that will allow affiliated users to connect to off-site resources. At UIUC remote access to e-resources is accomplished through a proxy server. The users authenticate with their NetID and then the proxy server brokers the connections, utilizing a set of instructions to access any title chosen. Problems can occur when the vendor changes machine addresses and, as often happens, the subscriber is not notified. If the proxy server instructions are not updated, then the user is informed that the proxy cannot handle it. Our programme lets users know that when access to a specific service is unavailable, an e-mail may provide a quick resolution.

FAQs

The FAQs are available at the programme website. Currently they serve to guide the users on how to manage such common problems as insufficient memory, long download times, frozen systems and printing problems. They will be updated as new problems and their resolutions emerge.

Take us with you!

The *Take us with you!* initiative attempts to address these issues of awareness and access. The 'product' of our effort is a website (see Figure 7.1) detailing available resources and services, and providing troubleshooting assistance.

Fig. 7.1 Take us with you! *home page*

Since relevant resources and services are scattered throughout the Library Gateway, we pulled them together under the rubric of 'Off Campus Library Services' to call attention to their utility for the distance users. The site will be linked from our Library Gateway and also from stakeholders' websites: International Programs and Studies, Area Studies Centers, and others. A brochure detailing resources and services has also been developed and will be widely distributed.

Merely developing and promoting a website is not sufficient, however. As described above, cultivating campus partnerships is a critical component of this initiative. As a result of meeting with International Programs and Services, we will participate in their orientation programme for study-abroad students. Though we targeted IPS as a logical constituency, other campus programmes can benefit as well. The Executive Development Center and Agricultural Extension Service, for example, both involve significant off-campus work. Part of our outreach efforts will therefore include identifying and working with these units to raise their awareness and enable us to become integrated into their programmes. We anticipate working closely with the aforementioned Computing and Communication Services Office and with the Division of Academic Outreach to keep abreast of issues and developments in telecommunications and distance education. Though it is more difficult to do so, we would also like to reach out to individual stakeholders. Faculty members who have been awarded sabbatical leave, for instance, will receive an electronic letter of congratulations from the library inviting them to 'take us with them' if they leave campus, and providing links to the website.

Evaluation

We need to hear from users to continue to evolve the programme and to be sure to alert CCSO to ongoing problems. We want to know who uses the service and how they heard of it, to evaluate our outreach plan, then determine what they used and any problems that they encountered. Prominent on the main web page is a feedback form, which we ask all users to complete. The form questions are reproduced in the appendix below. All the data are collected in a library database and will be analysed for future service development and evaluation.

Summary and conclusion

Take us with you! represents a natural extension of the movement to make library use more open and seamless to users, regardless of their physical location. In developing the programme we have identified the needs of our users and helped to expand our role as librarians, as technical advisors and as partners with agencies on campus. One result of our programme will be to improve the use of library services and the users' knowledge and use of them – on-campus as well as off. At UIUC we encourage users to keep us in mind and take us along wherever they go.

Appendix

Take us with you! Feedback Form

Please answer the questions below. The information collected will be critical in evolving this service to best help researchers in the field. Thank you in advance for your help in filling this out.

1. How did you find out about the *Take us with you!* Program?
   a. Brochure
   b. Library website
   c. E-mail message
   d. International Programs and Studies
   e. Colleague

2. Did you find out about the Program before leaving campus or after?
   a. Before
   b. After

3. Did you find the website useful?
   a. Yes
   b. No

4. Please comment on the format and content of the website:
   a. Easy to understand
   b. Understandable, with mild effort
   c. Difficult to understand
   d. Very difficult to understand

5. What UIUC Library services did you use while away? (check off all that apply.)
   a. Reference
   b. Article and chapter delivery from the UIUC's collection
   c. Article and chapter delivery from non-UIUC collections (ILL)
   d. E-reserves
   e. Guide to using resources

6. What UIUC Library resources did you use? (check off all that apply.)
   a. Illinet Online Library Catalog
   b. Article databases
   c. Full text resources

7. Did you experience technical problems and, if so, please comment:
   a. No
   b. Yes, check all that apply below:
      • Equipment
      • Software
      • Connectivity
   Comments on these problems are appreciated:

8. What could the library do differently to have made remote access easier for you? Feel free to add any other comments on the *Take us with you!* programme.

   Comments:

8

VLEs AND INFORMATION SERVICES: REDEFINING DISTANCE LEARNING AND THE ROLE OF INFORMATION SERVICES WITHIN THE VIRTUAL LEARNING ENVIRONMENT

Sue Roberts and John Davey

Introduction

The emergence and growing significance of virtual learning environments (VLEs) within the higher education (HE) learning process offers information professionals new opportunities for tailored and user-responsive services, strategic repositioning and role development. This paper explores the role of central learning support services in supporting distance learning through VLEs, and in particular through the integration of the hybrid library. The focus is on one specific case study and explores the development process from the original conception, with the emphasis upon organizational rather than technical issues, such as collaborative working arrangements and the emergence of hybrid academic teams.

Information and media services (IMS) staff at Edge Hill College of Higher Education have worked collaboratively with the Teaching and Learning Development Unit (TLDU) and academic staff to integrate resources, support and information skills within the Postgraduate Certificate in Teaching and Learning in Clinical Practice Programme (PCTLCPP). This case study provides a microcosm for VLE and hybrid library developments and illustrates the strategic issues relating to a holistic approach. This was the first fully online course at Edge Hill and consequently provided insights into delivering and supporting online learning, enabling IMS to explore the challenges and requirements involved in linking VLEs with hybrid library and information services.

Undoubtedly VLEs are leading to a redefinition of the learning process and the services, infrastructures and skills required to support lifelong and flexible learning.

Context

Electronic information sources and VLEs

The impact of electronic information sources on the work of information service professionals has been recognized by research projects such as IMPEL (**http://ilm.unn.ac.uk/impel**) but many of the services currently available are not being used to their full potential. This view has been reinforced by the recent first-cycle annual report for the JISC, *JISC user behaviour monitoring and evaluation framework* (Rowley, 2000). Initial findings from this snapshot of electronic information use within the HE sector question information services' ability to promote and embed electronic services within learning and teaching. In a survey of over 100 first-year undergraduates, only 0.98% used electronic journals, with this figure rising to 3.87% for other student years.

In order to embed these electronic resources and develop student skills, JISC recommends liaison between all stakeholders and the embedding of electronic information sources course design and delivery. This pitifully low usage is a wake-up call for information professionals within HE, and VLEs can be seen as a great opportunity to integrate resources fully within the learning experience and develop information-literate graduates.

Interest in VLEs, particularly the interlinking of the digital or hybrid library, is developing rapidly across higher education, with examples of JISC-funded projects leading the way. INSPIRAL (INveStigating Portals for Information Resources And Learning, **www.inspiral.cdlr.strath.ac.uk**) is a JISC-funded research project examining the institutional challenges and requirements involved in linking VLEs and MLEs (managed learning environments) with digital and hybrid libraries and is already beginning to raise interesting issues around roles, collaboration and barriers. Further grass-roots developments can be seen across HE institutions in the UK, although the picture is extremely variable in terms of information services involvement and integration. The profession is now asking 'How can libraries support and work with academics using VLEs?' We also need to be asking how we can harness the potential of VLEs to develop truly flexible and accessible services and learning support.

The local context

Edge Hill is a higher education institution in the North West of England, with 7000 students on a range of degree and diploma courses and a further 5000 on professional development programmes, particularly in education and health-related areas. Edge Hill has 'many benefits in being small enough to seek out and encourage co-operation and collaboration between staff, and to embrace institution-wide approaches to teaching and learning development' (Edwards and Jenkinson, 1998, 180). Information and Media Services (IMS) is a converged learning services provider encompassing communications and information technology (C&IT), library and media facilities with a strong focus on electronic information sources and learning support. A strong culture of curriculum involvement has been developed in keeping with the learning support ethos at Edge Hill. IMS wishes to integrate the use of electronic information sources and information skills within learning programmes in order to promote full and relevant use and to enhance the student learning experience. The Teaching and Learning Development Unit (TLDU) at Edge Hill is concerned with assisting and supporting students and staff, and provides support in a variety of disciplines, including education and teaching and learning, learning technologies and online learning, inclusive student support and provision, dyslexia and specific learning difficulties support, study skills and key skills.

IMS works in close collaboration with TLDU under the umbrella of Learning Support Services. The two departments are delivering co-ordinated student and staff development and support programmes to satisfy the needs of a rapidly changing HE environment. The rapid development of VLEs and the integration of electronic information sources at Edge Hill can be attributed to the close working relationships between the two departments.

The WebCT context

WebCT was adopted as Edge Hill's VLE for distance course delivery in 1999. Typically, VLEs will include course materials, assessment facilities, conferencing and chat, as well as management tools for student administration and monitoring. The VLEs in existence now number in their hundreds. Some have been developed by individual institutions for use in-house, whilst others like WebCT are commercial packages, although WebCT itself was first developed in-house at the University of British Columbia, Canada.

The tools and facilities in WebCT fulfilled the requirements of the initial distance learning course at Edge Hill, and the system offered the availability of a free trial software download with no cost implications until students were installed into the programme. In addition, licences could be purchased in small numbers (rather than as a campus-wide licence), thus satisfying the need, initially, for only one programme using WebCT.

Programme context

The Postgraduate Certificate in Teaching and Learning in Clinical Practice was developed following the identification of a need for teaching and learning training for medical and dental practitioners. Although it is usual for practitioners to be assigned students and to 'teach' them, very few have undergone any formal training in teaching and learning. Two members of the programme team had already developed and delivered short, face-to-face development workshops to medical professionals, on subjects such as 'the role of the supervisor' and 'teaching small groups'. Responses from these workshops, combined with recent changes within medical education, provided the direction for the programme. The aim of the programme is to 'support and accredit the professional development of clinical practice staff in respect of teaching and providing learning support' (course participants' handbook, 2001).

The programme has been developed co-operatively by three institutions: Edge Hill, Mersey Deanery, and Chester College of Higher Education. A multi-disciplinary programme team of six was assembled to provide skills and expertise in education, health, teaching and learning, online learning and design, and electronic information services. This hybrid, inter-departmental and inter-institutional team can be seen as one of the key success factors of the course.

Online development work began in August 1999, and the programme went live in February 2000. The first cohort finished the programme in December 2000, with 20 of the original 21 participants successfully completing. The current cohort (of 25 participants) started the programme in January 2001, and is due to complete at the end of 2001. The decision to deliver most of the programme online, and hence the need for team members with skills in online learning and electronic information sources, was prompted mainly by the fact that it would have proved very difficult to bring together a cohort of busy and committed clinical professionals for regular face-to-face sessions. There was also a recognized need for seamless access to course materials, learning resources and support, with currency a crucial factor given the rapidly changing context of the medical and educational sectors.

Programme design

WebCT allows the customization of courses in the types of tools and functions which can be put in place, where they are located within the site, and their visual design. In terms of overall design, the team set out to integrate the programme material, the activities and interaction which would take place between participants, and the learning resources to help meet the aims of the programme in a user-friendly environment. The design had to allow participants to research and work independently, but also encourage them to share their experiences and knowledge and to work proactively with fellow participants.

It should be noted that although most of the programme is accessed online via WebCT, the team still considered face-to-face interaction with the participants to be a vital element of the programme design. There are five face-to-face sessions during the course of the programme, positioned at relevant points, such as the start of the programme and the start of each module. The detail and timing of these sessions has changed (following evaluation from the first running of the programme) for the current cohort, with the development of an introductory module. This has been crucial to participants' successful use of the electronic information sources, and will be described in detail later.

Learning resources and support

VLEs and hybrid libraries are important current developments in online learning, yet their evolution has thus far proceeded along largely separate lines (Currier, 2001). At an early stage in the development process of this first online programme at Edge Hill, the need to fully integrate electronic information sources, support and information skills was identified as necessary to support the learning outcomes and contribute to an effective student experience. A holistic approach to embedding learning resources was taken to ensure maximum and most appropriate use. As a result, integration was planned at various levels, which can be summarized as:

- a tailored resources and support section (see Figure 8.1 overleaf) providing access to selected quality resources (from individual journal titles to full-text, fully searchable databases), e-mail support, online guides, information and advice on the physical resources and facilities available, postal loans and inter-library loans, the aim being to provide a one-stop shop within WebCT that provided seamless access to all relevant information services whether virtual or real
- support via the discussion area to answer specific problems and questions relevant to the wider group (so not one-to-one)
- printed materials, e.g. study guide, information skills handbook with activities to encourage use
- help desk support, e.g. for password changes, authentication issues
- face-to-face sessions to introduce resources and develop skills
- introductory module
- specific resources embedded within the actual content.

These diverse means of embedding and supporting electronic information sources ensure that different learning styles are met. The student feedback supports this assumption – a survey revealed that 97% of respondants used electronic journals, with 85% accessing online databases (Ashcroft, 2001). Students were also asked to comment on the most important advantages of studying and accessing electronic resources online. Here is a sample of their responses relating to the embedding of electronic resources:

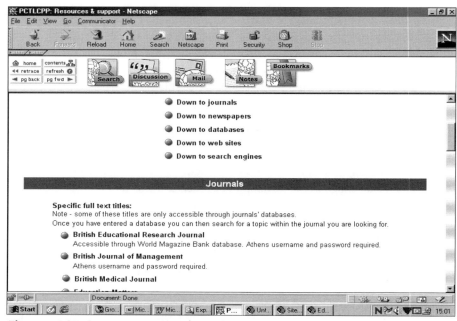

Fig. 8.1 *PCTLCPP: resources and support*
Reproduced with permission of Edge Hill College of Higher Education.

'Access to good quality current information without having to travel'
'Electronic resources excellent'
'Anytime anywhere access to plenty of full text information'
'Truly online nature liberating in terms of working when I wanted to'.

The findings from this small sample questionnaire suggest that the parallel needs of acquiring information skills and accessing quality resources are being met through the adoption of a range of different strategies, all offering embedded and flexible access and support. Embedding resources within the VLE does raise certain concerns, particularly around the issue of spoon-feeding and narrow focus. This can be minimized by emphasizing resource discovery through the use of the world wide web and online databases. The introductory module and activities throughout the course attempt to do this by encouraging independent research and critical evaluation of resources. As part of the programme assessment, each participant produces three assignments on negotiated topics relevant to their area of practice, and can use this resources section for independent research into programme-related topics. These resources are crucial in providing participants with the scope of research material they require, without leaving them unaided to lose their way in the mass of material available via the world wide web.

Introduction to the programme

Following evaluation from the first cohort, there have been significant changes to the introductory elements of the programme. For the second cohort, the initial face-to-face session concentrates on introducing the programme (in general terms) and on the use of WebCT and electronic information sources. In contrast, the first cohort's initial session introduced all of these elements plus the first module of the programme. Evaluation showed that first-year participants felt overloaded after this first session, so the second cohort was only introduced to module 1 at the second face-to-face session, following completion of the introductory module (as described below).

The introductory session is reinforced by the introductory module, lasting for two-and-a-half weeks. During this period, participants are encouraged to read introductory programme information (e.g. detailing what would be expected of them, how the online study would be delivered and facilitated, etc.), and to undertake a number of activities to familiarize them with using WebCT and the online learning resources. In contrast, members of the first cohort began module 1 immediately following the introductory session, thus having to familiarize themselves with WebCT and the online learning resources *and* tackle the first module at the same time. Also, members of the first cohort had no activities built in to explore use of the online learning resources, whereas activities for those in the second cohort have helped to ensure an understanding of their potential and how to make best use of them.

The introductory module provides the second group of participants with an invaluable opportunity to highlight and resolve the problems they encounter in using the online resources. Most issues have been voiced using the WebCT discussion facility (where messages can be posted for all participants and tutors to view and respond to). This is not only beneficial in giving all participants access to any issues and their solutions, but also for the reassurance, especially in the early stages of a programme, when they realize others are experiencing problems similar to their own!

During the two-and-a-half weeks of the introductory module, 34 discussion messages were posted relating to use of the electronic information sources. Here is an example of one of these messages:

```
Message No. 23: posted by ANNE B.
on Mon, Jan. 29, 2001, 21:04

Subject: Online resources

Re. activity D made access to 'Do continuing
professional...learning' have done as instructed
```

(re. click 'full text') and so far it has asked me for
credit card details 3 times?? Would be grateful for a tip
on this as this is annoying!

Was I meant to enter the Medical Education site as a guest?
that is, after entering ID and password was I meant to click
on guest?

Anne B

The introductory day sessions are also now 'hands-on' – that is, participants receive their usernames and passwords at the sessions, are guided through the log-on procedures and have the opportunity to access and explore some of the electronic information sources. This hands-on element has helped the participants, along with the introductory module, to a much better understanding of how to best use WebCT and the relevant electronic information sources.

Changes to the programme introduction have been central to improving electronic information sources integration. The large number of queries regarding electronic information sources this year has been prompted by the introductory module and its activities. This highlights how electronic information sources activities must be embedded at an early stage to ensure engagement and the development of skills and confidence.

It is important to highlight that the embedding of electronic information sources is not just limited to the introductory module. A number of the general programme activities have electronic information sources elements and part of one module's content is actually about online resources and their effective use in learning and teaching. In addition, participants are provided with printed materials and handbooks as a comfort blanket. The support offered to the participants (in various forms) is crucial to the success of the programme. Most of the participants have had little or no experience of learning online prior to starting the programme, and many have not been students themselves for 20 or 30 years! A discussion message (shown below) from one of the second cohort, and echoed by other participants, supports this view. The message was posted in response to one of the introductory module activities, which was aimed at familiarizing participants with using the discussion facility, and providing the team with feedback on the introductory day of the programme:

Message No. 4: [Branch from no. 2] posted by KAREN G. on
Thu, Jan. 25, 2001, 22:40

Subject: Re: Activity B - Introductory day feedback

```
Today was very informative. Very impressed by the
technology! Very, very glad to have some paper help i.e.
the Technology & Resource Handbook. Having taken a long,
long time to even begin to customize my Homepage this is
going to be very slow I think!
```

Activities

The use of activities, and the interaction between participants and tutors using the discussion and mail facilities, is important for a deeper understanding of the topics within the programme, and is one way of encouraging active learning. This is reflected in the section on electronic information sources in the introductory module, into which three related activities have been integrated. These activities are designed to help participants master the step-by-step process of using online learning resources, but also to give them an understanding of independent research and its benefits to their study. One of the introductory module activities is shown in Figure 8.2.

Activity F
Use a search engine to search for a subject you are currently interested in. Find one web page that you have assessed for accuracy, authority and quality.

Post the URL (eg. http://www.edgehill.ac.uk) of your web page in the 'Discussion' area with your views as to its use and value.

Fig. 8.2 *Example of an introductory module activity*

Ensuring the quality and authority of information discovered on the world wide web is an important issue in independent research. To address this, the programme study guide and resources and support sections contain resource links to some clear and simple online courses concerned with assessing the validity of material found on the web.

Staff roles and development

This new learning environment raises a whole new set of issues and challenges for both teaching and learning support staff. These challenges demand the establishment of partnerships – technological, personal and organizational. IMS staff are now working within hybrid academic teams in relation to curriculum development, and online learning in particular. The diversity of their roles can be seen in the following suggested remit:

- role in strategic development
- helpdesk support (face-to-face, telephone, e-mail)
- technical support and design
- design of own courses/key skills integration
- electronic resources integration and support
- distance learning support
- promotion.

It should be stressed that IMS staff at Edge Hill are engaged in these activities in close collaboration with TLDU staff and that the range of skills and involvement varies according to role. It is clear that information services staff roles in the VLE arena are not just about supporting academics in their use, and not even just about embedding electronic resources as we are now becoming e-tutors, e-writers, e-designers and e-collaborators. As Slade (2000, 13) highlights, the issue of collaboration and strategic alliances is now a major theme in distance learning and this is clearly visible in relation to VLE developments.

'In all this we must not lose sight of the importance of human resources' (Brophy et al., 2000, 3) and in order to support and develop IMS staff, a multi-stranded strategy for staff development in online learning has been implemented. This has encompassed general awareness sessions for all staff, guidance for helpdesk staff on support issues, and design and specific skills development for staff involved in learning and teaching. Edge Hill is also developing two online modules on online learning – so the medium is also the message. These modules are developing and delivering online learning for staff wishing to deliver online learning, and supporting online learning for all those staff who are supporting students but are not involved directly in design and delivery. IMS staff will participate in both depending on their role.

What is clear is the continuing need to work in partnerships, and to continue to review roles as boundaries become increasingly blurred. There are no new positions within IMS with an expressed focus on VLE work, but it is becoming a part of all staff roles at a certain level and a central part of the changing skills portfolio.

Strategic issues

Since the successful implementation of WebCT for the Postgraduate Certificate in Teaching and Learning in Clinical Practice, WebCT developments have flourished at Edge Hill – both for distance learning and for mixed-mode approaches. There are now over 30 different courses using WebCT and over 2000 students registered as WebCT users. IMS has been involved directly in a range of these courses and has been instrumental in the development of specific initiatives such as WebCT for Postgraduate Certificate in Education English students. IMS is also currently developing policies and standards on embedding and supporting electronic resources. It is clear also that VLEs are not just relevant to distance learning in a conventional sense but can offer flexible modes of delivery for all students.

The strategic issues for VLE development and the information services role are too great to explore here but the following snapshot offers an indication of the challenges to consider:

- institutional commitment and direction
- strong central learning support services
- close collaboration between the above and with academic areas
- commitment to learning and teaching developments and not just technical developments
- strategic positioning of information services within the VLE arena
- issues to do with authentication and seamlessness to electronic resources
- staff skills and role development.

The key must be collaboration and INSPIRAL is astutely asking: 'How will academics, librarians and IT professionals begin to work together as partners in these endeavours? Is a reassessment of everybody's role and remit necessary?' (Currier, 2001)

Conclusion

Undoubtedly, 'Learning networks are transforming teaching and learning relationships, opportunities and outcomes' and as a result 'students need new and different information resources, skills, roles and relationship' (Harasim et al., 1995, 271). Information professionals also need new skills, roles and relationships particularly in relation to VLEs and the integration of the hybrid library.

This case study has illustrated an approach to embedding that has led to an enriched student learning experience and seamless (or as seamless as is possible at the moment) access to resources and support. This seamlessness is made possible for all students (whether distance or mixed-mode) by a collaborative approach towards online learning and electronic information sources. The development of relationships within the new academic team is the major critical success factor, and not the technological advances, which are simply the tools to make it happen. IMPEL research suggests that the aim of information services is to 'encourage formal and informal links between information services, computing services, academic staff and students' (Edwards and Walton, 1998). In order to engage successfully with online learning and to play a significant role in emerging learning environments, information professionals need to do far more than 'encourage'. They need to be proactive in seeking out and initiating new relationships and opportunities for collaboration as the emergence of VLEs offers new avenues for user-focused, tailored and embedded services.

References

Ashcroft, R. (2001) *Case study: supporting a distance learning course through WebCT*, EHCHE, unpublished.

Bartle, C. and Walton, G. (1998) Effective use of electronic information sources. In *Impact of electronic libraries: IMPEL guide*, University of Northumbria at Newcastle, available at
http://ilm.unn.ac.uk/impel

Brophy, P. et al. (2000) Introduction. In Brophy, P., Fisher, S. and Clarke, Z. (eds) *Libraries without walls 3: the delivery of library services to distance users*, London, Library Association Publishing, 1–5.

Currier, S. (2001) *INSPIRAL stakeholder consultation: stakeholder interviews summary report*, available at
http://inspiral.cdlr.strath.ac.uk/documents/documents.html

Edwards, C. and Jenkinson, R. (1998) Case study: managing change at Edge Hill University College. In Day, J. and Hanson, T. (eds) *Managing the electronic library: a practical guide for information professionals*, Bowker-Saur, 167–84.

Edwards, C. and Walton, G. (1998) Change and the academic library: understanding, managing and coping. In *Impact of electronic libraries: IMPEL guide*, University of Northumbria at Newcastle, available at
http://ilm.unn.ac.uk/impel

Harasim, L. et al. (1995) *Learning networks: a field guide to teaching and learning online*, The MIT Press.

Rowley, J. (2000) *JISC user behaviour and monitoring framework*, available at
www.jisc.ac.uk

Slade, A. (2000) Keynote address: international trends and issues in library services for distance learning: present and future. In Brophy, P., Fisher, S. and Clarke, Z. (eds) *Libraries without walls 3: the delivery of library services to distance users*, London, Library Association Publishing, 6–48.

Theme 2
Online enquiry services for remote users

9

GLOBAL CHAT: WEB-BASED ENQUIRIES AT THE UNIVERSITY OF LEICESTER

Lou McGill

Introduction

This chapter describes the experiences of the University of Leicester Library Distance Learning Unit in offering a chat-based enquiry service for a trial period of three months from October to December 2000. Whilst it was essentially aimed at providing an enquiry service, it became obvious that this type of facility was also a powerful tool for user education, at the point of need. Targeting skills support is a significant challenge for those providing services to distance learning students. A chat service offered a useful mechanism for providing this support when it was most needed, and therefore most likely to be effective.

Background

The University of Leicester has over 7000 students based throughout the world studying at postgraduate level by distance learning. Many of these students work full time and have significant time constraints which affect their information retrieval activities. Students present a wide range of cultural and language differences and have varied access to IT and internet facilities. They tend to be mature students with competing demands from work and families, and they often feel isolated from the university. Many courses are sold as 'self-contained' and students have not traditionally been encouraged to look for information from sources other than the comprehensive course packs.

   In September 1999 the University Library established the Distance Learning Unit to support all distance learning students studying with the university. In addition to a range of services, the unit developed a comprehensive website providing access to many electronic resources, and a range of pages to support students' information skills development.

Types of enquiries

Most distance learning student enquiries are related to the services offered by the unit and to utilizing electronic resources effectively. Many enquiries reveal a need for both information skills support and help in making the most effective use of the website. Subject enquiries are few (3%) and are incorporated into the 'other' category listed below. Enquiries are often multi-faceted and an extensive knowledge of procedures, services, electronic resources and website content is required in order to respond appropriately.

Categories of enquiries are:

- service information (60%)
- help in using electronic resources (13%)
- library registration (12%)
- other (15%).

Methods of enquiries are:

- telephone (42%)
- e-mail (41%)
- personal visit (14%)
- post/fax/web form (3%).

What is a chat enquiry service?

Web-based chat enquiry services offer students the opportunity to 'talk' to a librarian using text messages in 'real time', as opposed to the delayed response with e-mail. Enquiries take the form of a 'conversation', similar to a reference desk person-to-person interaction. Librarians have the opportunity to question students in order to find out the full details of their enquiry and can also direct them to appropriate resources on the internet.

Why chat?

Several factors led to considering chat software as an additional method for dealing with enquiries. The most significant of these were the limitations of existing methods.

The telephone offers students important personal contact and seems to provide a sense of reassurance that someone is dealing with their request for help. The telephone is, however, less useful for enquiries related to using the Distance Learning Unit website or internet resources. If students are using a home modem to connect to the internet, they often have to disconnect their telephone line to ring up for support. Staff cannot then guide the student through the problem, as they are no longer connected to the internet.

E-mails are an excellent enquiry method, particularly for students based outside the UK. This method can allow staff to respond to enquiries in a more methodical and comprehensive manner. Web page links can be included with detailed instructions of how to proceed. One limitation of this method, however, is the time delay. A student sending an e-mail enquiry from outside the UK may not receive an answer until the next day due to time-zone differences. If questions are not expressed well in the first e-mail, there may be a series of clarifying e-mails over a period of several days. Students with tight deadlines can find this frustrating and often require an immediate response.

Experience in the Distance Learning Unit has shown that students prefer several different options for contacting us. Some methods suit some people more than others. Students who are confident using computers are happy using e-mail, but may still prefer to use the telephone. A student based at work may use a different method from a student at home.

Another significant factor in deciding to trial chat software was the presence in the University Library of a project officer, Danielle Hinton, with a brief to investigate electronic communication methods for distance learning students. This post was funded for one year to help establish the Distance Learning Unit. Danielle identified various software packages and evaluated their potential. She also provided support during the trial period. The trial would not have been possible without this support.

In summary, we expected a chat-based enquiry service to offer students the following advantages:

* a web-based alternative to traditional enquiry methods
* immediate response
* 'real-time' interaction
* support whilst using the internet
* staff who could open appropriate web pages on the student's desktop.

Software choice

The following criteria were applied to a variety of software packages to help identify the most appropriate that:

* were free for the library and students during the trial period
* did not require students to download any software or plug-ins to operate the service
* provided an option to send an e-mail if no one was staffing the service
* had user-friendly and adaptable interfaces

- provided good support from the supplying company
- allowed us to track the web behaviour of visitors to the site.

The free services considered were:

- AOL Instant Messenger
- Human Click
- Livehelper.

AOL Instant Messenger was rejected because it required students to download software to access the service. Livehelper was excluded on account of a cumbersome operator interface and limited user support from the supplying company. Human Click met our main criteria and was selected as the preferred software.

Implementation

The operator software was downloaded onto all eight computers in the Distance Learning Unit. This was to enable all unit staff to undergo some training and to observe interactions during the trial period. The university web pages were prepared with chat icons and tracking html code on most of the Distance Learning Unit pages (see Figure 9.1).

The service was demonstrated to the unit staff, which included two qualified librarians. We decided to use the two qualified librarians to staff the service, with library assistants observing until they felt confident enough to take an enquiry. They were able to respond to an enquiry at any time as they had the software loaded on their machines.

The software was available free for a period of three months, which was the main consideration affecting the length of the trial. Since the unit deals with many courses that do not mirror the usual academic year, we anticipated that there would not be any significant variation in results by conducting the trial from October to December, as opposed to another time slot in the year.

One decision to be made during the implementation stage was whether to accept enquiries on demand or to insist on an appointment system. Although we suggested, on the supporting pages about the service, that students made an appointment to avoid disappointment, we were also prepared to accept enquiries on demand. We decided to offer the service during our normal office hours of 9.00 a.m. to 5.00 p.m. Monday to Friday. Whilst this may appear to present problems for some students based outside the UK, it is interesting to note that many distance learning students work at home in the evenings. A student in Sydney,

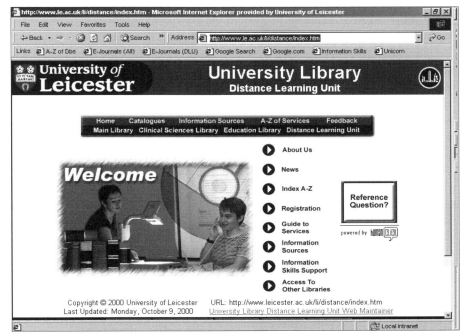

Fig. 9.1 *Distance Learning Unit home page with chat icon*
Reproduced with permission of the University of Leicester.

Australia, working to this pattern would find the service operating if they tried to open a chat session.

The trial

Staff operating the service had the option to choose three states of readiness by clicking on bell icons, which in turn affected the wording on the chat icons. These were:

- online – librarian available to chat
- offline or away – librarian away from office; students invited to send an e-mail
- away for five minutes – librarian unable to chat for a brief time; students invited to send an e-mail.

Chat sessions were generally initiated by students rather than the librarian. The librarian could track a visitor to the site and send an invitation to the visitor asking them if they wanted to chat. Although we tried this approach a few times, we did not receive a positive response and felt that it was perceived as intimidating. If a web visitor clicked on the chat icon when the service was staffed, they would see a welcome screen (Figure 9.2), and have the opportunity to start a dialogue.

During the three-month trial period, a total of 43 chat sessions took place. None of these were by appointment. Twelve e-mail messages were received as a result of the service being offline. Many more sessions were initiated by visitors to the website, but were not included in the statistics as the person did not respond or left the site. The reasons for this are not known, but we suspect that it may have been a mixture of curiosity, causing them to click on the icon, and panic when confronted with the welcome screen.

Anyone visiting the website could have initiated a chat session regardless of whether they were a distance learning student with the university or not. The breakdown of enquiries into category of user revealed that the majority of sessions were with legitimate distance learning students. The sessions were with:

- 29 University of Leicester distance learning students
- 11 librarians interested in this type of service
- 1 University of Leicester academic staff member

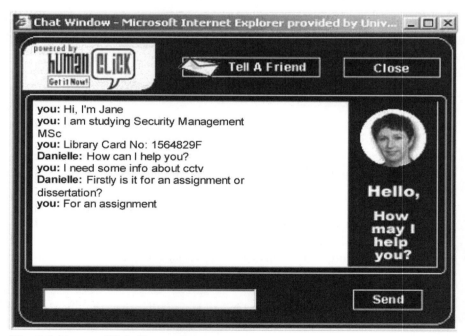

Fig. 9.2 *Human Click Chat welcome screen*
Reproduced with permission of the University of Leicester.

- 1 distance learning student from another university
- 1 potential student needing course information.

During a chat session, librarians can observe the current web behaviour of the student. They can also access the history of any previous chat sessions with that person. This kind of information offered useful non-verbal clues to the enquirer's level of competence with the service and with using electronic resources.

The librarian was able to view three different screens of information during a session. The navigation screen shows which web pages the student has already visited (see Figure 9.3). The info screen shows any history of previous chat sessions, and the chat screen is where the librarian types in answers to student text messages. Thanks to the time delay whilst waiting for a response as students typed in their information or questions, it was possible to switch between screens comfortably during a session.

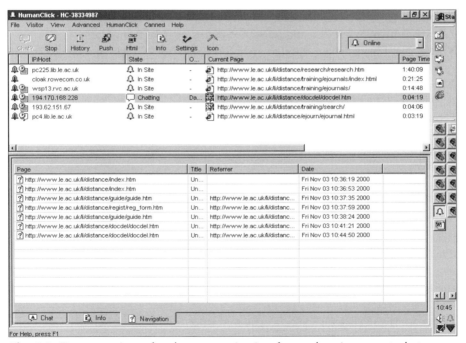

Fig. 9.3 *Operator view of web page navigation for student in current chat session*
Reproduced with permission of the University of Leicester.

Sample chats

Chat 1 A simple chat transaction

Librarian: My name is Lou. Please allow reasonable thinking and typing time . . . following a sentence means there is more to follow. How can I help you?
Visitor: What time do you close tonight please?
Librarian: The library closes at 10 p.m. Issue desk finishes at 9 p.m. Distance learning office closes at 5.
Librarian: Can I help you with anything else?

Chat 2 Extract from a more complex chat session showing examples of 'pushing' web pages to the enquirer

Visitor: Hi Lou, I'm not sure whether this is reaching you. My name is *** *** and I'm partway through my MSc in Training with CLMS, I sent an e-mail yesterday evening asking about joining the library facilities. Can you provide details?
Librarian: Hi ***
Librarian: Have you already filled in a library registration form?
Librarian: Here is an online form...
Librarian: http://www.le.ac.uk/li/distance/regist/reg_form.htm#form
Visitor: No, I have looked through my information from CLMS and do not appear to have one. I can only find a computer centre registration form.
Librarian: Have you looked at this page of links to databases and electronic journals for CLMS students? . . .
Librarian: http://www.le.ac.uk/li/distance/subjects/clms/index.html
Librarian: You will need the ATHENS password for some of these – fill in the computer centre form for that...

Chat 3 Extract from a very long (20-minute) session, which happened early in the trial

Both the operator and user were unfamiliar with this method of communicating. The outcome of this session was a phone call, which solved the problem of the user being unable to find the 'catalogue button'. This was only possible because the user had two phone lines and was guided around the web site by the librarian.

Librarian: If you click on the catalogue button you should be taken to a catalogues page . . .
Librarian: Click on the WEBCAT button and then click on the distance learning button . . .

Visitor: I wasn't.
Librarian: http://www.le.ac.uk/li/catalog.html
Librarian: Has it worked now?
Visitor: OK thanks, I will try but can I phone if it doesn't work . . . this takes ages?
Librarian: Of course you can – 0116 252 5051 for us or 0116 252 3737 for the education library team.
Visitor: I can't do anything with this window in the way.
Librarian: OK – let's log off now and you try again. If it doesn't work please ring us. I hope you get it to work. Thanks for perservering with this new method of communication . . .
Visitor: I can't find a webcat thing at all.
Visitor: I have got a red line of options and then a blue line but none say webcat.
Librarian: Do any say 'Catalogue'?
Visitor: Yes.

What we learned
Chat as a method

This method of responding to student enquiries presented its own unusual challenges and benefits. The absence of non-verbal clues that are present in a face-to-face encounter, and lack of tone of voice clues that you have with telephone enquiries, were to some extent balanced out by the advantage of being able to see exactly where the student had already been on the website, or seeing what ground had already been covered in previous chat sessions.

The time delay proved to be frustrating for both staff and students, as it frequently resulted in unsynchronized dialogue, with several different threads running at the same time while each person typed in their responses. With time and patience the librarians learned to direct the conversations more effectively, minimizing the time delay effect.

Chat sessions worked very well for enquiries requiring a quick, simple answer. They were most effective in helping students find information on the internet for themselves, since the software allowed the librarian to open any internet page on a student's own screen. This type of enquiry method was less useful for some multi-faceted enquiries or enquiries about the status of user requests for photocopies or book loans. Service operators occasionally encouraged students to use a more appropriate method to contact the unit.

Once the librarians became familiar with the new service it became possible to respond to several different enquiries simultaneously. It also became apparent that other members of staff working close by required some form of signal that the librarian was involved in a chat enquiry, since this was not immediately obvious to them. Telephone or personal interruptions had to be dealt with by other team members as chat sessions could be very intensive and prolonged.

One of the most useful functions of the software was the option to 'push' web pages to the enquirer. This greatly enhanced the service, as librarians could open relevant web pages and tutorials on the student's screen at the most appropriate time. Another useful feature was the ability to set up 'canned responses', which were standard greetings and messages that we used regularly. This prevented retyping the same information and resulted in fewer mis-spellings – a particular feature of this type of interaction.

Staffing issues

During the trial we did not restrict the times the service was available, apart from periods when the librarians had other commitments. The ideal way to staff this type of service would be to operate a rota similar to those used on enquiry desks. This type of method offers great potential to provide an enquiry service outside usual office hours. It does not have to be operated from within the library itself as the operator software could be loaded onto any PC.

The need for staff to have both multi-tasking abilities and extensive knowledge of the services, the electronic resources, the website and the tutorials, meant that not all staff would have been able to answer all enquiries. The enquiries covered a range of issues at a variety of different levels. Whilst it is also true for enquiries received through other channels, some of the benefits of this method would be lost if the operator did not know which web page to send or which tutorial might be the most relevant. One notable failing of this software was the inability to transfer enquiries to an appropriate person, as once an enquiry was accepted on one computer it had to be dealt with from that machine.

Although the software was easy to use, it took several weeks for staff to feel confident with this method of enquiry. Many early transactions were less successful because staff and students were unfamiliar with the time delay and synchronization difficulties. Eventually staff discovered that they could help students with this problem by resisting the temptation to type during a long pause. Patience and calmness had a significantly positive effect on the quality of interactions. Chats often ended on an unsatisfactory note for staff, however, as students sometimes terminated sessions suddenly or without completing the interaction.

Software limitations

The Human Click software had fulfilled our original criteria but during the trial we developed additional needs that were not met by this software.

The invaluable history and chat transcripts were held on the Human Click server. This meant that we could not access the web tracking history or information that would have been important to help improve our service. The history of a previous enquirer only became available if that person engaged in a subsequent chat.

Enquiries in academic libraries often need to be passed to a more appropriate person. The trial software does not allow operators to forward an accepted chat session to anyone else. This would be a required function for any chat software that may be used in the future.

MAC users had a problem using this software, which effectively excluded those users from accessing this service.

At the end of the trial period the software would have cost £50 per month. We decided to stop the service while we evaluated the trial and investigated other software and staffing options within the University of Leicester Library.

Ways forward

This method of enquiry service is a potentially valuable tool for the Distance Learning Unit and for the University Library as a whole. The unit is not currently offering this service while we continue to evaluate the trial and deal with the implications that have emerged. Before proceeding several key decisions have to be made regarding:

- software choice
- extent of service.

Software choice

Several factors affect the choice of software. The software needs to fulfil our original criteria and overcome the limitations of Human Click discovered during the trial. Cost would be a significant factor as well as the impact of the university's move towards selecting software to manage virtual learning environments (VLEs). The University Library needs to ensure that choices made in relation to chat software are compatible with wider policy and sustainable in terms of subscriptions and staffing.

Extent of service

During the trial the service was intended for distance learning students and was staffed by that team. The potential of this type of service for any off-campus user means that the University Library needs to consider how this type of service could be offered as an additional method to enhance its existing enquiry service. The University Library needs to define which users the service is intended for and how to target it. This has implications for staffing, training, advertising, recording use statistics, and deciding where and when the service is offered.

Initially the library would need to evaluate the effectiveness of this type of service for different categories of user and identify which time periods were most popular. This initial assessment could then be used to shape the service in the longer term. The undoubted potential of this method to enhance information retrieval skills support offers the University Library a way to extend its current facilities for all off-campus students. The University of Leicester Library, in the forthcoming year, will continue actively to review and investigate the most appropriate way to offer a web-based chat enquiry service.

Useful sources

From our experience the following sources would be useful to anyone wishing to explore the possibilities of providing a chat service:

Eichler, L. and Halperin, M. (2001) Liveperson: keeping reference alive and clicking, *Econtent*, (November), available at
www.ecmag.net/awards/award13.html
Hinton, D. and McGill, L. (2001) Chat to a librarian: 21st century reference for distance learners, *VINE*, **122**, 59–64.
www.le.ac.uk/li/distance/eliteproject/elib/chat.html
www.aol.com/aim/imreg_download_template?pageset=aol&promo=106695
www.humanclick.com/
www.livehelper.com/
www.rrc.usf.edu/pres/chat/
www.wdvl.com/Software/Applications/Chat/

10

THE ONLINE PERSONAL ACADEMIC LIBRARIAN (OPAL): A VIRTUAL LIBRARIAN FOR A VIRTUAL STUDENT COMMUNITY

Gill Needham and Evelyn Simpson

Background

The Open University (OU) is the largest distance teaching university in the UK, with around 180,000 students each year. The OU method of delivering courses is called 'supported open learning' – students work essentially on their own at home, with high-quality course materials mailed to them. These materials typically include print materials, audiotapes and videotapes. Every student has support from a tutor (employed part-time by the university), who provides optional face-to-face group tutorial sessions (once or twice a month) and marks assignments. More and more OU courses now have online elements, and some are now taught entirely online, using an electronic conferencing system called FirstClass. There are currently 120,000 members of this virtual community using conferencing for teaching and learning, support and both course-related and social discussion groups.

In recent years, students' increasing access to the internet has allowed the gradual introduction of remote access to library resources into many courses. The OU Library has developed an extensive electronic library for students – Open Libr@ry. The library has a Learner Support Team of ten staff who deal with enquiries from students by telephone, post and e-mail. However, a major weakness in the service is the fact that it is currently restricted to the library's opening hours.

As the majority of OU students (75%) are in full-time employment, much of their study takes place in the evening and at weekends. An analysis of e-mailed enquiries during 2000 showed that more than 50% were received when the library was closed. The greatest proportion of the enquiries received by the team each week are sent over the weekend. Students who may need help on a Friday evening, for example, do not receive a reply from the Learner Support Team until Monday morning.

All this evidence suggested that the service offered was failing to meet the needs of OU students. A number of approaches were considered for the provision of a 24/7 enquiry service. These fell into three categories:

• extended staffing to increase the hours to include evenings and weekends
• collaboration with libraries in other time zones to provide a round-the-clock service
• an automated 'virtual' service.

It would prove extremely expensive to increase the staffing sufficiently to offer a 24/7 service and may not be cost-effective. It would also be difficult to recruit sufficient numbers of suitably qualified staff prepared to work unsocial hours.

While collaboration with other libraries seems attractive, the analysis of enquiries to the Learner Support Team indicates that the majority are specific to the services and systems at the OU and could not be easily answered by colleagues elsewhere. This is likely to be the case for potential collaborators also.

It was therefore decided to pursue the automated model. This has the added attraction that it could potentially help with an increasing number of straightforward enquiries received during staffed hours also, should the volume become problematic. The preliminary analysis revealed that 60% of enquiries are straightforward and could be answered by information available within the library's web pages or electronic conferences.

The university agreed to fund an 18-month research project to investigate alternative technical solutions and develop and test a prototype system. The library is working in partnership with the OU's Knowledge Media Institute (KMi), which specializes in the development of near-term future technologies for sharing, accessing and understanding knowledge, such as the use of organizational memory and the use of intelligent agent systems. The project has been able to build on previous work in KMi like the 'virtual participant' (Masterton, 1997) – a virtual member of a business studies course which engaged in virtual discussions and drew its fellow students' attention to relevant information elsewhere.

The project has two further partners – the university libraries at Birkbeck College London and the University of Leicester, both of which will be involved in testing the prototype system. This was particularly important as the intention is to develop a system which is transferable to other libraries in both the academic and public sectors.

The project

The objective of the OPAL project (**http://oulib1.open.ac.uk/wh/research/opal/**) is to research the development of an online, 24-hour, fully automated enquiry service capable of handling routine natural-language questions and providing a near-immediate response to the user, leaving library staff more time to deal with complex enquiries. The five key stages of the project are:

1 To develop an operational requirement for the proposed system/service.
2 To explore the user perspective re enquiry systems.
3 To identify the range of possible technical solutions and review previous experience as recorded in the literature.
4 To develop a prototype system and test this with the OU student community and those of the two partner institutions.
5 To make recommendations for the development and implementation of a longer-term solution.

Developing an operational requirement for the proposed system/service

To help determine the operational requirements for the OPAL system, a group of information professionals from academic, public and research libraries was invited to share their ideas and expertise at a focus group held on 12 February 2001. As it is planned for the OPAL concept to be extended for use in libraries beyond the Open University, input from a range of information professionals is of importance throughout the project to ensure the system meets the needs of a diverse user base. The focus group of 13 information professionals was invited to the Open University Library to discuss the patterns underpinning reference enquiries and to describe the functionality and capacity of an ideal automated reference enquiry system. In particular, the focus group emphasized the need for understanding the whole enquiry context, usually ascertained during face-to-face enquiries via the reference interview process.

The enquiry context includes all the verbal and non-verbal clues which gives librarians the information they need in order to select the appropriate answer, such as the manner, language and terminology in which an enquiry is expressed. This context also includes users' previous library experience, their level of information and IT literacy, their expectations concerning the level of service available, their cultural and professional background, the specific course being studied, and the urgency of the information needed.

All impact upon the answer selected by a real librarian, and where possible the OPAL system, will need to be able to identify these differing user contexts by means of user profiling in order to deliver a more specific answer to the user. In the case of universities, much of the information required for user profiling is already held on centralized university student authentication systems, or could be gathered via the development of a personal information environment (PIE). The PIE concept has already been tested through the UK HeadLine (Hybrid Electronic Access and Delivery in the Library Networked Environment) project (Gambles, 2001). The PIE presents the user with an information environment that is tailored to their needs, also allowing user personalization. The Open University Library is now planning a 'My Open Libr@ry' PIE style facility, alongside which the OPAL system would sit. Public libraries, with their particularly wide user base and remit, pose greater problems for user profiling, and represent a further area of research for the OPAL project.

Exploring the user perspective

In addition to understanding the iterative nature of the reference interview process and the importance of the enquiry context, another key part of the OPAL project is to get a clear picture of the system's users, and an understanding of the way they interact with web-based applications. To this end a series of experiments was conducted at an Open University psychology residential school held in July 2001. The aim of these experiments was:

- to gather a clean data set for the analysis of question types and potential keywords
- to see if there are any significant differences between the types of questions asked, depending on the nature of the agent answering the question (see the details of the experimental design set out below)
- to see if there is any correlation between the types of question asked and the level of experience that the student has in using internet applications.

In total, 60 students took part. Participants were read a scenario explaining about the introduction of a new Open Libr@ry question-and-answer service called OPAL. In the scenario they were told they were about to begin a new course assignment and had decided to see if the OPAL service could be of assistance. They were then invited to put a question to OPAL. The scenario was read to participants, as opposed to them being given a written version, so as to avoid giving cues that might bias their responses. Each student was allocated to one of three groups. Each group undertook a slightly differing experiment:

1 In the first group participants were *not* given any information about the nature of the agent who would be answering their query – i.e. they were not informed whether they were dealing with a human agent or a computer agent.
2 In the second group participants were told that an artificial agent – in other

words, a computer system – would be answering their query.

3 In the third group participants were told that a human being would be answering their query.

Each student was then asked to put a question to the system, and to phrase it in three different ways. This was done to ensure that a wide variety of requests was obtained. Finally, the participant filled out a short questionnaire detailing which web-based applications they had used. Each enquiry was automatically archived into an Access database.

Our hypothesis was that the nature of the agent participants believed they were interacting with would make a significant difference to the length of the question they asked. Specifically, if the participants thought they were interacting with a human being they would ask questions in grammatical sentences (e.g. 'What Psychology journals do you have in stock?'), whereas if the participants thought they were interacting with an artificial agent they would ask questions in the form of a list of ungrammatical keywords (e.g. 'psychology, journals') in much the same way as a person would use a search engine.

In fact our results showed there was no significant difference between any of the three experimental groups in terms of the length of the query that was submitted. Table 10.1 illustrates this by showing the mean length of query in terms of numbers of words.

Table 10.1   *Word length of queries submitted to three agents*

Type of agent answering the query	Mean length of query (in words)
No information given	4.35
Software	4.83
Human	4.9

Another possibility was that there was a correlation between the experience a person had in using web applications and the nature of the question that was asked. For example, this correlation could be in terms of the length of the enquiry, the subject matter, or the manner in which the question was posed, i.e. keywords or natural language. Each participant was given one point for each of the various web-related activities they had undertaken. Again there seemed to be no correlation between query type and experience of web applications with a score of –0.04.

From keyword analysis of the data, it was also found that the majority of participants formulated subject enquiries using subject-specific keywords drawn from within the psychology knowledge domain, such as 'model', 'modelling', 'cognitive', 'cognition', 'memory', 'psychology', and 'neuropsychology'. This is as opposed to resource- and access-specific keywords, such as 'journal', 'password', and 'database'.

From these results it is clear that neither the nature of the agent with which they were communicating, nor the participants' level of experience, made any significant difference to the length of query they submitted to the system. This is largely counter-intuitive – one might question what could cause the participants to behave in such a way. One possibility is the nature of the visual clues given by the online form itself. Despite the text box being much larger than those used in typical search engines, the interface still had the general appearance of a search engine and this could have been the determining factor in many cases. Another aspect of natural-language-based search engines is that many of them (see, for example, **www.askjeeves.com**) have an avatar as part of their look and feel. This helps to personalize the system so that people feel asking a question in a natural language is a natural thing to do. Again this need for an avatar could be part of our visual heritage and literacy, and will be researched by the OPAL team.

With respect to the participants' keyword usage, the dominance of subject-related rather than resource-specific keywords could be an indicator of the participants' subject- and course-centred perspective. It could also indicate a general lack of awareness about the types of electronic library resources available via the web, e.g. databases, e-books and electronic journals. This indicates the need to research user perceptions and expectations about online library services in order to understand how best to develop and convey library services to the user. It also indicates that the OPAL system should be built from the user's subject- and topic-oriented perspective rather than from the librarian's often resource-orientated perspective, and this will be an approach investigated in the OPAL prototype.

Possible technical solutions

There have already been several attempts in both the UK and the USA to build automated library systems capable of handling natural-language enquiries. In 1997, Newcastle University, UK, created NERD (Newcastle Electronic Reference Desk, **www.ncl.ac.uk/library/**) (Gleadhill, 1997), a database of common enquiry questions and answers searchable in natural language powered by Orbital Organik Knowledgeware (**www.orbitalsw.com/**). Through NERD users can ask a question of the automated system and, if an answer is not on the system, can then choose to e-mail the question to a librarian. The librarian then answers the enquiry and chooses whether or not to add the new question–answer pair to the NERD database. The concept behind NERD was derived from Mark Ackerman's work at MIT on the Answer Garden (Ackerman, 1994 and 1996). In the Answer Garden new questions – i.e. those not already included in the knowledge base – were fielded to a group of experts who could then add their answer to an ever-growing database of questions and answers, hence the name Answer Garden. While providing obvious benefits, the OPAL team also felt this question–answer model posed possible issues surrounding maintenance and quality control, with the potential for record overlap as the knowledge base grew. Nor did it take into account the user's enquiry context or reflect closely enough the iterative, diagnostic nature of the reference interview process between the librarian and student.

Fully automated question–answer services have also been developed in the USA, the most successful of which include the Indiana University Knowledge Base (**http://kb.indiana.edu/**) and the Massachusetts Institute of Technology's START Natural Language Question Answering System (SynTactic Analysis using Reversible Transformations) (**www.ai.mit.edu/projects/infolab/**) (Katz, 1997). These systems do provide reliable answers to user questions and also have good quality control mechanisms in place, but could also represent high-maintenance or complex development, particularly in the case of START, whose natural-language processing and artificial intelligence capacity is beyond the scope of the OPAL project.

Recently there has also been an emergence in the use of web-based virtual assistants for the delivery of customer service (Lees, 2001; Chartrand, 2001; Denison, 2001). These virtual assistants, also known as conversational bots and vReps, can receive and respond to questions submitted by the user in natural language. They are programmed to recognize and respond to questions within their predefined knowledge domain, and this knowledge domain is usually based upon topic hierarchies. Most often these virtual assistants take the form of a text box accompanied by an avatar, where the avatar is used to make the service seem more personable and human. There are several software developers now creating bespoke conversational bots for a number of big name companies. The OPAL team is also investigating and testing this style of conversational bot software, which could offer diagnostic possibilities if programmed correctly.

It should be remembered that one aim of the OPAL project is to free up staff time to concentrate on more complex tasks while the OPAL system handles routine enquiries on their behalf. It is important that any system developed does not absorb all free staff time with the maintenance of the new OPAL service.

Developing the OPAL prototype

In the first phase of the project, we aim to build a prototype capable of handling routine enquiries submitted in natural language. The system will answer questions about the library itself such as those about opening hours and core services, and secondly the system will point users towards Open Libr@ry website resources relevant to their query. It has been found that around 70% of all enquiries received by the library's Learner Support Team can be answered using information already on the Open Libr@ry website. Initially the system is being developed to answer enquiries within two subject domains – social science and management and business – and will also aim to answer non-subject specific and general enquiries.

The OPAL prototype will draw on a wide range of current and emerging software technologies. With respect to the first iteration of OPAL, we are currently experimenting with an open source content management framework system called Zope (**www.zope.org**). As well as facilitating dynamic content, searching and connection to external relational databases, Zope is also extensible with either Python (**www.python.org**) or Perl (**www.perl.com**). In the current OPAL prototype, students will be able to submit their enquiry in natural language to a Zope-based system, where a Python pre-processor will strip the text of stop words and filter out keywords to provide a series of search terms. Using the Zope content management framework, we are looking at the creation of a topic hierarchy containing the knowledge domains of social science, management and business, and also a topic hierarchy for generalist enquiries. The search terms will filter and descend through this topic hierarchy and its associated metadata, mapping the search terms onto relevant subject and general information resources available on the Open Libr@ry website. When a set of matches has been found, a results page will be built on the fly for the student, who will then be asked if the results are suitable. Students can then choose to accept the first set of results or choose to search for broader or more detailed information, and hence descend or ascend within the topic hierarchy structure. The OPAL prototype will use concepts drawn from the topic hierarchy technology used in commercial virtual assistants. This will give the system a diagnostic element, with the possibility of some degree of reference interview process between the student and the system. However, rather than just delivering a single response, as is the case with many online virtual assistants, the OPAL prototype will offer the student a list of suitable options, more in the manner of systems such as NERD and the Indiana University Knowledge Base. In short, the OPAL prototype will aim to guide students to a suitable set of information resources for their needs using the Zope topic hierarchy as a guiding knowledge map.

Further development and implementation

It is then hoped to move into an implementation stage. During this stage the system will be scaled up and integrated with existing university systems, such as the planned My Open Libr@ry personal information environment. This will enable user profiling and help deliver answers more readily geared to the user's enquiry context, possibly incorporating a recommender system where pages could be pushed to the user given the previous pages they have visited. Finally, the team envisages the possibility of an 'artificial librarian'. This would be a far more advanced addition to the Zope topic hierarchy system, and would involve building a community of intelligent mobile software agents capable of traversing Open Libr@ry's network of databases in order to answer more specialized questions.

Conclusion

It is hoped that during the life cycle of the OPAL project there will be opportunities to experiment with a range of new and emerging technologies and technical solutions. Indeed the project itself may help to shape some of these and to influence developing standards. The project team is keen to share knowledge and experience as widely as possible both within and outside the library community.

References

Ackerman, M. S. (1994) Augmenting the organizational memory: a field study of Answer Garden, *Proceedings of the ACM Conference on Computer Supported Cooperative Work*, available at
www.ics.uci.edu/~ackerman/pub/94b12/cscw94.html

Ackerman, M. S. (1996) Answer Garden 2: merging organizational memory with collaborative help, *Proceedings of the ACM Conference on Computer Supported Cooperative Work (CSCW 96)*, Boston MA, November 1996, available at
www.ics.uci.edu/~ackerman/pub/96b22/cscw96.ag2.html

Chartrand, S. (2001) New customer service software, *The New York Times* on the web, 20 August 2001, available at
www.nytimes.com

Denison, D. C. (2001) Bots for business, *Boston Globe*, (13 May 2001), available at
www.artificiallife.com/publications_us/2001_05_1.asp

Feldman, S. (2000) The Answer Machine, *Searcher*, **8** (1), available at
www.infotoday.com/searcher/jan00/feldman.htm

Gambles, A. (2001) The HeadLine personal information environment: evaluation

phase one, *D-Lib Magazine*, **7** (3), available at
www.dlib.org/dlib/march01/gambles/03gambles.html

Gleadhill, D. (1997) Electronic enquiry desk: does NERD have the answer?, *Library Technology*, **2** (2), 35–6.

Katz, B. (1997) From sentence processing to information access on the world wide web, *AAAI Spring Symposium on Natural Language Processing for the World Wide Web, Stanford University*, Stanford CA.

Lees, J. (2001) The gift of the gab: virtual assistants, *InternetWorks*, **48** (September), 12.

Masterton, S. (1997) The virtual participant: lessons to be learned from a case based tutor's assistant, *Computer Support for Collaborative Learning '97, University of Toronto, Canada, December 10–14, 1997*, available at
www.oise.utoronto.ca/cscl/

THEME 3
VIRTUAL LIBRARIES AND NATIONAL INITIATIVES

11

A DISTRIBUTED NATIONAL ELECTRONIC RESOURCE FOR LEARNING AND TEACHING

Caroline Ingram and Catherine Grout

Introduction

JISC and the DNER

The Joint Information Systems Committee (JISC, **www.jisc.ac.uk/**) has responsibility for the provision of network and data services to the whole of the UK's higher and further education communities. The Distributed National Electronic Resource (DNER, **www.jisc.ac.uk/dner/**) aims to bring together much of the JISC's service provision in an information environment allowing easy access to quality-assured learning, teaching and research resources.

The DNER initiative includes development programmes. In total, £13 million has recently been distributed to projects across the UK for the development of the DNER. The majority of funding (about £9 million) was allocated to the enhancement and development of materials for learning and teaching. The 26 projects in this area are concerned with the generation of a range of new digital content for learning and teaching, including tailored learning materials. In addition, seven projects were funded to enhance existing JISC service provision of learning and teaching materials.

Electronic resources in the academic context

Network technology has made it possible for electronic resources to be provided and accessed throughout the UK. It enables the exploitation of the rich diversity of resources available to the higher and further education community and the development of various delivery modes, interfaces and accompanying support services. The JISC's resources have been used heavily in research for a number of years. Increasingly students are able to turn to the internet and digital resources when seeking material to support their studies. Networked access to digital resources greatly expands the amount of material open to them and can do much to reduce inequalities in resource provision between institutions. Teaching and research staff, apart from being heavy users of digital resources, are also creators.

A DNER should allow them not only to create resources that are accessible within their own institution but also to manipulate electronic resources to enhance learning, teaching and research.

These resources are very rich and include textbooks, journals, monographs, theses, abstracts, manuscripts, maps, music scores, still images, geospatial images and other kinds of data, as well as moving picture and sound collections.

This information environment must be fit to serve the needs of students, teachers and researchers in further and higher education into the future. The development of a robust and appropriate platform to provide access to educational content for learning, teaching and research purposes is a key component of the JISC five-year strategy, which includes a commitment to: 'build an on-line information environment providing secure and convenient access to a comprehensive collection of scholarly and educational material' (JISC, 2001). The development of this information environment is being led by the DNER team.

Development activity is essential for the JISC across all of its various initiatives and programmes, as it defines the process for moving forward and allows appropriate investment to take place. The JISC's development activity is clearly pivotal for a leading-edge initiative such as the information environment, which is an innovative vision for service provision. It is, however, also worth noting that the information environment rests upon a conceptual and abstract framework that is somewhat in advance of what it is currently possible to offer to students and teachers who access digital resources.

However, as it aims to stay 'ahead of the game', the JISC needs to provide active evidence of what the landscape of the future will look like. The information environment is about providing real resources to real students now, and in ways which appeal to them and those who teach them. It needs to be able to demonstrate the range of significant services and resources funded by the JISC to a diverse constituency of users, while providing evidence, particularly to teachers and information mediators, of the validity of new approaches to teaching – for example, allowing teachers to interact with demonstrators which show the potential of the new range of portal services envisaged and the power of searching across a diverse range of information resources.

These new developments are not only technically innovative, they also have the power to transform the process of learning and research. By transforming and informing the currency of how information and learning resources are accessed, they will bring fundamental change to the process of learning and research. For example, the JISC Information Environment will provide new opportunities for interrogating aggregated resources supporting the discovery and the presentation of items in new contexts, so pushing back the boundaries of knowledge.

The Information Environment

The current information environment can be characterized as the set of network services that support publishing and the use of information resources. At the moment online services providing digital resources tend to operate in a standalone manner. The user is therefore required to navigate a complex set of different websites with different interfaces in order to locate relevant resources. It has been recognized that this is one of the key factors limiting take-up of digital resource. The JISC is now looking to a broader information environment, which supports web-like integration for richer, structured content.

It is acknowledged that the information environment envisaged for the JISC is ambitious. This is primarily because it has evolved to embrace two key concepts which are by nature semantically and technically complex to advance through a process of investment. These are:

- the view that information resources are inherently distributed and will never be provided by a single service provider
- the view that users do not all want to access information in the same way but will require a diverse range of views of that information in order to satisfy their needs; for example, a web portal is essentially a window upon a set of distributed resources, which can be defined in different areas (e.g. subject, bibliographic).

This inherent complexity is a common feature of the emerging e-learning culture, and the national and international infrastructures which are being required to support it. The development strategy for the JISC Information Environment articulates how the JISC can progress this distributed model, based upon the foundation made by the JISC's investment and research over the past five years. Further development of the Information Environment will rest on directed development programmes.

A collaborative environment

The DNER development is part of a national and global agenda for developing environments for lifelong learning. Other initiatives, in the UK particularly the People's Network, the National Grid for Learning and the Research Grid are, like the JISC's Information Environment, intending to provide information and resources for new generations of adult learners, who will increasingly rely on accessing information and training through virtual, networked environments. The DNER strategy recognizes that key to pursuing the development of the information environment is working in partnership with other agencies who are also looking to find solutions to the challenges of distributed information resources and ways of presenting it to new audiences.

For example, the JISC Information Environment needs to progress in such a way that it fully acknowledges the needs of the post-16, as well as the higher, or university, education constituency. It needs to be geared up to the delivery, discovery and presentation of appropriate learning materials, and needs to support the submission and exchange of individual learning objects. It is worth pointing out that the needs of the higher education sector are far from resolved in terms of what the JISC currently offers, and much further work is necessary. However, it is essential for the information environment to engage directly with post-16 learning requirements.

One of the fundamental issues in building national and international environments for accessing shared educational content is the recognition that these activities need to be based on common standards to ensure maximum exchange of resources. These apply to the creation, access, use, preservation and interoperability of networked resources. In order to progress this process, the DNER office has produced a set of standards and guidelines intended to underpin the Information Environment and to support the activities of current and future development programmes (**www.jisc.ac.uk/dner/programmes/guidance/DNERStandards.html**). Moreover, the DNER team is actively participating in the process of sharing and building standards for educational resources in a national and international context.

Goals for the JISC/DNER Information Environment

The JISC/DNER strategy indicates that the Information Environment should achieve the following:

1 It should be fit to serve all kinds of digital content. Kinds of electronic content are increasingly diverse, and may be based on rapidly evolving and non-standard technologies. It has to be able to accommodate all types of content, from streaming video to electronic books to learning objects. It must be able to deliver these efficiently to users, and must allow them to be accessed in a series of useful and satisfying ways which progress learning, teaching and research.

2 It should support fully the submission and sharing of research and learning objects. Activity will focus on methods and toolkits to allow members of the community to build content that they will access, and to share this in meaningful ways with colleagues and peers. This activity will build a framework for leveraging our mutual community resource, the significance of which is emphasized in the JISC five-year strategy and elsewhere.

3   It should provide a range of meaningful and innovative methods of accessing electronic materials, to enrich learning and research processes. This is achieved through developing portals relevant to the needs of end-users, and which can also be embedded in institutional websites. These also create a presentation layer, which provides windows on the rich content available through development projects, the collections of the national data services and, increasingly, community-leveraged resources.

4   It should be a collaborative landscape of networked national service providers, who work together to cater seamlessly for the needs of the community. This will be achieved through the developing sophistication of shared services, which will enable the information environment to operate in a truly joined-up fashion.

5   It should be underpinned by interoperability, based upon a common standards framework and common semantic for digital resource description and access. It has become clear that enhanced interoperability for users will not be achieved without the agreement of some common semantics supporting cross-searching. As part of developing the Information Environment, the JISC will strive for the cross-sectoral adoptions of standard terminologies – for example, for subject or resource type.

DNER development programmes

The JISC has been successful in developing a portfolio of online digital information and data resources that are an important component of the DNER. To date these data have been used primarily for research purposes, although existing content should also be of great value for learning and teaching. Much content, however, needs to be repurposed for learning needs. Alternatively, routes into datasets can be developed to aid their use.

Development activity for learning and teaching purposes should enable some of the goals above to be met and the products offered through JISC services to be used in different ways from those originally envisaged. The current development programmes arose out of the need to integrate learning environments with the wider information landscape, aimed at increasing the use of online electronic information and research datasets in learning and teaching processes. Following the Comprehensive Spending Review (CSR), funds were allocated to the JISC to improve the applicability of its collections and resources for learning and teaching (see below, Learning and Teaching Programme). JISC also allocated funds, as part of the ongoing development of the information environment, to an initiative enhancing the infrastructure of JISC services to support the DNER (Infrastructure Programme).

A number of management and co-ordination mechanisms are already in place or are being developed which will feed directly into, and support, development activity. These include the standards and guidelines document mentioned above, and the DNER team's involvement in national initiatives to meet the goal of ensuring that development is underpinned by interoperability.

The projects funded under the Learning and Teaching Programme and the Infrastructure Programme have been clustered according to themes. This encourages efficient use of resources for collaborative training and events, sharing of metadata and dissemination of the project results to the relevant learning and teaching communities. A number of successful synthesis events have been organized by the DNER team, bringing together all projects in the programme, as well as project staff from other initiatives. These meetings are useful not only for disseminating operational information (on topics such as accessibility and interoperability) but also for exchanging ideas on development activities and future direction and for providing feedback to the JISC.

As has been emphasized, development is one of the key strands of activity for the JISC for the foreseeable future. Development activities are currently taking place within a number of related JISC-managed areas. It is clearly important for DNER development activity to be developed actively with cognate areas. Of particular relevance are managed learning environments (MLEs), authentication and authorization, and content delivery architecture developments.

The Infrastructure Programme

The Infrastructure Programme was funded to contribute to the technical infrastructure of the Information Environment. The projects involved are clustered in three areas:

- z-projects (investigating use of the search protocol Z39.50)
- Article Infrastructure Services (or 'Join-Up', concerned with enhancing access to serials and articles)
- the Resource Discovery Network development projects (improving and increasing access to quality internet resources for the learning, teaching and research community using the RDN); most RDN projects are building subject-specific portals.

The Learning and Teaching Programme

The Learning and Teaching Programme (L&T) has the following complementary aims:

- to enhance service provision and re-orient it to provide for learning and teaching
- to carry out research on the information environment
- to enhance access to networked resources through research into, and development of, the semantic challenges posed by achieving interoperability of information resources.

The projects are clustered according to media type (images, moving image and sound) or aim of project (enhancing JISC data services and access to L&T or museum resources), as well as a number of miscellaneous projects linking MLE/VLE developments in a related programme and others in the e-books and pricing strategy areas.

Exploiting the potential of subject-based resources online

The Virtual Norfolk project is clustered with projects using museum and archive content to create learning and teaching materials. The project aims to create a website providing access to original historical documents and image material (**www.uea.ac.uk/his/virtualnorfolk/**). The overall objective of the project is to create a web-based history L&T resource which can expand its provision by exporting its structure and encouraging collaboration between institutions and regional record offices.

The importance of using historical documents as a core element in teaching history has long been recognized. However, there are problems in providing wide student access to such materials. Recent educational and technological change may provide the potential for widening access. The Virtual Norfolk project builds upon earlier work seeking to provide students and tutors with access to historical documents.

Until the end of the 18th century Norwich was one of the pre-eminent cities in England, and for much of that period was the 'second city' after London. What is more, the region was one of the most densely populated, and therefore closely governed, in the British Isles. Thus the resources for this period archived at the Norfolk Record Office are unparalleled outside the capital, and permit exploration of the major themes of historical study. Furthermore, the documents are a resource of national and international interest. The problems in utilizing these rich materials are exacerbated by Norwich's present comparative geographical isolation, making electronic access ideal.

The core of Virtual Norfolk will be a database consisting of transcriptions and digitized images of original documents (c.1200–1850), and other relevant images (maps, engravings), music and video footage. The database will also include reference maps, a bibliography, a timeline, glossary terms and a biographical section devoted to notable characters from the source material. The database will be indexed and fully searchable.

Constructed around this database will be learning and teaching packs, providing organized pathways through the material. Each pack will focus on a theme, issue or topic and will be suitable for use as either an individual seminar or as the foundation for a complete module. A library of such packs is envisaged, allowing flexibility for users. The inclusion of well-researched metadata will enable the site to attain its goal of providing flexible learning and teaching resources capable of delivering primary materials to students and teachers of history across a broad spectrum of the educational sector.

Finally, Scalable Vector Graphics (a sub-set of XML) will be used to create interactive historical mapping of Norfolk. The aim is to link as many geographically determined files to their locations as possible. In the long term users will be able to click on a village and receive a menu of associated object files and links to related material.

To encourage students to reflect critically upon the process of creating history it is intended to include learning pathways, facilitating the acquisition of basic skills. Students will be able to begin to grasp the complexities of translating raw historical materials into contemporary English. Virtual Norfolk's use of these learning pathways, and the inclusion of skills-based tutorial packs, will allow tutors to impress upon students the fragility of representations of the past and historical narratives.

Exploiting the potential of media-based resources online

Other projects in the programme have similar aims in terms of integration of materials, facilitating access to physical materials of whatever media type, and linking resources more widely for learning and teaching purposes.

Digital images have a rich potential as learning and teaching resources and are currently under-utilized in support of pedagogical activities in many subject areas. The FILTER (Focusing Images for Learning and Teaching – an Enriched Resource, **www.jisc.ac.uk/dner/programmes/projects/filter/**) project aims to address this under-use and encourage uptake of visual resources. Categorizations will form the basis of the project deliverables: a generic image dataset, a set of subject-specific image datasets, and supporting documentation such as 'how-to' guides and case studies. A framework for the production and utilization of digital image exemplar datasets and materials will also be developed.

A high level of expertise in image use exists in some subject areas, but often using a limited range of image types. The FILTER team aims to enable, through working with a variety of Learning and Teaching Support Network Subject Centres (LTSNs), a cross-fertilization of knowledge across subject disciplines, so that there are multiple learning opportunities for all involved. The transferral of expertise will have a major role in the development of the subject-specific datasets. The approach should permit the team to identify and explore common factors of image in a range of subjects. The synthesis of these factors in the exemplar database will ensure maximum benefit to the widest possible potential user-base. The project will also identify, investigate and establish standards for issues underlying the creation and use of image databases for wide dissemination to the learning and teaching community.

The project fits closely within the aims of the DNER Learning and Teaching development programme by providing exemplar digitization and supporting materials to directly inspire use of images in learning and teaching, with particular emphasis in subject areas not normally accustomed to using digital images as learning and teaching tools.

Conclusions

The JISC has a high level of responsibility for ensuring that its products enhance education. JISC services need to be proactive to ensure that what is produced by projects has an impact on education and will be used and useful into the future.

Organizations adopt information and communications technology because it offers them perceived net benefits offset against costs. It may be that the same rules of adoption apply to learners and teachers in higher and further education institutions. However, many tutors see online learning as a threat to established educational values, partly because in many institutions managers and inter-mediaries direct investment into new electronic resources and teachers are not getting involved deeply enough in the choices available (Bentham, 2001).

Criticism has been levelled at the resources available to the learning and teaching community. A recent JISC-funded study (Rowley, 2000) reported the following barriers to development of appropriate and adequate learning and teaching resources:

- the diversity of the community (FE/HE, range of qualifications taught)
- changes in institutions for widening access
- collection development policies (libraries versus departments)
- subject-based differences.

The JISC/DNER needs to address these barriers, to get teachers to see past the individual and institutional barriers to uptake. Teachers and learners also need to be encouraged to lose their concern about the technology, and instead to see the tools integrated seamlessly into their teaching. At one level the JISC is improving access to, and use of, its resources through the programmes described above. The JISC is also working to improve the infrastructure that sits behind the delivery of services to universities and further education colleges.

In other recent developments in JISC services the Resource Discovery Network (offered online and free at point of use) has been enhancing what it can offer, seeking to embed the RDN into university home pages and also to offer value added services rather than just lists of links to quality resources. All of the RDN's c.30,000 resources are selected, catalogued and described by subject and information professionals drawn from over 60 UK education institutions and related organizations. A new 'Behind the Headlines' service offers users background information on the latest news stories via pre-set searches of high-quality internet resources.

The RDN also offers the Virtual Training Suite, funded through the Learning and Teaching Programme, which currently consists of 27 subject-based online tutorials, directing users to the best sites in their subject or to further information on how to find quality-assured information in their subject on the internet. In the next few months, another 11 tutorials will be written, specifically aimed at courses taught in FE colleges.

A study on advancing the use of electronic learning and teaching materials through routes to assisted take-up is to be carried out under funding from the current JISC Learning and Teaching Programme. The study team will be asked to explore innovative ways to ensure uptake of resources where appropriate. In addition the study will need to consider:

- improving familiarity and confidence
- offering the best subject-based tools
- encouraging creative applications
- the responsibility for take-up
- publicizing best practice.

The study should elicit innovative ways in which the JISC/DNER can develop its activity to account more for the needs of users.

The Information Environment aims to offer the user a more seamless and less complex journey to relevant information and learning resources. The Learning and Teaching Programme is, in particular, intended to advance a common fabric of information use and learning opportunity. It is hoped that this will both support and influence institutions and individuals in the future.

References

Bentham, M. (2001) Web learning: threat, panacea, or enrichment?, *Library Association Record*, **103** (5), 294–5.

JISC (2001) *JISC five year strategy 2001–2005*, available at
www.jisc.ac.uk.pub01/strat_01_05/

Rowley, J. (2000) *JISC user behaviour monitoring and evaluation framework: first annual report*, available at
www.jisc.ac.uk/pub00/m&e_rep1.html

12

ACCESS TO LARGE AMOUNTS OF ELECTRONIC SCIENTIFIC INFORMATION ON A NATIONAL LEVEL

Bo Öhrström

Introduction

The name of the national Danish project is Denmark's Electronic Research Library, which is abbreviated to DEF in Danish. DEF is the realization of a vision of one virtual research library focused on the need for easy access to scientific information for researchers and students in Denmark. The project aims to help the transition from purely paper-based services to electronic services in the library sector and focuses on organizational changes as well.

This chapter will describe the background and the present status of the project and explains the planning methods for achieving the goals of the project. The project is heavily based on co-operation at national and international levels, and the strategy behind this is put forward. One of the important tasks is to establish a technical national infrastructure, which primarily contains a portal, a number of subject portals or subject-based information guides, an access control system and a service for accessing journals in full text. This infrastructure is based on modern technical principles, and the development work aiming at a common national solution will be presented. Finally the chapter will discuss challenges in a national project as seen from a Danish perspective.

Background

Denmark's Electronic Research Library aims to move Danish libraries from a state of automated, conventional, co-operating individual libraries to a state of a single large, coherent, electronic library structure providing integrated information services.

The project was defined in a project description of September 1996 by the three ministries involved, which were:

- the Ministry of Culture
- the Ministry of Research
- the Ministry of Education.

A governmental agency, UNI-C, and the management consulting firm Ernst and Young then conducted a study, which resulted in the publishing of a report in early Spring 1997. The report described a vision for the development of research libraries in Denmark.

On the basis of this work the three ministries decided to develop the Danish research libraries over a five-year period (1998–2002) in order to get them to function as one integrated research library: Denmark's Electronic Research Library. The ministries made funding of 200 million DKr available for the project. The project was a part of the government's initiative for research and IT, and it is still part of the present political planning for the IT and knowledge society in Denmark.

The project teams created for the implementation of DEF comprised the following:

• a liaison group consisting of members from the three ministries involved
• a steering committee with 11 members appointed by the ministries and organizations
• a secretariat integrated with the Danish National Library Authority.

The steering committee represents various skills such as library management, research, IT and commercial work. The role of the secretariat in the Danish National Library Authority is to execute the decisions of the steering committee in general.

After approximately one year's work, the roles of the steering committee and the secretariat were changed from traditional steering committee and secretariat to something more akin to a board of directors and managing director in a private company. This was the result of the chairman of the steering committee's demand for speed and minimal interference in the work of the secretariat between the committee meetings.

The goal for the secretariat and the steering committee is to realize the vision of the 1997 report, taking into account that global changes will impact on conditions and opportunities for the project.

From vision to action

Some key points from the report are:

1 A network of electronic libraries. The aim is not to build one huge central library, but instead to use an internet-based networking structure. The physical libraries and information centre must be linked to one another and establish several virtual libraries.

2 Virtual access to all information resources in Denmark. Access to the electronic library should be possible from any location, whether from work, home or a mobile telephone. The goal involves access to all Danish resources – but this should not be limited to purely Danish resources.
3 New standards and working relations. New standards must be devised in order to build an open structure that enables the use of existing subsystems and easy interoperability with other systems. The new working relations are a very interesting and important area, since old boundaries have to be removed and new relationships established, mostly due to the new media and its possibilities.

The four areas of activity

The project is divided into four areas of activity:

* national infrastructure
* library infrastructure
* digital resources
* user facilities.

National infrastructure

The national infrastructure is the IT network and facilities enabling the libraries and the users to communicate efficiently.

The Danish Research Network has been chosen as the IT network, and this high-speed network has the advantage that a substantial proportion of the libraries and the users are already linked to it.

This national infrastructure is, however, more than technology. The overall infrastructure includes creating common guidelines for national licensing agreements, exchange of information, use of international standards, unified user access, etc. The regulations for user administration must also be uniform and agreed by all the libraries.

Library infrastructure

For each library to become part of the virtual library, they need to be modernized in a number of ways. Until now it has been acceptable for each library to use its own individual IT systems and organizational procedures. In the virtual research library, the technology and a number of organizational issues must be standardized.

Increasing co-operation between the research libraries will require overall common management and co-ordination. Co-operation across ministerial borders should be established, but the local participants must retain their independence in order to preserve the dynamics of the system.

Digital resources

Digitization of some parts of various collections is under consideration. For the digitized materials the challenges are:

- efficient management
- wide access
- protection against damage and misuse
- migration to future technological platforms.

National principles and a strategy for digitization are being developed by the steering committee. This involves the establishment of standards, methods and competence centres – and a plan for the selection of collections to be digitized.

National licensing agreements are negotiated and signed by the Danish National Library Authority on behalf of DEF. A better term for these agreements might be common licences or DEF licences, since most of them do not cover the whole nation but only the users of the essential institutions. As usual any library can co-operate with another library or institution, form a consortium and negotiate licences. The consortium can apply for financial backing from DEF or just hand over the licence to DEF, thereby ensuring that more relevant institutions are invited to share the licence. In this case the licence will be transferred to the Danish National Library Authority as holder of the licence.

Other digital resources are the Danish Research Database, which is being transformed into a new web-based architecture, and a large number of retro-converted card catalogues, the conversion of which was financed by DEF.

User facilities

For the digital library user, facilities will be a major issue, especially in economic terms. It will be crucial to provide the user with sufficient facilities and electronic services.

This area of activity focuses on projects such as user services in subject searching (subject portals or subject-based information guides, SBIGs), tools for web-based education, and tools for the annotation of web-based research and studying.

DEF statistics

A precise way to express the current status of the project is to show numbers for several key activities. These numbers are for August 2001 – updated figures are posted on the DEF website (**www.deflink.dk/eng/default.asp**).

1 The DEF portal involves 29 libraries, comprising 12 large and 17 medium-size libraries, all of which have submitted information about their subject areas, participated in the harvesting of their websites, and provided guidelines for the DEF portal.
2 The DEF catalogue of catalogues gives access to more than 400 electronic net resources (catalogues and information databases). This is a function in the DEF portal which points to selected resources at the libraries.
3 Three SBIGs are in operation; two more are opening in Autumn 2001 and a further two are under development.
4 DEF has enabled 55 libraries to install new library systems according to DEF technical standards, and 30 more libraries received funding for this in June 2001.
5 DEF gives access to 30 DEF licences, including approximately 6800 journals in full text. DEF licences are defined as licences negotiated and held by the Danish National Library Authority on behalf of the libraries.
6 DEF provides 104 libraries with access to between one and 40 DEF licences.
7 There are 14 projects working with user education, skills development, user statistics/user satisfaction, digitizing, e-learning, etc.
8 Retroconversion of approximately 2.5 million catalogue cards from the card catalogues of 14 research libraries is in progress at a total cost of 19 Million DKr.

Co-operation is crucial

The philosophy of the project development reflects the importance of national co-operation and consensus. No lasting solutions can be implemented without the participation and acceptance of the libraries. Therefore the key words for all activities are co-operation, co-operation and co-operation. After some time everybody realized that pooling resources gave a better result than everybody working individually. This opinion is obviously easier to obtain with some central funding.

Another way to support co-operation in projects like DEF is to achieve good results. Therefore it is advantageous to choose activities which quickly lead to improved conditions for the libraries and their users. Planning according to the line of least resistance gives quicker results, but it is not the same as dealing with confrontation. Conflict is part of the process and the resolution of conflicts results in a peaceful and lasting consensus.

In order to achieve results, co-operation and effort from the biggest libraries are of great importance. These libraries control most of the financial resources and materials, they already have an organization which can deal with common issues, and they are ready for changes. The DEF project started co-operating with these libraries early on, and their efforts have been of value for the smaller libraries.

National co-operation is not enough, since international co-operation is often the key to solving general problems in building a digital library. DEF's existing international relations can be divided into the commercial and non-commercial sectors.

Commercial relations

Commercial links primarily involve direct contact with multinational suppliers of electronic journals and databases with a view to guaranteeing efficiency and minimizing costs. Because of the complexity of the market the options available for the inexperienced purchaser are limited. Consequently it is necessary to establish a professional liaison or partnership with the supplier in order to secure the continuity of reasonable favourable deals and contracts.

Non-commercial relations

This area mainly involves other projects or national initiatives similar to DEF, and provides a valuable network of inspiration, knowledge and information.

In practice this involves:

- research on, and purchase of, electronic licences
- the development of the technical architecture and user interfaces.

A joint initiative for purchasing electronic licenses was established primarily through close Nordic co-operation and through membership of the International Coalition Of Library Consortia (ICOLC) and the European Coalition Of Library Consortia (ECOLC). The Nordic co-operation covers all aspects of purchase, renewal, service and filing of electronic resources, and serves to underpin a joint Nordic effort in negotiations on prices and services with the suppliers. At an early stage DEF joined in the work of ICOLC in order to be able to participate in international efforts concerning contracts and purchase of electronic resources.

The European equivalent of the American ICOLC – ECOLC – also has Denmark's Electronic Research Library as a member and active participant. Both organizations play a leading role in relation to suppliers of journals, and the collective pressure from ICOLC and ECOLC is a valuable factor when trying to negotiate reasonable prices and contracts.

The development of technical architecture and user interfaces primarily takes place within the framework of the Nordic countries. Here models of interfaces, access control systems, methods of cross searching in catalogues and standardization issues are discussed.

Planning for the success of the DEF project

The project went through different stages in the first two-and-a-half years. The first year was used for staffing the secretariat, making routines for the steering committee and the liaison group and, most importantly, to translate the vision of the report and the ministry expectations into concrete plans. The project gathered speed during the next 18 months and a lot of experimental work was done. In August 2000 a new chairman of the steering committee was appointed, and being a Deputy Director of IBM Denmark, he quickly organized the project plan, with deliveries, milestones and project success criteria. This thinking narrows the possible activities and sub-projects and focuses on successful completion, which ultimately should transfer the project into a permanent activity. Furthermore it optimizes the use of the remaining funding and gives a solid basis for prioritizing.

Examples of general success criteria for the project are:

- a single main portal with unified log-on procedures and a personalized web interface
- cross-searching in library catalogues, electronic journals and reference databases
- tools for information handling either alone or in groups
- access to a large amount of scientific information from work, home and when travelling
- a national digitizing policy combined with projects based on accepted technical standards, which is well used and of interest to the media and the Danish population
- a new organization and model for funding in order to continue existing areas of co-operation
- close co-ordination with the Danish Virtual University project.

These success criteria are detailed in precise quantitative and qualitative criteria for each area of activity. For example, for 'national infrastructure' the success criteria are:

- 1000 unique visitors per day at **deff.dk** (the DEF portal)
- 500 daily personal logins using the DEF key (the access control system)
- 2000 daily searches via the DEF search service for electronic journals
- 1000 daily downloads via the DEF search service or directly from publishers
- five libraries using the DEF key (the access control system)
- single sign-on established to 10 DEF licences
- making available a toolkit which is user-friendly and faultless for building SBIGs; each new SBIG uses as a maximum 20 hours' support each year on the toolkit.

Development of a Danish national infrastructure

In order to provide a solid basis for 24-hour access to the content in the digital library, a system architecture project was launched. The project follows three main principles:

1 The architecture will be the concrete practical implementation and realization of the DEF vision.
2 The vision is a system of systems, meaning that no single central standalone system will be built. A decentralized approach will govern the project.
3 The system architecture project will be the main project for five sub-projects:
   - the DEF portal
   - the DEF key
   - the DEF catalogue
   - the DEF SBIGs
   - the Danish Research Database.

Important milestones for the system architecture project were:

- to have libraries connected to the Danish Research Network in 1998
- for the system architecture project to start in February 1999
- a call for projects in February 1999
- a project seminar in May 1999
- for international co-operation to start in June 1999
- for five SBIGs, a user service and a user education project to start in July 1999
- a key (access control system) report in August 1999
- a DEF portal version 1 (catalogue of catalogues) in operation in October 1999
- a cross-searching test to start at the beginning of 2000
- the first system architecture (Z39.50-based) description in April 2000
- the second system architecture (three-layer architecture) description in October 2000

- for two new SBIGs to start in January 2001
- for the tender for the key system etc. in February 2001
- for three SBIGs to open in April 2001
- that the tender for the key system was called off in July 2001
- that there was new planning for tenders in August 2001
- that the DEF portal version 2 (journals and cross-searching) should be opened in September 2001.

DEF portal development

One access point to the digital library is the DEF portal (**deff.dk**). The DEF portal has passed through two main versions in the development process.

The first generation was a catalogue of catalogues for the 12 large libraries. It was purely based on harvesting, and besides giving access to the libraries resources, the project was the basis for a fundamental co-operation process between the 12 large libraries.

The second generation portal is a catalogue of catalogues for 27 libraries. It is based on cataloguing in a common database, and it gives Z39.50 cross-access searching to more than the 12 large libraries. Furthermore it is possible to order material through the Danish union catalogue and to access the licensed material in DEF.

Further development of a national infrastructure

The next generation of the DEF portal will be based on a new modular technical solution. The existing portal has been less concerned with the technical structure than with gaining experience and results for the project and its users. The new solution will separate different functions in different software modules, which are arranged in a three-layer architecture (see Figure 12.1).

The architecture has three layers, the portal layer; the common service layer and the dataservice supplier layer. The layers are separated (and connected) by XML interfaces.

The portal layer contains only user interface functionality and can provide a personalized interface to the individual user.

The common service layer holds different modules with different primary capabilities. Examples are a search module for the journals and a metadata module for SBIGs.

The dataservice supplier layer will mostly contain existing data suppliers such as journal publishers.

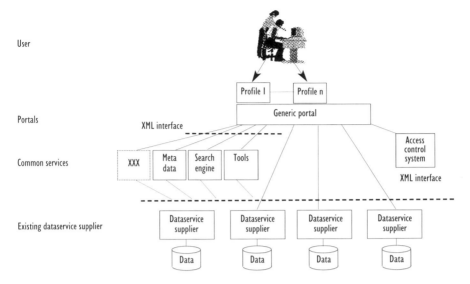

Fig. 12.1 *Three-layer architecture*

Parallel to these three layers is the access control module. This module verifies the user logins and undertakes the authentication and authorization, whereby the user identification and rights will be decentralized and stored in the participating institutions. In this way only the right users can get access to the allowed functions and data.

This architecture has several advantages. It effectively separates user interface discussions from work concerning other functionality, which will improve the final result, since user interface discussions tend to stall much development and progress. It allows a thorough use of the common services, which in the end will provide the users with the necessary functionality for using the data. Furthermore, the data suppliers are separated from the development of user functions. However, the biggest advantage is that the libraries can take the modules they like, change or build their own interface or add local functionality. In this way the libraries share common necessary modules but can still add their own.

The architecture described shows the ideal solution. However, the existing DEF project ends on the 31 December 2002, and this puts a limit on the level of development for the required functionality and number of modules. From a project management point of view, this puts pressure on the involved parties to make decisions and deliver results. The modules will be acquired through a tender process, which allows both academic and commercial suppliers to deliver, provided they can comply with normal commercial rules. Furthermore, it would appear that XML will be replaced by Z39.50 and http protocols for a while, until more effort can be put into XML.

The access control system has already been through an EU tender process together with the Danish Virtual University project. This combined tender reflects the need for a common access system and the close connection between the two projects. This tender was based on the three-layer architecture already described, and was supposed to give the Virtual University project a portal as well. Unfortunately the Virtual University project had to cancel the tender due to lack of funding and poor co-ordination with its users, which means DEF has to start all over again with the access control system – alone.

Experiences in managing a national project

During the first three-and-a-half years a lot of experience has been gained in managing a national digital library project. The most fundamental issue is that national and international co-operation is the gateway to success. It is impossible to be successful unless the national players are co-operating, and the only way to avoid duplicating work is to co-operate internationally.

Another important area to control is increasing project complexity. With many project focus areas, and the decentralized structure in Denmark, progress tends to be slow unless decisions are made at a reasonably quick pace.

The different backgrounds of the steering committee members are both a strength and a weakness. It is valuable to have many experts participating in the group, but it can certainly be a challenge for a chairman to control. Furthermore, it is of great importance to divide the responsibilities and work between steering committee, secretariat and libraries. Specifically it is necessary to give the secretariat financial flexibility and mandate in negotiations and project management, and this has been one means of keeping up to speed in the DEF project.

Development work has been done with both academic and commercial partners. Their ways of working are very different and both have their pros and cons. Put simply, academic work seems to be more effective in the experimental phases, while commercial work fits better into a production system. One difficulty is the need to resort to EU tenders, which is time-consuming and doesn't seem to result in optimal solutions.

Finally, a project manager coming from outside the library sector has gained a lot of experience with libraries. The following points illustrate the meeting between the world of a librarian and that of a computer engineer:

- decisions are necessary – prolonged discussions do not make much progress
- librarians are used to independence – in every aspect
- librarians lack a lot of commercial experience and skills
- librarians are believed to be experts – there are also IT experts
- there are no secrets in the library world or in its surroundings – not even commercial secrets.

13

Library consortia and their educational dimension: the HEAL-Link experience

Claudine Xenidou-Dervou, Sassa Tzedaki,
Anna Fragkou and Marina Korfiati

Introduction

One of the major problems for most academic libraries over the past 30 years has been the high cost of print subscriptions. According to the Association of Research Libraries (ARL), from 1986 to 1998 the unit cost of serials rose by 207% and serial expenditure by 170%. The prices vary for different subject areas, with science, technology and medicine (STM) journals being by far the most expensive ones. Libraries are being forced to cancel their subscriptions to expensive and rarely used journals as periodicals absorb a higher percentage of their budget, and have responded to this situation by relying increasingly on interlibrary loans.

Libraries in several countries have a long history of co-operation, especially for co-operative cataloguing and interlibrary loans. But success in the co-operative development of print collections has been limited and marginal (Shreeves, 1997). Although libraries have long been joining consortia, it seems that consortial arrangements have recently become more popular than ever before. Many of these co-operative efforts have been mandated by governing bodies for the sole purpose of saving money by sharing a core of electronic products. In other cases, older consortia have gained a new lease of life by taking on the challenge of co-operatively developing electronic or virtual libraries. Whether old or new, today's most successful consortia provide three basic functions: sharing physical resources, providing connections to the internet and the world wide web, and providing access to electronic resources.

The most important factor in the success of the new consortia has been the ability to obtain more favourable pricing for products than libraries have been able to obtain individually (Kohl, 1997). Furthermore, by having access to a large pool of funds, consortium directors have been more easily able to attract the interest of producers/publishers, who can now negotiate for larger sums of money with fewer customers (Thornton, 2000). Yet one more reason for the success of consortia is their ability to provide greater access to core materials needed by the smaller libraries within the group, improved level of service, and convenience to users previously excluded from expensive resources which their individual libraries could not provide, plus the possibility that consortia will be able to contain future costs.

Co-operation among Greek libraries

In Greece, libraries do not have a long history of co-operation. With the exception of a national programme for interlibrary loan of journal articles that was initiated in the early 1990s by the National Documentation Centre, libraries in Greece for a long time operated in isolation both at national as well as international level. Any co-operation that existed in earlier years was mainly based on personal initiatives. The area where academic libraries suffered most was the reality of stagnant budgets which, in combination with double-digit inflation and double-digit price increases, had forced libraries to keep cancelling journal subscriptions every two or three years in order to survive. With a limited national collection, libraries turned to the British Library Document Supply Centre for interlibrary loan services at a high cost, which they were unable to contain and therefore passed directly to the users. As a result library services were suffering, since in Greece there is no national body like the British Library to supplement the limited national collection and subsidize the diminishing journal subscriptions with interlibrary loan.

According to the Greek constitution, higher education is offered strictly by government-funded institutions that operate under the auspices of the Ministry of Education and Religious Affairs. There are 33 academic institutions including the recently founded Open University: 18 of these award doctorates, while 14 are technology education institutes which offer only undergraduate studies. Higher education (HE) is free to all and no tuition fees are charged. Enrolment is on the basis of participation in national examinations. Not only are no tuition fees charged, but every student at every level of public education in Greece, including HE, receives one textbook free of charge for each course attended. As a result, there seemed to be little need for library services for undergraduate students in the past. Thus, academic libraries were mainly catering for the needs of the faculty staff members.

In 1995 the Greek Ministry of Education and Religious Affairs requested proposals for funding from the HE institutes for upgrading their services. Ultimately all institutions (and libraries) received funding which came in part from the European Union's Structural Funding Programme. Most institutions purchased library automation systems, undertook retrospective cataloguing, established CD-ROM networks, created web pages and supplemented materials (primarily journals) budgets. While such individual funding was useful, it did not really address the huge potential of library co-operation, so it was suggested that in addition to the vertical actions (i.e. funding and developing individual libraries) there should be a horizontal action in support of collective library activities. One of the horizontal activities was dealing with the problem of escalating serial costs.

HEAL-Link

In a report which was submitted by the Serials Cost Working Group in December 1997, the focus was shifted from co-ordinated collection development in print publications to the exploration of national licences for online databases. To achieve this, the establishment of a consortium, as the international practice suggests, was deemed necessary. Setting priorities, the group submitted a report suggesting that action should concentrate initially on STM journals, since they are the most expensive and subject to the highest price increases. In December 1998 HEAL-Link (HEllenic Academic Libraries Link), after long negotiations, signed a licensing agreement with Elsevier for access to all journals in ScienceDirect, and with OCLC for access to 12 databases through FirstSearch. Before the end of 1999 the consortium had also signed agreements with Springer, Kluwer, MCB and Wilson for OMNI Mega File – a bibliographic database which includes 1,500 full-text journals.

Although all academic institutions in Greece are members of HEAL-Link, in the earlier days of the consortium less than half were interested in accessing its services. Nowadays, not only have all the academic institutions access to these services but the consortium has also expanded to include more institutes within the public sector. These are the 18 research institutes that operate under the auspices of the General Secretariat for Research and Development. The effect on library services has been enormous for all academic institutions. Libraries, especially in small institutions in remote places like the regions of Ipiros and Western Macedonia – considered to be the poorest regions in the European Union, with only a few tenths of print subscriptions – now have access to about 4000 electronic journals and 12 bibliographic databases.

HEAL-Link is governed by a 32-member committee with one representative from each academic institution, large or small. The decisions on the electronic resources which are to be made available through HEAL-Link are based on the perceived needs of the academic institutions, namely the expensive STM journals. HEAL-Link cannot cover all the needs of its members for electronic resources with its limited budget. What the consortium can do is try to spend its budget as effectively as possible. For this reason the role of the steering committee for electronic resources does not end once a licensing agreement is signed. The main concern is to make sure that the electronic resources are used by a large base of users. If not, the committee has to examine if indeed the most-needed electronic resources have been selected and if the resources are user-friendly. So far not all the publishers have provided workable monthly statistics for HEAL-Link usage, but they are gradually improving over time. From the statistics that have been gathered, it does not come as a surprise to see that even journals for which there is no print subscription at the national level are heavily used. For example, the statistics for Academic Press IDEAL indicate that the majority (62%) of the downloaded articles are from non-subscribed journals.

Co-operative collection development

Back in December 1997 the Serials Cost Working Group suggested that, along with the shift to exploration of national licences, a pilot project be undertaken in three disciplines (physics, chemistry and informatics) in five universities to examine the possibility of co-operation at a national level on collection development of the print journals' subscriptions. The Conspectus software was purchased from WLN (which was later bought by OCLC). The project lasted for over a year. It entailed a detailed study of the syllabus of the faculties involved, the specific research areas of these faculties and evaluation of the journals collection, against the perceived needs of the departments. The needs of the departments depended on the level of study (undergraduate, graduate, research level) and specific areas of research interest among the faculties. It proved to be a difficult and time-consuming exercise. It also entailed the development of core lists of journals for the three subject areas selected for study. These lists were the model journal collections against which the faculties' collections were compared.

The aim was to decide which model of co-operation in print collection management to choose to follow: either the centralized model (like the one in the UK with one library, namely the British Library, building a comprehensive collection); or the decentralized model, where each co-operative library adopts certain titles and cancels others that are more pertinent to the syllabus or research needs of other universities. It was not easy because standards had to be set against which the collections could be evaluated. Upon completion of the study it was realized that most libraries in the disciplines under study were down to the core collections, so these titles were impossible to cut in favour of another university. The savings in money from cancelling some peripheral titles would be marginal, not to mention the reaction of the faculty staff members who are suspicious of co-operative initiatives and accept cancellations only if there is no more money and no other way out.

HEAL-Link usage

Any new service has to be actively marketed to become known to its prospective users. The means for marketing new services are mailing leaflets with pertinent information, the professional or daily press, conferences, meetings etc. In the case of HEAL-Link, owing to a very limited budget, no promotional material has been produced. Unfortunately there are hardly any professional journals for librarians in the Greek language and the cost of advertising through the daily press is prohibitive. It is left to the 32 members of the governing body to inform their libraries, and each institution is responsible for informing the corresponding academic community. Bibliographic instruction is rather limited in Greek HE institutions and university newsletters are infrequent, if they exist at all. In spite of all the above, the news about HEAL-Link services has spread, largely by word of mouth, as is obvious from the statistics of usage.

The figures in Table 13.1 compare the HEAL-Link members' usage of Elsevier's ScienceDirect with that of OhioLINK (Sanville, 1999) and indicate that ScienceDirect is more heavily used from HEAL-Link, although OhioLINK is a bigger consortium.

Table 13.1   *ScienceDirect usage statistics: HEAL-Link and OhioLink*

	Number of requests	Downloaded articles
OhioLink (Elsevier, Academic Press) April 1998–March 1999	10,000,000	280,000
HEAL-Link (Elsevier e-journals) September 1999–August 2000)	1,923,183	329,000

So far we have seen that HEAL-Link has consolidated the buying power of the Greek academic institutions and selected services which are used by an academic community that has a never-ending need for more scientific information. But how does this information become available to the users? Does each library have to have a website to link its users to these resources? Do users have to become familiar with several different platforms? And do they have to search each platform separately to find the information they want?

HEAL-Link portal

Here we come to the role of the portal, one of today's biggest web trends. The fastest growth is occurring in vertical portals, which can more efficiently match topic-oriented users and information than can general portals like *Yahoo!*. The purpose of any library portal is to direct the user to specific information sources amongst the vast mass available. Librarians and readers are now beginning to confront, more than ever before, the blessings and the difficulties of abundance. The flood of new electronic resources released in the last several years has been too powerful to moderate. The result is a world in which electronic information is still poorly integrated, one where multiple interfaces need to be navigated in order to find information, and one where the interfaces themselves do not communicate. There is no shortage of possible standards for managing data at various levels, from SGML and its successor XML for structuring documents, to the Z39.50 protocols and the like for linking resources across multiple sites (Okerson, 2000). But, in practice, we are still far from the stage at which researchers will be able to focus their attention on the content of their enquiries and pursue them undistracted by difficulties of navigation and interpretation.

The web page of HEAL-Link (**http://heal-link.physics.auth.gr**) is the only marketing means of our consortium and it aspires to become a portal to its users. During the past year the efforts of the steering committee were concentrated on one target: the integration of our services. The first action was to sign an agreement with OCLC for ECO (Electronic Collections Online), thus enhancing the existing FirstSearch agreement with full text. The agreement for ECO has added extra security for perpetual access to the e-journals, even though all the licensing agreements that HEAL-Link has signed make it clear that the consortium has perpetual access rights. But this agreement was not sufficient, since ECO does not offer the journals of all the publishers the consortium has an agreement with. The main concern was that the 1500 journals from ScienceDirect would not be included in ECO. An agreement was also signed with Swets-Blackwell for Swets-Net Navigator. The reason for signing an agreement for another service similar to ECO was twofold. Firstly, ScienceDirect journals are included in SwetsNet Navigator and, secondly, users are familiar with this service since most of the Greek universities have individual agreements, using it as a platform for accessing their e-journal collections.

The second action was to establish an alphabetical list of all the journals offered, linked to the publishers' journals page, and the next step was to have some kind of keyword search. The system administrator, and webmaster for the HEAL-Link homepage, has developed a meta search engine which, when keywords are submitted, simultaneously searches all the journals of all the publishers and returns the results sorted by publisher with links to the article.

The reactions received from our users have been very positive, so it was decided to move ahead and try to develop subject search. A librarian was appointed with the task of finding classification and subject headings for all the journal titles accessed by HEAL-Link. This has proved to be a very time-consuming task. CONSER by the Library of Congress has been used for the project, and then the Union Catalog of Serials from OCLC for the journals that could not be found in CONSER. This service is targeted to the less experienced users, who need to be guided to be able to find the articles they need and feel lost searching in about 4000 journals, or who are not quite sure what the appropriate keywords for their search are. The HEAL-Link system administrator has developed a tree-like search facility (see Figure 13.1), which guides the user from the general subject category to the particular subject heading.

All the above actions have the aim of helping even the most inexperienced users to be able to search and find the information they need without being discouraged by different platforms and search engines for each electronic resource offered.

Conclusion

So far we have described the efforts of HEAL-Link to become more than a buying club that consolidates the buying power of the Greek academic institutions. HEAL-Link aspires to be involved in setting up a national policy for collection development and in building an integrated environment for its users. It is also concerned with archiving, copyright and related issues. HEAL-Link might not have saved any real money for its member libraries, but it has certainly expanded tremendously the access for all member institutions irrespective of their size.

The resources offered by HEAL-Link have obviously helped all faculty members, researchers and postgraduate students in their work. But what about the undergraduate students? Has HEAL-Link been able to attract them to use the library services? The licensing agreements that the consortium has signed with Elsevier, Springer, Kluwer, Academic Press and MCB for access to their electronic journals are of use mainly to researchers and postgraduate students. But the agreements for the 12 bibliographic databases of FirstSearch and the Wilson's OMNI Mega file are intended for use by undergraduate students. For a seven-month period from January to July 2000, and for the same period in 2001, usage statistics for the 12 FirstSearch databases show an increase of 232%. For Wilson's OMNI Mega file during the same time period the increase was an amazing 420%. It is hoped that by using the keyword meta search engine and the subject search services, undergraduates will start using all the electronic resources offered by HEAL-Link.

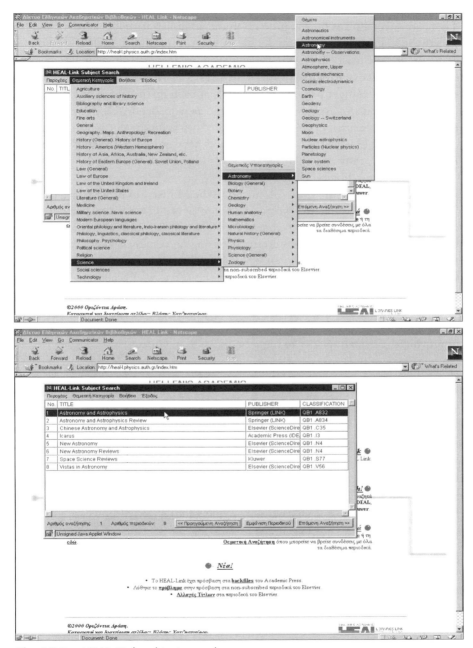

Fig. 13.1   *HEAL-Link subject search*
Reproduced with permission of Aristotle University, Greece.

There are several plans for the future. On the administrative level, a database has already been created containing details of the subscriptions of all the academic institutions, the cost and their providers. This information will be renewed annually and accessed by password. This database will be expanded to register usage statistics, contact persons and the IPs of each institution. For HEAL-Link users, future plans include alert services and personalized web pages reflecting their scientific research needs. Depending on future funding, it is also among the intentions of the consortium to expand the keyword search facility using the Z39.50 protocol, thus making it possible for a simultaneous search of the OPACs of Greek academic libraries.

In August 2001 HEAL-Link submitted to the Ministry of Education a proposal for funding for the next five years. Although it is known in advance that the consortium will not be able to expand its electronic resources significantly, it is hoped that, by preserving the current licensing agreements or by expanding in moderation, by monitoring the usage and by developing new services, HEAL-Link will play an important role improving the services of academic libraries. It will also support the distance learning programmes now under development at different academic institutions, as well as the programme of studies of the Greek Open University. In this respect, HEAL-Link is expected to contribute towards improving the overall quality of higher education in Greece.

References

Kohl, D. F. (1997) Farewell to all that . . . transforming collection development to fit the virtual library context: the OhioLINK experience. In Schwartz, C. A. (ed.) *Restructuring academic libraries: organizational development in the wake of technological change*, American Library Association.

Okerson, A. (2000) Are we there yet?: online e-resources ten years after, *Library Trends*, **48** (4), 671–93.

Sanville, T. (1999) Use levels and new models for consortial purchasing of electronic journals, *Library Consortium Management: an international journal*, **1** (3/4), 47–58.

Shreeves, E. (1997) Is there a future for cooperative collection development in the digital age?, *Library Trends*, **45** (3), 373–90.

Thornton, G. A. (2000) Impact of electronic resources on collection development, the roles of librarians, and library consortia. *Library Trends*, **48** (4), 842–56.

14

EVALUATING THE IMPACT OF THE UK's DISTRIBUTED NATIONAL ELECTRONIC RESOURCE

Shelagh Fisher

Introduction

The Distributed National Electronic Resource (DNER, **www.jisc.ac.uk/dner/**) is being developed by the UK's Joint Information Systems Committee (JISC, **www.jisc.ac.uk/**), which is a strategic advisory committee working on behalf of the funding bodies for higher and further education in England, Scotland, Wales and Northern Ireland. DNER is the working title for the concept of an electronic resource which appears seamless to the user. The intention underpinning the DNER is that staff and students in higher (HE) and further (FE) education will be able to access resources effectively and efficiently through intuitive and customized interfaces, unlike current electronic services, where the user needs to know the name of the service provider (JISC, 2001a).

In 1999, the UK's Higher Education Funding Councils gave JISC the remit to converge new learning environments with digital library developments. At the same time, funding was made available over three years to improve the applicability of information and communication technologies for learning and teaching and a call for proposals was issued in JISC Circular 5/99 (JISC, 1999b). As a first stage, this circular invited proposals from institutions for projects to develop the DNER, and thereby to extend the usefulness of JISC services for learning and teaching.

The three major foci of this call for proposals were (a) the implementation and development of the DNER, (b) JISC enhancements for learning and teaching, and (c) evaluation studies relating to both (a) and (b). Projects funded under the first two foci are described in the paper by Ingram and Grout elsewhere in this volume (see Chapter 11). The EDNER project (**www.cerlim.ac.uk/edner**) was funded under the third focus to undertake a formative evaluation of the developing DNER over a three-year period from 2000 to 2003. The project is being led by the Centre for Research in Library and Information Management (CERLIM) at Manchester Metropolitan University in partnership with the Centre for Studies in Advanced Learning Technology (CSALT, **www.comp.lancs.ac.uk/csalt/**) at Lancaster University.

This paper describes the evaluation methods being used within the EDNER project and presents some early findings.

The EDNER project

The EDNER project is utilizing a managed mix of methodologies which enable evaluation questions to be devised and explored from a number of perspectives. Methodologies are therefore selected on the basis of the questions which need to be answered and the locus of the available information and expertise. Techniques include:

- documentary analysis of a wide range of sources
- quantitative data analysis, e.g. of service usage, spread, etc.
- interviews with key individuals
- structured group discussions
- expert analysis on technical matters
- mapping between objectives/vision and evidence/projections
- questionnaires, circulated to end-users and service providers
- online discussion forums
- testing of service delivery issues
- development of case studies, including the highlighting of good practice
- feedback from workshops, which have a dual role in evaluation and dissemination.

As the DNER develops, the EDNER project is engaging upon a number of activities in order to address key questions as follows:

- developing definitions and models (What is the DNER?)
- investigating integration of the DNER within higher education institutions (Where is the DNER?)
- evaluating attributes relating to the quality of DNER resources and services (Is it quality-assured and fit for the purpose?)
- observing its use in learning and teaching (How it is it being used?)
- analysing quantitative measures (How much use is it getting?)
- observing stages of awareness and engagement by students and lecturers (What impact is it having?).

The evaluation framework, illustrated in Figure 14.1, has adopted a multi-stakeholder perspective and is organized into four related strands of activity. From a service perspective (strand A) the principal stakeholders include those charged

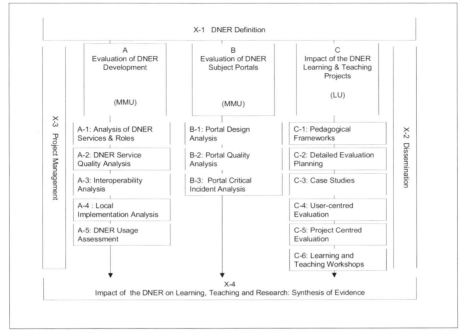

Fig. 14.1   *EDNER project structure*

with providing digital content and services, notably the funding councils and their agencies, publishers and third-party content suppliers, government agencies, research councils and libraries. An intermediary perspective (strand B) emphasizes the developing subject portals and fusion services in their role of drawing together services to present tailored landscapes and added value. Principal stakeholders in this context include the Resource Discovery Network Centre (RDNC), content providers and end-users. From a learning and teaching perspective (strand C) the principal stakeholders are learners, teachers and educational institutions. Strand X provides a framework for cross-project activity and an ongoing vehicle for collaborative analysis and synthesis of evidence from multi-stakeholder perspectives on the nature, requirements and impact of the DNER.

Because the DNER is a new and evolving concept, the EDNER project as a whole places considerable emphasis on the evolving views of stakeholders on scope, purpose and objectives, as well as the strategic direction, process, performance and impact evaluation of both contributory services and the service as a whole. The project contains a prominent element of synthesis in the belief that the whole is much greater than the parts and that a true picture of the value and impact of the DNER can only be achieved by looking at it as a whole. Results and insights from each vertical strand feed into the common work packages to enable informed iterative development, a combined approach to dissemination, cross-checking of findings and self-critical evaluation of the project itself. Good working relationships with the DNER programme team and with members of JISC Committee for Electronic Information have been established to enrich the evaluation and to enable the project to assist the development of understanding of the DNER and thus the development of its formal strategy.

In the initial stages of strand A of the EDNER project, primary objectives have been to determine exactly what the DNER is, what it is intended to become and how it is 'surfacing' in UK higher education institutions. The remainder of this paper focuses, therefore, on evidence pertaining to (a) defining the DNER and (b) local implementation of the DNER, and on issues and problems arising in the process of these investigations.

What is the DNER?

As stated earlier, in the initial stages of the EDNER project, a primary objective has been to determine exactly what the DNER is and what it is intended to become. Three lines of enquiry have so far been pursued in achieving this objective, utilizing both inductive and deductive techniques.

In the first approach, the views of DNER programme participants, potential users and other stakeholders were gathered. The findings suggested that there was a wide range of perspectives, from those who regarded the DNER as an e-university to those who perceived it as a large library or even a museum. This variety of views was confirmed by documentary analysis of the stated objectives of JISC services and projects. A second line of approach has been to make deductions by mapping the DNER to models of other services and environments and identifying common elements. Such models might include those of publisher, museum, traditional, hybrid and digital library, gateway, portal, managed learning environment and e-university (Brophy and Fisher, 2001).

A third approach within the EDNER project has been to undertake an analysis of the content of the emerging DNER. From an evaluation perspective, the analytical scope of the DNER comprises the portfolio of resources and projects funded through the JISC Committee for Electronic Information (JCEI). These include the JISC Collections, JISC Services, the Teaching and Learning and Infrastructure projects (funded under the JISC 5/99 circular), the Resource Discovery Network (RDN, **www.rdn.ac.uk/**) and projects funded within the Electronic Libraries Programme (eLib, **www.ukoln.ac.uk/services/elib/**). Types of service, collection and project have been mapped across subject areas. The findings are summarized in Figures 14.2 and 14.3. The 'explicit types' (e.g. finding

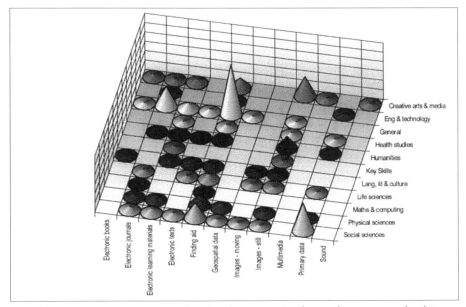

Fig. 14.2   *Composite view of the developing DNER by explicit type and subject*

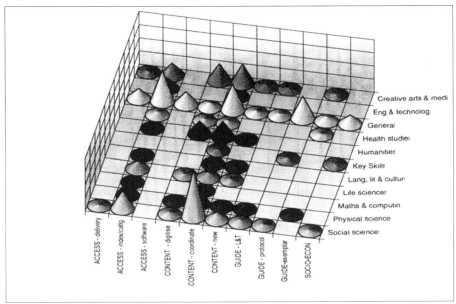

Fig. 14.3   *Composite view of the developing DNER by implicit type and subject*

aids, electronic books, electronic journals) and 'subjects' as represented in these figures are self-explanatory. However, an explanation of the 'implicit' typology represented in Figure 14.3 is necessary at this point.

From an inductive analysis of resources and projects, four broad categories of 'implicit type' were identified. These were 'content', 'access', 'guide' and 'socio-economic'. 'Content' is defined as the creation or organization of material for users, broadly analogous to the activities of authorship or publishing. A distinction was made between 'new content', where it appeared that there was creative intellectual input, and 'digitization', where, although the material had not existed in the intended form before, the process of creation was essentially a technical or mechanical one. Learning and teaching material was included in these categories if it was deemed to be generic in nature – for example, inculcating general information skills. Content which was primarily created to develop skills in using the resource to which it is related was categorized as 'learning and teaching guides'. Where the primary function of a service, resource or project was to identify and organize pre-existing digital resources, this was identified as 'co-ordination'.

The 'access' category encompassed mechanisms for facilitating access to content and included the sub-categories of 'developing software' 'delivery systems' or creating 'indexes or catalogues' to facilitate access to digital resources. The 'guides' category was defined as tools which assist users or developers of similar material. These were sub-divided primarily into guides on how to use resources (i.e. 'learning and teaching' guides), while others were intended to give guidance to those creating similar resources either by documenting processes (labelled 'protocol' guides), or by providing models of resource provision (labelled 'exemplar' guides). In addition, a number of JISC-funded projects have focused on socio-economic aspects of DNER development, either as a sole or as a parallel theme. Areas identified included, for example, IPR, economics, and ways to facilitate collaboration between institutions.

Although there are serious limitations to this approach, there are several conclusions which can be drawn – not least is that the spread of services and projects across domains appears to show that some are considerably less populated than others, for reasons that are not readily apparent. The approach was limited in that the identification of DNER resources and services rested largely on named services, collections or projects. These varied in scope, size, depth, comprehensiveness and extent of funding allocated. There were variations in levels of granularity in identifying resources. For JISC services, this meant drilling down to the second level of presentation to identify entities subsumed by that service. On the other hand, eLib projects were categorized at the project level, so that the UKOLN-based MODELS programme (**www.ukoln.ac.uk/dlis/models/**) was identified as a single resource, as was *Ariadne* (**www.ariadne.ac.uk/**), the electronic journal established for disseminating developments in digital library initiatives. Subject gateways (e.g. SOSIG, **www.sosig.ac.uk/**) were categorized as a single entity, despite the fact that a gateway may provide access to thousands of internet resources. It was necessary to impose such limitations because of the potentially unmanageable extent of activity required in categorizing individual resources encompassed by a gateway or service.

It is to be expected that there will be an uneven balance of services and projects across resource types and subjects. Indeed it would be astonishing, and a matter of deep concern, if funding had simply been spread as evenly as possible. However, the ways in which effort is being directed is worthy of comment, and the analysis generates some interesting questions which are worth debating. In saying this, it must be stressed that it is not the role of the evaluation team to make judgements on coverage; we do no more than raise some issues which programme and project personnel may wish to consider. There may be reasons for the 'empty' or heavily populated cells indicated in the figures, and indeed discussions have already taken place, or will take place in the near future, to achieve an overall balance in specific areas.

The analysis demonstrates a heavy emphasis on indexing and cataloguing. A major issue in networked spaces is the inadequate description of objects and collections, and it may be that in some areas (e.g. electronic texts) more is needed. Another outcome of the analysis was that little effort is being expended on digitizing primary data but a lot on co-ordinating primary data sources.

Initial attempts to categorize DNER entities revealed wide variation in the use of the labels used to present types of DNER resources. Although such variations can be discipline-related, it is more likely that the array of typologies has emerged due to disparate activities. Issues relating to semantic interoperability within and beyond the DNER are of course high on the JISC agenda, and a clear lead has been vested in the Interoperability Focus at UKOLN (**www.ukoln.ac.uk/interop-focus/**).

As yet, there is no single gateway, or portal, to identifiable DNER resources and services. The blurred boundaries are not only posing challenges in the EDNER project, but also, as noted by Breaks and MacLeod (2001), the multitude of access points, interfaces and search syntaxes is presenting major problems for academics. Valuable, and often expensive, subscription-based services may be under-used because potential users within subscribing institutions are unaware of their existence. Further activity within the EDNER project has therefore focused on how the DNER or its constituent resources are being promoted and presented within higher education institutions in the UK. The following section thus presents key findings from the EDNER project concerning the 'surfacing' of DNER resources within the UK higher education community.

Local implementation of the DNER

Two key questions have driven initial EDNER research concerning the integration of the DNER within higher education institutions: 'Where is the DNER?' and 'How is it being presented?' This recognizes that, even if academics are aware of the existence of valuable DNER resources, they may not know where to find them. Databases and other subscription-based services currently form part of what is sometimes described as the 'invisible web' in that they are unavailable for deep searching by commercial search engines such as *Google*.

The emerging picture reflecting the 'surfacing' of DNER resources within the UK higher education community is a complex one. Users may be led to a target DNER resource via a range of global, national and institutional access points such as a search engine (e.g. *Google*, **www.google.com**), via the list of JISC services (**www.jisc.ac.uk/services/index.html/**), via the JISC-funded Resource Discovery Network (**www.rdn.ac.uk**), via the local university library website, via the universities' departmental and course-related websites, or through paper-based or other publicity disseminated by the resource provider. The EDNER team has undertaken some initial exploration from different electronic access point perspectives and has analysed the 'surfacing' (location and presentation) of a number of DNER resources.

A key finding concerns the variation in description and surfacing context of resources. One argument supporting the use of a range of descriptions to present a DNER service is that the resource can be promoted in a way which is best suited to user needs and, at the institutional level, according to local availability. Another argument is that there should be a standard generic description used by all providers of access points, to which local information regarding access rights, restrictions and procedures may be added. The key issue here concerns the extent to which generic descriptions should be created locally or nationally, and the extent to which tailored descriptions are desirable. Where generic descriptions are being provided, there appears to be significant duplication of effort. Tailored descriptions are probably desirable for targeting resources to user needs, especially when the descriptions are supported by information on what is available locally. These issues are explored in the following account by illustrating the variety of access points to the Bath Information and Data Services (BIDS, **www.bids.ac.uk/**), which is a key bibliographic service, funded by JISC, for the academic community in the UK. In locating the BIDS service, the user is likely to be presented with a range of descriptions according to which point of access is chosen, whether global, national or institutional.

Global and national access points

A search on *Google* for 'BIDS' presents the searcher with a direct link to the BIDS service first in the list of hits. This shows that a very high number of other services are linking to the BIDS site. A description of the service provided by BIDS is shown in Figure 14.4, although this is not the service entry window, and a user must search for the specific resource description on the BIDS site. After authentication, the user is presented with the list of resources available, depending on the institutional subscription.

BIDS services

Our wide range of bibliographic services offer the research community a powerful source of online bibliographic information. All our services are free at point of use. We also provide linkages to our ingentaJournals full-text delivery service, allowing you to access electronic journals from some of the world's leading academic publishers.

GENERAL

ingentaJournals
Thousands of academic and professional journals online

UnCover@ingenta
Journal articles with fax and online delivery

BIDS Reuters Business Briefing Select
Full text news articles from over 1000 English Language sources around the world

SCIENCE AND ENGINEERING

INSPEC *
Data from the Institute of Electrical Engineers

RAPRA
Polymers, Plastics, Rubber, Composites, Adhesives & Additives

SOCIAL SCIENCES

BIDS IBSS *
Economics, sociology, politics and anthropology

PsycINFO *
Psychological literature from 1887 to present

EDUCATION

Education *
ERIC and British Education Index

MEDICINE & HEALTH

MEDLINE
Human medicine and related biomedical research

BIDS CAB ABSTRACTS
Extensive database on agriculture, forestry, aspects of human health, human nutrition, animal health and the management and conservation of natural resources.

Fig. 14.4   *Description of the BIDS service – BIDS website*

The link to the BIDS service provided by the DNER website is available only through a reference link to the JISC services, where a very brief description of BIDS is provided (see Figure 14.5).

Two descriptions of BIDS retrieved via the Resource Discovery Network's *Resource Finder* are catalogue records provided by the EEVL and SOSIG gateways (see Figure 14.6). EEVL (**www.eevl.ac.uk/**) provides a central access point to networked engineering, mathematics and computing information. The description of BIDS provided by EEVL has a bias towards engineering-related disciplines. SOSIG aims to provide a trusted source of selected high-quality internet information for students, academics, researchers and practitioners in the social sciences, business and law. The description of BIDS which is provided has a bias towards social-science related disciplines. Users of *Resource Finder* may come from any discipline, however.

JISC

BIDS

Bath Information and Data Services - provides access to a range of commercially supplied bibliographic databases.

Fig. 14.5   *Description of the BIDS service – JISC website*

Resource Discovery Network. Resource Finder

BIDS is a UK-based provider of bibliographic data services. It operates from the University of Bath and specialises in end-user access to a range of commercially supplied databases. Access to the services is generally restricted to the UK Higher Education sector; prospective users should enquire at their institutional library or computer service for details. Databases provided include the ISI Citation Indexes, ERIC, British Library's Inside Information, UnCover and IBSS - the International Bibliography of the Social Sciences.

(SOSIG)

BIDS is a UK-based provider of bibliographic data services. BIDS services are generally available on a site licence basis, allowing unlimited use by staff and students to services to which the institution has subscribed. In addition, there are some services that can be searched without a subscription. These include ingentaJournals , Medline, and Pascal. Other bibliographic services include BIDS BLII (multidisciplinary bibliographic database), BIDS Reuters Business Briefing Select, BIDS RSC (analytical science, chemical engineering, health and safety, chemical business news), INSPEC (data from the Institute of Electrical Engineers), and RAPRA (polymers, plastics, rubber, composites, adhesives and additives). Logging in to BIDS with your ATHENS username and password will show available services highlighted in the service selection page. The site contains information about and links to the services, user guides, FAQs, news, and contact details.

(EEVL)

Fig. 14.6   *Description of the BIDS service provided via the Resource Discovery Network*

Institutional access points

At the local (institutional) level, university libraries are providing general descriptions of the BIDS service which vary in style and depth of treatment. Three examples are given in Figure 14.7 to illustrate this point. In some cases, although not always, a general description is followed by information on what is available to institutional members and on access procedures. Edinburgh University's record, which includes a generic description and local information, is illustrated in Figure 14.8.

There is also strong evidence that lecturers are taking advantage of opportunities to incorporate information resources in web-based course delivery or in supporting materials. Departmental websites and lecturers' web pages commonly provide a 'related links' section. The advantages of embedding published information resources within the course delivery in a particular discipline, thus contextualizing resources for required reading or supplementary study, are obvious, but the context is not always readily apparent. For example, a researcher in the School of Computing Science at De Montfort University (**www.cms.dmu. ac.uk/~ac/**) offers a link to BIDS alongside Railtrack timetables, EastEnders updates, Leicester City Football Club and Tesco's online recipe collection. A

BIDS

Bath Information and Data Services

Description: BIDS is a gateway to a range of multidisciplinary bibliographic and full text resources. It provides access to the ingentaJournals full text service, both directly and also through links from database search results. BIDS is hosted by the University of Bath and performs an important role in the information strategy of the Joint Information Systems Committee of the Higher Education Funding Councils (JISC), and is one of three data centres funded by the JISC, along with MIMAS (located at Manchester University) and EDINA (located at Edinburgh University).

(King's college, London)

BIDS (Bath Information and Data Services)

Subject coverage: General, Social Sciences, Education, Medicine and Health, Science and Engineering
Date range: 1991 to date. **Updated:** Dependent on the database
Data retrieved: BIDS provides electronic access to a number of databases, including International Bibliography of Social Sciences, Medline, British Education Index and ERIC, and to full text databases such as IngentaJournals and ScienceDirect.
Service provider: Bath Information and Data Services (BIDS)

(Manchester Metropolitan University)

BIDS

BIDS (Bath Information and Data Services) is a leading UK provider of networked information for end-users in the higher education and research communities, offering a range of bibliographic databases and access to full-text electronic journals.

(Edinburgh University)

Fig. 14.7   *Generic descriptions of BIDS – UK university libraries*

BIDS

BIDS (Bath Information and Data Services) is a leading UK provider of networked information for end-users in the higher education and research communities, offering a range of bibliographic databases and access to full-text electronic journals.

The BIDS-ISI service terminated on 31st July 2000. The ISI Citation Indexes for Arts and Humanities, Science and Social Sciences are available instead from the ISI Web of Science service at MIMAS.

Edinburgh University Library also takes BEI (British Education Index), ERIC, IBSS Online (International Bibliography of the Social Sciences), Index to Scientific and Technical Proceedings and Embase from the BIDS services. BIDS also acts as a gateway to the Uncover database.

BIDS services are only available to matriculated students and staff of the University of Edinburgh. Access is controlled by the ATHENS national authentication service, by means of a personal username and password for each individual user. Self-registration instructions for setting up your personal account at the ATHENS web site are available. Use of BIDS is covered by the CHEST Code of Conduct for the use of software or datasets, the terms of which are encompassed in Edinburgh University's Computing Regulations.

User guide leaflets are available from Library service desks. A more detailed self help guide is available for purchase at the Service Desk, Ground Floor, Main Library and at the Faculty Libraries. HTML versions of user guides which describe the basics of using a database and give enough information to enable a beginner to get started are also available on the BIDS internet site

The BIDS service is normally available 24 hours a day, 7 days a week.

Fig. 14.8   *Generic description of BIDS with added local information (Edinburgh University)*

maths and statistics lecturer from Nottingham Trent University (**http://science. ntu.ac.uk/msor/dk/html/interest.htm**) offers a lengthy, randomly ordered, list of resources of personal interest where BIDS and COPAC sit alongside links to the BBC, museums, Celtic music, Shoe World and a dead cat certificate!

Labels used by academics to describe resources are also frequently inaccurate. For example, the University of Southampton's School of Medicine (**www.soton.ac. uk/~psychweb/linkpage.htm**) lists BIDS under 'www search tools' along with Yahoo! and NISS. The Department of Philosophy at the University of Lancaster (**www.lancs.ac.uk/users/philosophy/links.htm**) lists BIDS as a 'useful admin site' in between the Arts and Humanities Research Board and The Leverhulme Trust. Examples of other labels which describe BIDS on the websites of university academic departments and lecturers include:

- academic information
- bulletin boards and databases
- gopher services
- information links
- libraries, societies and organizations

- miscellaneous
- reference lists
- research admin
- searches
- web servers
- www search engines.

The manipulation of electronic resources to enhance learning, teaching and research has been envisaged as one of the key benefits of the developing DNER (JISC, 1999a). From an institutional perspective, however, there are strategic issues which need to be addressed in reconciling roles in the provision of information resources and facilitating an effective merger of the information and the learning environments.

Conclusions

From an evaluation perspective, defining and characterizing the DNER has proved more difficult than originally envisaged. What is more, the boundaries of the DNER are still somewhat blurred. There are questions surrounding what constitutes a DNER resource: is it one which is JISC-funded or quality-assured (and how) or both? For example, can resources catalogued by the RDN gateways, or links from HE library sites to free resources, or resources identified by academics creating course materials, be regarded as part of the DNER? In a networked learning environment, the rapid growth of published primary electronic resources such as e-journals, e-books, image banks and datasets, and secondary services such as bibliographic databases and abstracting and indexing services, has created opportunities for lecturers to offer such materials direct to students via personal or departmental web pages and virtual learning environments. There is strong evidence that lecturers are taking advantage of opportunities to incorporate these information resources by creating direct links to them in web-based course delivery or in supporting materials. In effect, lecturers are creating context-specific 'libraries' of electronic resources.

University libraries, meanwhile, are investing significant effort in providing web-based navigational aids to information resources, including resource descriptions, and in providing the means of access (e.g. authentication, authorization mechanisms). The context-specific 'libraries' being created by lecturers are by-passing such quality-assurance mechanisms. The JISC portals (**www.portal.ac.uk/spp/**) which are currently under development are intended to resolve some of the issues surrounding quality assurance and user awareness of resources by allowing a cross-search facility across targeted databases, so that the user will not need to be aware of the source provider, but can be confident about the quality of what they retrieve. JISC is also funding studies and development programmes on the organizational and technical issues in the effective use of large-scale, distributed digital content and advanced networking technologies in the context of the classroom (Currier et al., 2001; JISC, 2001b). The extent to which these developments bring coherence to the information landscape for the academic communities in the UK remains to be seen.

The evaluation methodologies being used within the EDNER project are providing a rich mix of approaches, which will enable the project team, JISC and the FE and HE communities to address such strategic direction, process, performance and impact factors. The idea of running an independent evaluation alongside a major development programme, so as to encourage it to learn lessons from implementation, is relatively new, yet recognizes the dynamic nature of the DNER, both in terms of rapid changes in technology and in terms of developing stakeholder experience, expertise and understanding. It is apparent that the task of building and evaluating national-level services is complicated by very different perspectives among key stakeholders, and by the lack of any single, clear model on which to base development and evaluative judgements. As it progresses, the EDNER project aims to contribute towards the development of representative models of large-scale digital initiatives such as the DNER, and to the development of a robust framework for associated formative evaluation activity.

References

Breaks, M. and MacLeod, R. (2001) Joining up the academic information landscape, *Library Association Record*, **103** (5), 286–9.

Brophy, P. and Fisher, S. (2001) Evaluating the distributed national electronic resource, *Proceedings of the first ACM/IEEE-CS joint conference on digital libraries 2001*, Roanoke, Virginia, USA, 144–5, available at **http://dblp.uni-trier.de/db/conf/jcdl/jcdl2001.html**

Currier, S. et al. (2001) *INSPIRAL: INveStigating Portals for Information Resources And Learning: final report to JISC*, Centre for Digital Library Research and the Centre for Educational Systems, University of Strathclyde, available at **http://inspiral.cdlr.strath.ac.uk/documents/INSPfinrep.doc**

JISC (1999a) *Adding value to the UK's learning, teaching and research resources: the Distributed National Electronic Resource (DNER)*, available at **www.jisc.ac.uk/pub99/dner_vision.html**

JISC (1999b) *Developing the DNER for learning and teaching*, JISC Circular 5/99, available at **www.jisc.ac.uk/pub99/c05_99.html**

JISC (2001a) *Five-year strategy 2001–05 executive summary*, available at
www.jisc.ac.uk/pub01/strat_01_05/exec.html#s3

JISC (2001b) *Digital libraries and the classroom: testbeds for transforming teaching and learning: a new international initiative funded by the JISC and the National Science Foundation*, JISC Circular 07/01, available at
www.jisc.ac.uk/pub01/c07_01.html

THEME 4
USER BEHAVIOUR AND USER TRAINING IN THE DISTRIBUTED ENVIRONMENT

15

BUILDING THE RDN VIRTUAL TRAINING SUITE TO TEACH INTERNET INFORMATION SKILLS VIA THE WEB

Emma Place and Heather Dawson

Introduction

The RDN Virtual Training Suite (**www.vts.rdn.ac.uk**) is a new national resource in the UK offering free web-based training in internet information skills for 40 academic subjects. There is a tutorial for most of the subjects taught in UK universities and colleges, with titles ranging from *Internet Philosopher* to *Internet Physicist*. The suite is intended to serve students, lecturers and researchers in higher and further education in the UK, enabling them to improve their skills in locating, evaluating and using information resources accessible over the internet. This paper describes the development of the RDN Virtual Training Suite and the way it is being adopted by librarians as a training tool to supplement traditional library user education programmes, both face-to-face and at a distance. The paper explains what the Virtual Training Suite is and why and how it was developed, describes the findings of two different forms of evaluation and concludes with a discussion of issues for the future.

What is the RDN Virtual Training Suite?

The Virtual Training Suite is just one of the services offered by the UK's Resource Discovery Network (RDN, **www.rdn.ac.uk/**) – a large-scale internet search service built by the academic community for the academic community. The suite comprises a series of tutorials delivered over the web, each offering 'teach yourself' training in information skills for a particular academic subject. The suite is freely accessible to everyone. Since May 2001 there have been 40 tutorials available (see Figure 15. 1 overleaf), with a further 11 planned for release in June 2002. The tutorials take around an hour each to complete, though users can work through them at their own pace. The tutorials can support self-directed learning from any networked computer with a web browser, but they are also designed for academics and librarians to incorporate into their curriculum.

Engineering and Mathematics (EEVL)
Internet Aviator
Internet Civil Engineer
Internet Electrical, Electronic and Communications Engineer
Internet for Health and Safety
Internet Materials Engineer
Internet Mathematician
Internet Mechanical Engineer
Internet Offshore Engineer

Health and Life Sciences (BIOME)
Internet for Agriculture, Food and Forestry
Internet Bioresearcher
Internet Medic
Internet for Nature
Internet Vet

Humanities (HUMBOL)
Internet for English
Internet for Historians
Internet for History and Philosophy of Science
Internet for Modern Languages
Internet Philosopher
Internet for Religious Studies
Internet Theologian

Physical Sciences (PSIgate)
Internet Chemist
Internet Earth Scientist
Internet Physicist

Reference (RDNC)
Internet Instructor

Social Sciences, Business and Law (SOSIG)
Internet Anthropologist
Internet Business Manager
Internet for Development
Internet Economist
Internet for Education
Internet Geographer
Internet for Government
Internet for Lawyers
Internet Politician
Internet Psychologist
Internet for Social Policy
Internet for Social Research Methods
Internet for Social Statistics
Internet Social Worker
Internet Sociologist
Internet for Women's Studies

Further Education (due to go live June 2002)
Internet for Art, Design and Media
Internet for Business Studies
Internet for Construction
Internet for Engineering (to include Motor Engineering)
Internet for Hairdressing and Beauty
Internet for Health and Social Care
Internet for Hospitality and Catering
Internet for Information and Communication Technology
Internet for Leisure, Sport and Recreation
Internet for Performing Arts
Internet for Travel and Tourism

Fig. 15.1   *List of tutorial titles within the RDN Virtual Training Suite*
© 2000 ILRT, University of Bristol, and reproduced with permission.

Tutorial learning objectives and design

All the tutorials have the same aim: to develop internet information literacy – the ability to effectively locate, evaluate and use information which is accessible via the internet for academic purposes – although each tutorial aims to cover the information needs of a different subject community. Subject specialists were commissioned to author the tutorials to ensure that they included information resources and examples that were relevant to different subject disciplines.

There are clearly defined learning objectives stated in the tutorials. These are, in brief, that after completion of the appropriate tutorial users should:

- be aware of the range of information resources accessible over the internet and be able to identify the key internet resources for their subject area
- know how to use effectively the main tools and techniques for internet searching
- be able to critically evaluate the internet resources that they find
- have practical ideas for incorporating internet information resources into their work.

All the tutorials share a common framework of four sections (TOUR, DISCOVER, REVIEW, REFLECT), which clearly structure the learning experience in line with the learning objectives. Users can choose to follow the whole tutorial sequentially or to select the section most suited to their individual needs.

TOUR

The TOUR section describes the range of internet information resources and provides a guided tour of key resources for the subject area. This highlights the range of materials available and directs users to the most important sites. For example, the Internet for Lawyers tutorial includes references to primary legal materials (legislation, treaties, law reports and judgements); secondary resources (journal articles, case commentaries and textbooks); finding tools (indexes to legislation, library catalogues and directories); organizational home pages (professional bodies, law firms, government departments and law departments in universities); statistical data and teaching materials (lecture notes and syllabuses).

DISCOVER

The DISCOVER section introduces the user to techniques for effective internet searching. It includes a comparison of the strengths and weaknesses of commercial search engines and information gateways, with guidance on when it is most appropriate to use each of these. This section also has a particular aim in helping students to use the RDN hubs effectively. For instance, the Internet Politician provides examples of how to use the advanced search form on SOSIG to truncate search terms and restrict searches to particular resource types.

REVIEW

REVIEW teaches skills for critically evaluating the quality of internet sites. This is an area of particular importance as the lack of quality control on the internet means that users must be careful to assess the value and authenticity of sources before they use them in their work. The tutorials highlight common pitfalls and offer tips on how to begin to assess quality. Internet Sociologist is one entertaining and effective example. This uses a site called Kill the Television to discuss issues relating to bias on the internet.

REFLECT

The final section summarizes the skills taught in the tutorial and provides scenarios describing how students, researchers and lecturers might incorporate use of the internet into their working practices. A good example is provided in the Internet Aviator, where the undergraduate scenario tells the story of Ryan Ayre who is looking for material about the military usages of unmanned aircraft for his essay. It takes him through the stages of research, showing how he can use the internet to find video footage, technical reports and relevant news items.

Special features

The tutorials have a number of special features designed to enhance the learning experience.

The **links-basket** feature enables users to collect their own personal list of useful URLs in their 'shopping basket' as they move through the tutorial. At the end they can pick these up and save them as a reference tool for the future.

Quizzes and practical exercises are offered at the end of each section and are designed to give students the chance to test their understanding of the material and deepen their learning (as well as to provide some light relief!). Each section contains a selection of optional multiple-choice, fill-the-gaps or more open-ended questions. There are also exercises that ask students to explore live websites to find answers to pre-set questions.

Additional features geared towards student needs include a **glossary** of commonly used internet terms and a **guide to citing internet resources** in essays.

A **resources for trainers** section includes an introductory PowerPoint presentation, a student workbook and handout, and lesson plans. Librarians can use the 'Print/Download' option to print out or download the whole tutorial or specific chapters within it. These can then be used as slides or handouts. **Free posters** may also be printed from the site.

Why was it developed?

Three major factors underpin the development of the suite. One is the need to provide training in internet information skills for higher and further education. The second is the need to provide this training to large numbers at minimal (i.e. no) cost. The third is the desire to enhance the value of the Resource Discovery Network for learning and teaching.

Internet information skills for higher and further education

Information literacy is an essential skill for academic work in all subject disciplines. It enables people to recognize when they need information, and to locate, evaluate and use relevant information for their work (American Library Association, 1989). As the internet increasingly becomes a major access point for information alongside the library, academics and students also need to develop their internet information literacy – the ability to use electronic and networked information resources to support their learning and teaching.

The potential of the internet to support education can only be met if people have the skills and inspiration to use it. Universities have their internet innovators, but there are still a great many internet novices. There is a considerable need and demand for training, not only in the technical skills required to operate machines and systems, but in the information skills required to make effective use of internet resources for academic work.

Training in information literacy needs to combine traditional information skills with IT skills (Standing Conference of National and University Librarians, 2000). A subject-based approach to training can make it more relevant to students and academics. In the UK the Quality Assurance Agency for Higher Education include 'information retrieval skills' and 'information technology skills' as key transferable skills in their benchmark standards for the content of degree courses in all subjects (Quality Assurance Agency for Higher Education, 1999).

Free training for large numbers

If you want to serve large numbers of users (e.g. students across the UK), then 'teach yourself' web tutorials are a practical option, as people can work in their own time, at their own pace, from any networked PC, without needing any personal support. The tutorials are designed to be incorporated into courses and training sessions at a local level, where librarians and lecturers can offer guidance, context, feedback and, ideally, formal assessment.

Enhancing the value of the RDN for learning and teaching

An additional aim of the Virtual Training Suite was to raise awareness of the networked resources available via the Resource Discovery Network (**www.rdn.ac.uk**) and to enhance the value of this service for learning and teaching.

How was it developed?
Timescales, funding and costs

The development of the Virtual Training Suite has been funded by the Joint Information Systems Committee (JISC, **www.jisc.ac.uk/**) under its Distributed National Electronic Resource (DNER) programme on behalf of the Higher Education Funding Councils of England, Scotland and Wales (**www.jisc.ac.uk/pub99/dner_desc.html**). The first phase of the project was completed in July 2000 with the launch of the first 11 tutorials. In May 2001, 29 more tutorials were launched. A further 11 tutorials covering subjects for further education are under development and due to go live in June 2002, which will bring the total number up to 51. It is worth noting that there has been a relatively small budget and time frame, which explains the simple and pragmatic approach adopted.

People

The tutorials were created by core project staff at the Institute for Learning and Research Technology (ILRT) at the University of Bristol (**www.ilrt.bris.ac.uk/**). The RDN hubs assumed a content management role, liaising with the authors, who were commissioned from the staff of 30 universities, museums and research organizations across the UK.

Tutorial software

CALnet tutorial software(**www.webecon.bris.ac.uk/calnet/**) was selected as the development tool for the RDN Virtual Training Suite. A number of software options were evaluated which could help build web-based tutorials, but CALnet was chosen largely because there were no costs associated with its use as it was developed in-house at ILRT. CALnet also builds a good navigation system and offered more interactive features than other packages considered (see Figure 15. 2 for a screenshot of a tutorial).

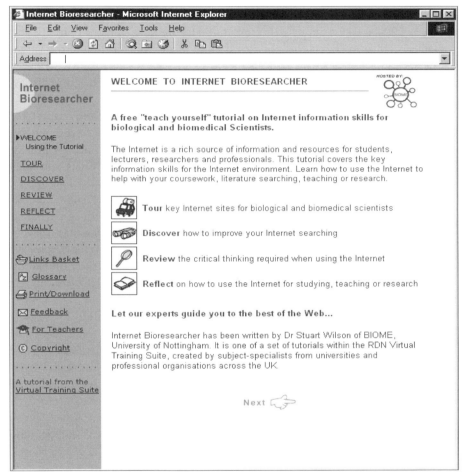

Fig. 15.2 *Front page of the Internet Bioresearcher tutorial*
© 2001 ILRT, University of Bristol, and reproduced with permission.

Evaluation – formal and informal

Formal evaluation

The first independent academic evaluation of the usage and value of the Virtual Training Suite was completed by Lin Amber of the University of Bristol Information Services in March 2001. This provides both quantitative and qualitative data on initial usage and is written up in a formal evaluation report, accessible on the website (**www.vts.rdn.ac.uk/evaluation.htm**).

In terms of quantitative statistics, initial usage was encouragingly high. In March to December 2000 there were over 43,000 log-ins to the site, with an average of 204 sessions per day. Interest in the future development of the project remained high as over 2000 people signed up to receive notification of the launch of the second phase of tutorials. This means that usage is likely to rise further in the future. One of the most popular options was to download the tutorial (739 sessions recorded) and to print off posters (1473 requests).

Analysis was also made from a total of 122 online feedback forms completed between December 2000 and March 2001. Although the number of respondents only represents a small percentage of the total number of users, it does provide some interesting information on the types of users of the tutorials and their opinions of the content. Of the users, 25% were librarians seeking material for inclusion in user education sessions, 14% lecturers, 11% undergraduates, 8% researchers, 10% postgraduates. The rest fell into other categories such as school students. A majority (56%) of users classified themselves as independent learners. This shows that the tutorials are reaching a wide audience, representing all the categories of user for which they were intended. The majority of the respondents felt that they had learned something from using the materials, which were thought to be particularly useful as starting points for novices.

The most common problems experienced were with functionality. These were often local problems related to the type of browser used and response time. Opinions were also divided on tutorial length. As a result of this feedback the authors of the second-stage tutorials were encouraged to adopt more concise styles of writing and the technical features needed to support the quizzes were revisited and streamlined.

Feedback remains an ongoing process. The DNER programme as a whole is being evaluated, and as one of the resources within the DNER the independent evaluation of the Virtual Training Suite is awaited with interest.

A case-study evaluation from The London School of Economics

The London School of Economics (LSE) is a renowned teaching and research institution for the social sciences with a student body of over 6000, of whom 93% are studying for postgraduate degrees. There are currently over 800 part-time students. Usage of the Virtual Training Suite tutorials was particularly attractive as the range and flexibility of the package means that it has been possible to incorporate them actively into the LSE library learning programme in a number of ways, which are described below.

Large-scale student inductions

At the start of each academic year, subject liaison librarians give presentations for new lecturers and students in particular academic departments. These presentation are large in scale and often take place in lecture theatres seating over 100 individuals. They are intended as overviews to the services offered. Slides have been taken from the tutorials and incorporated into PowerPoint presentations to demonstrate the types of training courses the library offers.

Hands-on workshops

Liaison librarians regularly offer small workshops for research and masters students from their departments. These sessions provide hands-on teaching for 10–15 individuals at a time. The tutorials have been incorporated into some of these as a useful resource for helping novice students.

Drop-in sessions

In addition to targeted workshops, the library also offers regular drop-in internet training sessions of around 90 minutes throughout term time. These are open to all staff and students without booking. The trainer usually demonstrates search techniques and important sites, and then the students are able to engage in hands-on exercises. As part of these sessions students are encouraged to work through the tutorial relevant to them. Trainers have found that while students are working independently at their own pace they have been able to offer them a supportive atmosphere, which encourages learning.

Training sessions for library staff

All new information desk staff at the LSE receive training sessions on internet skills so that they can assist users in finding information. There is also a regular ongoing programme of refresher training sessions to remind established staff of new services. The tutorials have been used effectively in these. Staff have been encouraged to explore the tutorials and to note key sites in the TOUR sections, as these often contain specialist subject directories or gateways which are of value in providing starting points for research. They are particularly useful in directing staff who do not have a wide experience of the subject area.

Inclusion in handouts

The library produces a number of guides for staff and students on electronic services. An example of these are quick reference guides for particular subjects, which are intended to offer an overview of starting points for research in the subject area. They contain a list of the main classmarks for the subject area, lists of locations of important journals and information on key electronic resources such as CD-ROMs, databases and internet sites. The Virtual Training Suite tutorials have been listed in the appropriate guides as a good starting point for beginning internet research.

Links on the library web pages

As the Virtual Training Suite is intended as an independent learning package, links to it have been placed on the library training web pages. This has encouraged the LSE Library to begin a process of redeveloping the information that is offered in order to provide more full-text, self-contained training materials.

Future plans for the Virtual Training Suite

There are a number of questions asked about future plans for the suite. Maintaining currency and the provision of more tutorials are the two most frequently asked.

Updating and maintenance over time

A stable curriculum for internet training is not possible in this ever-changing environment, and clearly changes will need to be made to keep the tutorials current. Future-proofing the content of the tutorials has been given priority when authoring, to keep the necessity for continuous editing to a minimum. Carefully chosen sites and examples can significantly reduce the need for maintenance and updating.

The resource has been firmly embedded into the organizational structure of its parent service – the RDN. The tutorials are all hosted by the relevant RDN hub, so all the social science tutorials, for example, are hosted by SOSIG (the Social Science Information Gateway). The hubs have assumed some responsibility for the upkeep of their set of tutorials by maintaining regular link-checking procedures.

However, there is, as yet, no long-term funding commitment from the JISC for this resource. The ILRT will be presenting arguments to become a JISC service with sustained funding, without which it is likely that this resource will have a shelf life of only a few years. DNER staff are aware of this issue and will no doubt be planning for it, but since the RDN is one of the first DNER projects to complete, it may be some while before a final decision is known.

Development of more tutorials

Users ask if the suite will be expanded as they have identified gaps in subject coverage (for example, in Art and Design, Music and Archaeology) and have asked for courses in these areas. One of the biggest demands has been for tutorials covering subjects taught within the further education sector, and these are now being built. Discussions are also taking place with the Learning and Teaching Support Network (LTSN, **www.ltsn.ac.uk/**) centres, some of which are keen to develop new tutorials to fill subject gaps.

International developments

The Virtual Training Suite has generated interest from outside the UK, and the potential to repurpose it to serve users in other countries has been recognized. ILRT is looking at ways of collaborating with developers in other countries to enable them to adapt the existing tutorial model rather than meeting the expense of starting their own model from scratch.

Conclusion

As the internet information revolution rages on, there is a pressing need for training to support users trying to make sense of everything. The web tutorials described in this paper are just one attempt to meet this need quickly and efficiently. It is likely that e-learning technologies, methods and industries will develop very fast, and that we'll be talking about new solutions in the years to come. Meanwhile, we hope that the free training we are offering now helps to fill an immediate need.

References

American Library Association (1989) *American Library Association Presidential Committee on Information Literacy: final report*, available at
   www.ala.org/acrl/nili/ilit1st.html
Quality Assurance Agency for Higher Education (1999) *Benchmarking academic standards*, available at
   www.qaa.ac.uk/crntwork/benchmark/benchmarking.htm

Standing Conference of National and University Librarians (2000) *Information skills in higher education: a SCONUL position paper*, available at
www.sconul.ac.uk/publications/99104Rev1.doc

16

30,000 DIFFERENT USERS, 30,000 DIFFERENT NEEDS?: DESIGN AND DELIVERY OF DISTRIBUTED RESOURCES TO THE USER COMMUNITY

Jenny Craven and Jillian Griffiths

Introduction

This paper identifies aspects of information-seeking behaviour in an electronic, distributed environment by sighted and visually impaired users, and addresses some of the potential problems this diverse population of users may face. The '30,000 different users' in the title refers to one such user population – the (approximate) student population of one UK HE institution – Manchester Metropolitan University (MMU). This comprises a mix of 'traditional' students (that is, those who have entered higher education straight from school or college), mature students, part-time and distance-learning students, and students with special needs. It could be argued that all users have special needs, as a consequence of different learning styles, cognitive styles, access to technology, disabilities, etc. Suffice to say that potentially there could be 30,000 different needs in just one institution, and that these needs should be taken into account in the design of resources for distributed delivery.

This paper, therefore, is a contribution to the development of enhanced understanding of design features and user behaviour relating to information provision and information retrieval in the current context of information-seeking theories. It is primarily based on the findings of two research projects that have been undertaken in the Centre for Research in Library and Information Management (CERLIM) at MMU. DEvISE (Dimensions in Evaluation of Internet Search Engines, **www.cerlim.ac.uk/projects/devise.htm**) and NoVA (Non-Visual Access to the Digital Library, **www.cerlim.ac.uk/projects/nova.htm**) are projects which have examined information-retrieval issues amongst users and look at approaches to the search process which can be used to inform developers and designers of online and web-based services such as courseware, distance learning packages and other distributed services.

Context of resource delivery

The library in the 21st century can present its user community with increased choice in the way services are provided. Users can choose to visit the library in person or may prefer to visit remotely, from their place of work, study or home. The delivery of resources continues to be a combination of print and electronic – what is commonly referred to as 'hybrid' services – although the move forward is towards a more technological resource base, particularly in relation to provision of services to distant or remote users.

Information seeking in electronic environments can present the user community with a range of problems, both navigational and conceptual (Marchionini and Komlodi, 1998). Technological developments have, in many respects, driven the evolution of information seeking towards a process which is dynamic and interactive as the user directs the search, interprets results, reflects on progress and evaluates the efficiency of continuing. Online searching behaviour has been studied through the analysis of searchers' decisions and search acts (Fidel, 1984; Pejtersen et al., 1999) or tactics (Bates, 1979, 1990) but, whilst these studies have informed information retrieval (IR) design, few recommendations have been posited regarding interface design for such systems.

The move to multimedia, parallel with approaches using frames, tables, graphics, sound and animation, has increasingly led to users retrieving information using a combination of different search and retrieval options, often presented in just one interface, which can prove problematic to some users (Griffiths, 1996). Although work is continuing to make interfaces more accessible by, for example, applying accessibility features such as text alternatives, descriptions of hyperlinks, consistent layout and contrasting colours (*World Wide Web Consortium accessibility guidelines*, 1999; Buultjens et al., 1999; Brophy and Craven, 1999), further consideration needs to be given to the different information-searching behaviours of users and how an understanding of these behaviours may influence the design of interfaces to electronic resources.

Information retrieval and information-seeking theories

Evaluation of comparative systems has a long tradition of improving the state of the art in IR technology. The criterion for the evaluation of performance effectiveness has largely been based on the overall goal of a retrieval system, i.e. the retrieval of relevant documents and suppression of non-relevant items. Such evaluations adopt the Cranfield experimental model based on relevance, a value judgement on retrieved items, to calculate recall and precision. These dual measures are then presented together where recall is a measure of effectiveness in retrieving all the sought information and precision assesses the accuracy of the search.

Many and varied criticisms and concerns have been levelled at the validity and reliability of a Cranfield approach to IR evaluation (e.g. Ellis, 1984). The core concern centres on the compromise necessary in defining relevance for such experimentation. That is, it is necessary to assume that relevance judgements can be made independently, that users will assess each document without being affected by their understanding of any previous items read. In addition, there is a basic assumption that relevance can ignore the many situational and psychological variables that, in the real world, affect relevance (Large et al., 1999). Despite such concerns this approach to IR evaluation has become the traditional approach of retrieval testing, embodied more recently by TREC (Text REtrieval Conferences).

The appropriateness of this traditional model, however, is also being questioned when applied in the internet environment, the major limitation being that internet search engines (SEs) and the internet do not provide for a controlled environment. As a result many studies in this area use the precision measure only (Clarke and Willett, 1997; Leighton and Srivastava, 1999). Further difficulty is observed in the lack of standardization of the criteria for relevance judgements (Tomaiuuolo and Packer, 1996; Chu and Rosenthal, 1996). Furthermore, the requirement that queries should be kept constant across SEs results in test queries of the most basic form, which may not reflect real use. Additionally, there has been a shift from batch processing, where the end-user has no direct involvement with the system or results, to interactive systems, where the end-user directly interacts with both.

Jansen et al. (2000, 208) posit other concerns, primarily that whilst 'Internet search engines are based on IR principles, Internet searching is very different from IR searching as traditionally practised and researched in online databases, CD-ROMs and OPACs'. They base their argument on findings of transaction logs of *Excite* users, where they report that there is little use of advanced searching techniques and that users frequently do not browse results much beyond the first page.

The shift from trained intermediaries to novice end-users of interactive IR systems has resulted in research which seeks to understand the impact of individual differences on searcher behaviour and performance (e.g. Saracevic and Kantor, 1988; Marchionini, 1993). Information-seeking behaviour has important links with electronic information retrieval in that novice searchers 'may rely more on basic learning styles to guide their behaviour when online. Experienced searchers may rely on learning styles and more on acquired techniques' (Logan,

1990, 509). As Marchionini et al. (1993), have posited, novice searchers can be seen as *domain* experts and experienced searchers as *search* experts, so that it is not just the learning style or acquired technique which affects searching behaviour, but also knowledge of the information being sought.

A previous research project (Griffiths, 1996) sought to evaluate use of full-text CD-ROM by untrained end-users. This project investigated success, or failure, of information retrieval on nine different CD-ROMs and was informed by other studies in the areas of IR, information-seeking behaviour and human computer interaction (HCI). To this end 180 searches were gathered and analysed from two communities: public and academic library users. Results showed that a number of interface features affected IR. The most critical of these were:

- the inclusion of on-screen prompts and instructions
- users being kept informed during the searching process
- help always being available and context-sensitive.

Use of Boolean logic operators was often problematic, proximity operators were rarely used, and truncation was never used. Presentation of features had a significant affect on success, sometimes leading users away from the information they required. Increasing the users cognitive burden, by requiring them to undertake more actions and decisions, often led to increased numbers of errors and less effective information retrieval.

Although much work has been undertaken on general information retrieval in traditional formats and now web-based environments, there are relatively few studies on the information-seeking behaviours of blind and visually impaired people. The few studies in this area which can be identified (Astbrink, 1996; Williamson, 1995, 1998; RNIB, 1998; Carey and Stringer, 2000) tend to focus more on information needs. They demonstrate that sight-impaired users need to be provided with a variety of methods for meeting their information needs and that, like everyone else, they form their own set of strategies for finding information.

A study of the information needs of blind and sight-impaired people (Williamson et al., 2000) revealed that, although people were generally positive about the potential of the internet for information seeking, they often experienced access problems, mainly relating to the poor design of websites. They also expressed a desire to be able to choose a format for delivery which was appropriate for them, thus revealing that, as for users in general, independence appears to be 'rooted in the freedom to choose'.

The structure of a web page is a particularly useful navigation aid for blind and visually impaired people, as information can be retrieved more easily if the sequence of the layout is consistent and the page uses standard accessible design features such as contrasting colours and appropriate font sizes. Increasingly, however, information is displayed out of sequence or in a way that loses sequence altogether. The use of frames, for example, can be confusing if the user is unsure which frame should be examined first. Regarding the number of links to a page, Brazier and Jennings (1999) found that visually impaired people tend to prefer the narrow and deep approach in which fewer links are attached to a page but with more pages to the site, rather than the wide but shallow approach (i.e. many links, fewer pages), which can be time-consuming and requires more cognitive load.

The concept of 'getting lost in cyberspace' may of course be a problem for all users (Dillon et al., 1993). In paper environments the chances of getting lost are reduced as navigation typically consists of a number of moves such as jumping ahead or back, using an index or contents page, or simply by paging serially through the text.

Navigating in electronic environments can follow a similar framework to printed works, but the same amount of information is less likely to be available. Page numbers, indices or publication details, for example, are rarely included, if at all. Users must therefore develop different ways of interacting with electronic documents to aid navigation. This could include the use of landmarks such as links to the home page, or non-serial structures such as menus and groups of categories. For a blind or visually impaired person, the use of landmarks and menus to navigate through web pages is particularly important, as they have difficulty viewing a web page as a sighted person would – and probably as the designer would have intended.

Descriptions of DEvISE and NoVA

The DEvISE (Dimensions in Evaluation of Internet Search Engines) project

The aim of this project was to develop a framework for the evaluation of internet search engines with an emphasis on a user-centred perspective and an understanding that evaluation is a multi-dimensional construct. Thus a dimensional approach was adopted, whereby the search engine's effectiveness, efficiency, utility and interaction were evaluated by the user.

Internet search engines have proliferated with the growth of the internet itself. These search engines are often categorized as robot-driven – responding to a user query, or directory-based – guiding users through classified lists. Whilst this distinction is increasingly blurred, with catalogues and full-text indexes coming together in a single service, the popularity of query-based systems is evident. In a study commissioned by RealNames (Sullivan, 2000), 75% of frequent internet users used query-based search engines. As a result of this evidence, the DEvISE project focused on query-based search engines.

The results of analyses of participants' searching behaviours are presented below. Further details can be obtained from the DEvISE final report (Johnson, Griffiths and Hartley, 2001).

The NoVA (Non-Visual Access to the Digital Library) project

The development of networked distributed resources enables a wider range of possibilities in the way resources and services are delivered to users, for both learning and teaching activities. This includes users who need to use appropriate accessible formats and systems in order to read and interact with information on screen – for example, users with a cognitive, audio, motor or visual impairment. Access to digital resources is seen as an important factor in combating social exclusion, as an inability to access learning materials excludes people from taking part in a learning society.

The overall objective of the NoVA project is to develop an enhanced understanding of the retrieval of information by blind and visually impaired people – in particular, how serial searching and retrieval can be optimized in non-serial environments and how this can influence the design of digital library resources for all. To achieve this, a series of search and retrieval experiments was undertaken in order to map serial and non-serial approaches.

The experiments were conducted with a sample of sighted users and a sample of blind or visually impaired users (in other words, users who were not able to view a standard size screen without the aid of access technology or by viewing at very close range). Both groups were asked to perform the same semi-structured tasks using four web-based resources: a search engine, a library online catalogue, an online directory of internet resources and a commercial website.

The initial results of the search engine information-seeking tasks by the visually impaired sample have been analysed and are described below. A project final report will be available in 2002.

Results of the DEvISE and NoVA projects

The results of the DEvISE and NoVA projects are described here, and then the findings from both projects are compared to ascertain similarities and differences of user behaviour between the sighted and visually impaired participants.

DEvISE: user behaviour across three search engines

Twenty-three participants were recruited from second-year students of the Department of Information and Communications, MMU. No restrictions were placed on the type of information they required or the purpose for which it was intended. Participants were asked to search for an information topic of their choice, to use as many reformulations as required and to search for as long as they would under normal conditions. This task was to be repeated on two further search engines. The researchers specifically chose the three search engines used in the test. A summary of key results is given in Table 16.1.

Table 16.1 *DEvISE searching behaviour results*

Search stage/process	DEvISE
One formulation only	59%
Maximum number of reformulations	7
Phrase search – Yes	26%
No	74%
Simple search – Yes	90%
No	10%
Average number of query terms (formulation 1)	4
Maximum number of query terms	12 (in formulation 3)
Average number of pages evaluated	1st page (81%)
Time taken	15–19 mins (27%)
General feelings overall:	
Satisfied	30%
Neutral	34%
Dissatisfied	36%

On average, 59% of users only used one formulation, with 41% reformulating their query. The maximum number of reformulations was seven, which was undertaken by two participants.

A quarter of participants used phrase searching, whilst the majority entered their query in the form of keywords.

An overwhelming number of participants used the simple search option, with very few using the advanced search option and Boolean operators. Some participants used more than one option when reformulating their query. Other options used by participants included Advanced Search (20%), Precision Search (12%), Search Smarter (6%), Power Search (4%) and News Search (4%).

The average number of terms used in formulating the query in iteration 1 was

4. The maximum number of query terms used was 12 (used in formulation 3). As many as 81% of the sample looked only at the first page of results retrieved (i.e. the first 10). A further 12% went on to examine a second page, 3% looked at three pages and 1% at four, five, six and eight pages.

The average time taken to search was between 15 and 19 minutes, with 27% of the participants completing their task in this time. The longest time taken to search for information was between 60 and 65 minutes (4%). General feelings about the success of their search and their satisfaction with the search engine were mixed, with 36% stating that they were dissatisfied, 34% expressing neutral feelings and 30% feeling satisfied with their experience.

NoVA: user behaviour in the distributed environment: analysis of searching behaviour using a search engine

The user sample for the NoVA analysis comprised a sample of 20 blind or visually impaired people ranging from 21 to over 50 years of age. Of the 20, 10 had no vision at all or none of any use (i.e. a small degree of light perception), nine had some vision ranging from degenerative conditions to involuntary eye movements, and one user could see print but needed access technology to be able to interpret it.

The majority of the users (90%) needed access technology to be able to read a screen. Access technology included screen readers, an electronic Braille bar and screen magnification. The remaining 10% of the users could look at a regular-size screen but needed to be extremely close up to the screen to be able to read it (and then only with some difficulty).

For the search engine task, users were asked to find out the national weather forecast for the UK and then the most recent forecast for Manchester. They were required to use the UK *AltaVista* search engine but were given a free rein as to whether they used the search facility or the categories and links provided on the home page. Half the users (50%) chose to use the search facility only, 40% chose to follow categories and links from the home page and 5% tried a combination of both. The remaining 5% found difficulty in reading anything on screen, so were unable even to begin to search or browse. This paper concentrates on the users who chose the search facility, with summary results presented in Table 16.2.

Table 16.2   *NoVA searching behaviour results*

Search stage/process	NoVA
One formulation only	45%
Maximum number of reformulations	6
Phrase search – Yes	55%
No	45%
Simple search – Yes	100%
No	
Average number of query terms (formulation 1)	3 (in formulation 1)
Maximum number of query terms	8 (in formulation 1)
Average number of pages evaluated	1st page (100%)
Time taken	16.5 mins
General feelings overall:	
Satisfied	9%
Neutral	36%
Dissatisfied	55%

The maximum number of query reformulations was six. Reformulations tended to be either repeating the same search as before or adding another term or terms, for example, first query – weather, second query – UK weather. Stated reasons for repeating the same query were a lack of confidence that the search had worked at all, or because the user had got confused and decided to start the query again.

Phrase searching was used by 45% of users, while 36% used a keyword search, 9% used search strings such as 'Manchester, weather, UK, BBC' and 9% used a combination of keyword, phrase and string searches. Boolean operators were used by 9%, but had not been applied in a way that achieved helpful results.

Of the users who chose the search facility, almost all used the simple search function. The one user who chose the advanced function did so on account of being unable to activate the simple search function (in fact, the user was in a different function altogether but could not see this because the access technology did not provide enough clues) and applied simple search strategies to the advanced function. The average number of query terms used in formulation 1 was three and the maximum number of terms used overall was eight.

All users looked at only the first page of returned results, and then usually just the first two or three hits, before pursuing one of these links further or reformulating the query. The tendency not to look further than the first page of results is a behaviour found in other studies on the use of search engines (Jansen et al., 1998; Silverstein et al., 1999; Jansen, 2000). Reasons for this are unclear, although with regard to the NoVA sample it may relate to the users' perception of the efficiency of the system. The visually impaired users in the sample tended to relate efficiency with how easy the results displayed were to find. Users who were using magnification generally located the results without too much of a problem. However, those using speech technology (the majority) found that, because a screen reader generally starts reading from the top of a page, they were not always sure that there were any results displayed at all, or whether the search had even been activated successfully. Users commented that they found the results 'difficult to find' and 'hard to read', also that they were 'not sure if results are there, the top of the page is the same as the last one'.

The number of results returned also seemed to influence behaviour. A screen reader will read out the number of results – 26 million in one case – but does not indicate clearly that only the first 10 are displayed per page. One user simply gave up at this point because of finding this kind of information 'frightening' – perhaps worried at being forced to listen to 26 million results being read out!

The average time taken for the task was 16.5 minutes, with a minimum time taken of two minutes and a maximum of 45 minutes. General feelings about the success of this task were quite negative, and 50% did not manage to complete the task. As a result, 55% were generally dissatisfied, 36% neutral and only 9% satisfied. Comments included [that it took] 'too long, would give up or go direct to a weather site', 'found information eventually', 'it is a visual system not designed for non-visual use', and [it took] 'a lot of action to get some simple information'. Finally, users were asked what type of resource they would have used to find out this information if they had been given the choice. Apart from some exasperated answers such as 'I would just switch on the radio' or 'I'd go outside', users showed a strong preference for simple search engine interfaces such as *Google* and *AlltheWeb*.

Summary and conclusions

From a comparison of results in Table 16.3, it can be seen that there are a number of similarities in the searching behaviours of sighted and visually impaired users. Just over half of the DEvISE sample used one formulation only when searching, compared to just under half from the Nova sample. Of those participants who reformulated, the maximum number of reformulations was seven for DEvISE and six for NoVA.

Table 16.3   *Comparison of searching behaviour results*

Search stage/process	DEvISE	NoVA
One formulation only	59%	45%
Maximum number of reformulations	7	6
Phrase search – Yes	26%	55%
No	74%	45%
Simple search – Yes	90%	100%
No	10%	
Average number of query terms (formulation 1)	4	3
Maximum number of query terms	12 (in	8 (in
	formulation 3)	formulation 1)
Average number of pages evaluated	1st page (81%)	1st page (100%)
Average time taken	15–19 mins	16.5 mins
General feelings overall:		
Satisfied	30%	9%
Neutral	34%	36%
Dissatisfied	36%	55%

The phrase searching results are quite different, with 26% using phrase searching in DEvISE and 45% in NoVA. This may, in part, be due to the differences in criteria for definitions of what a phrase search is, which in itself has arisen from the different approaches taken by the two projects.

Perhaps unsurprisingly, most participants, whether sighted or visually impaired, used the simple search option. The average number of query terms was also very similar, with four for DEvISE and three for NoVA, although the maximum number of terms used by a participant for DEvISE was 12 – noticeably more than the eight for NoVA.

Overwhelming numbers of both sets of participants looked at only the first page of results. This is consistent with other studies in this area (Sullivan, 1998). Time taken to search was also very similar, with a search for DEvISE taking, on average, between 15 and 19 minutes, and for NoVA 16.5 minutes.

From these results it is clear that users do not appear to like complex search functions, tend to use few search terms, spend less than 20 minutes searching and will most often only look at the top 10 results returned by the search engine. Users appear to rate ease and speed of searching most highly. This can certainly be seen in the results from DEvISE, which showed that general satisfaction correlated most strongly with efficiency and with effectiveness slightly less strongly. This suggests that the amount of time and effort required from the user matters more than traditional recall and precision – a trend which is also apparent in the initial NoVA findings.

Importantly, the greatest area of difference can be seen in the satisfaction levels of sighted and visually impaired users. Some 30% of DEvISE participants were satisfied with their results and searching, compared with 9% of NoVA participants. Clearly questions must be raised as to why visually impaired users are so unhappy with their searching experiences.

In light of the work of programmes such as the eLib subject gateways, and now the Distributed National Electronic Resource (DNER), questions may be raised about the provision of streamlined and user-friendly versions of commercial services. However, the increasing popularity of simple search engines, such as *Google*, should not be underestimated, and the design of distributed services should perhaps move towards similar design features, i.e. a simple one-stop search interface to cover a variety of distributed resources.

Better understanding of users' searching behaviour in electronic environments is therefore necessary in order to inform the designers of distributed resources how best to present their services to a diverse and changing audience. There are many good information sources available – the trick is not only to make people aware of them, but also to get people to use them. Users know what they like and will not use a service – no matter how good the service may be – if, in its presentation and organization, it does not meet their needs and requirements. Finally, it should be noted that the question mark in the title of this paper is there for a reason. Without a doubt, people are individuals each with their own set of needs, but are the basic needs of people really so different? The findings in this paper suggest that, whilst it is important to consider the possible requirements of individuals when designing and delivering distributed resources, what *all* people want is information delivered to them in an efficient, accessible, consistent and user-friendly way.

References

Astbrink, G. (1996) Web page design: something for everyone, *Link-up*, (December), 7–10.

Bates, M. (1979) Idea tactics, *Journal of the American Society for Information Science*, (September), 280–9.

Bates, M. (1990) Where should the person stop and the information search interface start?, *Information processing and management*, **26** (5), 575–91.

Brazier, H. and Jennings, S. (1999) Accessible web design: how not to make a meal of it, *Library Technology*, **4** (1), 10–11.

Brophy, P. and Craven, J. (1999) *The integrated accessible library: a model of service development for the 21st century*, British Library Research and Innovation Report 168, Manchester, Centre for Research in Library and Information Management.

Buultjens, M. et al. (1999) Size counts: the significance of size, font and style of print for readers with low vision sitting examinations, *British Journal of Visual Impairment*, **17** (1), 5–10.

Carey, K. and Stringer, R. (2000) *The power of nine: a preliminary investigation into navigational strategies for the new library with special reference to disabled people*, Library and Information Commission.

Chu, H. and Rosenthal, M. (1996) Search engines for the world wide web: a comparative study and evaluation methodology, *ASIS 1996: Proceedings of the 59th ASIS annual meeting* (33), Medford NJ, Information Today, 127–35.

Clarke, S. and Willett, P. (1997) Estimating the recall performance of web search engines, *Aslib Proceedings*, **49** (7), 184–9.

Dillon, A. et al. (1993) *Space – the final chapter: hypertext: a psychological perspective*, Ellis Horwood Ltd, 169–91.

Ellis, D. (1984) The effectiveness of information retrieval systems: the need for improved explanatory frameworks, *Social Science Information Studies*, **4**, 261–72.

Fidel, R. (1984) Online searching styles: a case study based model of searching behaviour, *Journal of the American Society for Information Science*, **35** (4), 211–21.

Griffiths, J. R. (1996) *Development of a specification for a full text CD-ROM user interface*, MPhil Thesis, Department of Library and Information Studies, Manchester Metropolitan University.

Jansen, B. (2000) The effect of query complexity on web searching results, *Information Research*, **6** (1), available at **www.shef.ac.uk/~if/publications/infres/paper87.html**

Jansen, B. J. et al. (1998) Real life information retrieval: a study of user queries on the web, *SIGIR Forum*, **32** (1), 5–17.

Jansen, B. et al (2000) Real life, real users, and real needs: a study and analysis of user queries on the web, *Information Processing and Management*, **36**, 207–27.

Johnson, F. C., Griffiths, J. R. and Hartley, R. J. (2001) *DEVISE: a framework for the evaluation of internet search engines*, Resource: The Council for Museums, Archives and Libraries (Library and Information Commission Research Report 100), available at **www.cerlim.ac.uk/projects/devise.htm**

Large, A. et al (1999) *Information seeking in an online age: principles and practice*, Bowker-Saur.

Leighton, H. and Srivastava, J. (1999) First 20 precision among world wide web search services (search engines), *Journal of the American Society for Information Science*, **50** (10), 870–81.

Logan, E. (1990) Cognitive styles and online behaviour of novice searchers, *Information Processing and Management*, **26** (4), 503–10.

Marchionini, G. (1992) Interfaces for end user information seeking, *Journal of the

American Society for Information Science, **43** (2), 156–63.

Marchionini, G. and Komlodi, A. (1998) Design of interfaces for information seeking, *Annual Review of Information Science and Technology (ARIST)*, **33**, 89–130.

Marchinonini, G. et al. (1993). Information seeking in full text end user oriented search systems: the roles of domain and search expertise, *Library and Information Science Research*, **15**, 35–69.

Pejtersen, A. M., Dunlop, M. D. and Fidel, R. (1999) A use centred framework for evaluation of the web, *Proceedings of SIGIR 1999 workshop on evaluation of web document retrieval*, edited by M. Agosti and M. Melucci, August 1999, available at **www.cs.strath.ac.uk/~mdd/research/publications/99pejtersendunlopfidel.pdf**

RNIB (1998) *The internet and how to access it*, RNIB. Updated version *Access to the internet*, available at **www.rnib.org.uk/technology/factsheets/internet.htm**

Saracevic, T. and Kantor, P. (1988) A study of information seeking and retrieving II: users, questions and effectiveness, *Journal of the American Society for Information Science*, **39** (3), 177–96.

Silverstein, C. et al. (1999) Analysis of a very large web search engine query log, *SIGIR Forum*, **33** (3), 6–12.

Sullivan, D. (1998) Counting clicks and looking at links, *Search Engine Report*, available at **http://searchenginewatch.com/sereport/9808-clicks.html**

Sullivan, D. (2000) Survey reveals search habits, *Search Engine Report*, available at **www.searchenginewatch.com/sereport/00.06-realnames.html**

Tomaiuuolo, N. and Packer, J. (1996) An analysis of internet search engines: assessment of over 200 search queries, *Computers in Libraries*, **16** (6), available at **http://neal.ctstateu.edu:2001/htdocs/websearch.html**

Williamson, K. (1995) *Older adults: information, communication and telecommunications*, PhD Thesis, Department of Social Sciences, Melbourne, RMIT.

Williamson, K. (1998) Discovered by chance: the role of incidental information acquisition in an ecological model of information use, *Library and Information Science*, **20** (1), 23–40.

Williamson, K. et al. (2000) Information seeking by blind and sight impaired citizens: an ecological study, *Information research*, **5** (4), available at **http://informationr-net/ir/5-4/paper79.html**

World Wide Web Consortium accessibility guidelines (1999), available at **www.w3.org/TR/WCAG10/**

17

LIBRARY RESEARCH INSTRUCTION FOR DISTANCE LEARNERS: AN INTERACTIVE, MULTIMEDIA APPROACH

Betty Ronayne and Debbie Rogenmoser

Background

This chapter describes the process of implementing and publicizing a programme of new library services for distance learners, considers effective web page design, and concludes with an experiential account of library research instruction delivered via live cablecast, interactive television (ITV).

The California State University, Sacramento (CSUS), is one of 23 campuses in the California State University (CSU) system which share the primary mission of teaching. CSUS is a state-supported institution with 25,000 students enrolled.

The library received grant funding to develop, implement and publicize a pilot programme of new services for 200 distance learners in teacher education courses in the fall of 1998. A year later the programme was expanded to serve all CSUS distance learners.

There are nearly 4000 distance learner students of whom:

- most are juniors and seniors taking 10–16 units per semester
- 65% live within 20 miles of campus
- more than 65% work 20–40 hours per week
- 90% say they feel comfortable with technology
- 98% have internet access.

Implementation

Identifying campus resources, stakeholders and key players early on is crucial to the success of any new academic enterprise. A system-wide mandate from the CSU Chancellor, plus the CSUS president's directive to expand distance education, provided validation of our new programme. Moreover, the library dean had written the grant proposal for the pilot project, which was funded by the CSUS provost. Therefore we could expect internal and external support from several levels of administration with a vested interest in the project's success.

Collaborations with other campus departments quickly developed: University Distance Education; Department of Continuing Studies; Registrar; University Computing; Publications Office and University Media Services. By the second year, a partnership evolved which included the distance education librarians as members of a team that provided workshops and support for distance faculty (teaching staff).

Promotion

Faculty staff attitudes toward distance education varied from sceptical to enthusiastic. Concerns included pedagogical effectiveness, intellectual property rights and labour union issues. Some faculty embraced the technology but ignored the library. Gaining faculty support for the new library services was important to the project's success. We used traditional media to publicize the distance education services, placed articles in the faculty newsletter and student newspaper, contributed a chapter for the faculty handbook, made presentations at departmental meetings and faculty workshops, and persuaded the College of Education to include information about the new services in course syllabuses. Highlighting the chancellor's mandate and the recently revised accreditation standards for distance education helped to get the faculty's attention – often the greatest hurdle.

To reach our targeted students in education, fliers, information packets and a brochure describing the new personalized services were mailed to students or delivered by faculty. From a brief survey which we designed to assess student needs, it was clear that most had access to the internet. Creating a website to act as a primary source of library information for distance learners became a top priority. 'Here's the DEAL: distance education access to the library' was online within two months, and in 1999 it received the Highsmith Innovation Award for 'creatively connect[ing] students with the faculty and resources of the Distance Education program at CSUS'. It is a dynamic resource which is continuously monitored, updated and enhanced. In addition to providing current information on new services and procedures, the DEAL links students to the library home page and other campus resources, as well as research tutorials and content-rich databases.

Web page design and maintenance

Before beginning the creative process, we needed to define 'distance learners' and set parameters for the personalized services the website would provide. A variety of editing software is available to facilitate production of web pages. We used HomeSite, adding few graphics and limited automation. The pages are text-based as opposed to the entire page being one graphic, making them easy to update. Simple additions or corrections can be made quickly without major changes to the format itself.

Accessibility should always be part of web page design, with careful consideration of issues such as mobility, visual and hearing impairment. Using text equivalents for graphics is one method of addressing these concerns. The goal is to provide content that, when presented to the user, conveys essentially the same meaning whether auditory or visual. Text content can also be presented as synthesized speech or in Braille. Because the DEAL pages are text-based, scanners can 'read, speak or print in Braille' almost everything in the pages. Web Content Accessibility Guidelines and a checklist are available from the *World Wide Web Consortium* (W3C, **www.w3.org/TR/WCAG10/wai-pageauth.html**).

Hints for designing web pages include:

- Be sure to check your pages in different browsers.
- Always make sure each page has contact information, the date it was updated, and a logo or other identification indicating the source of the page.
- Avoid long pages – try to keep users from scrolling more than one page, and consider breaking up the information into two pages instead of maintaining a long one.
- Limit graphics and animation – remember that graphics and animation take longer to load, and the wait can be annoying.

Jakob Nielson, an expert on web usability, offers a variety of guidelines (**www.useit.com/alertbox/9605.html** and **www.useit.com/alertbox/990f30.html**).

'Maintenance is nowhere as heroic, inspiring, or remarkable as creation, yet it represents the bulk of activity that's needed to keep a document alive and well' (Tittel and James, 1998).

The time required for maintenance, and keeping the page accurate, current, relevant and useful, was surprising. It is important to develop a regular mainten-ance schedule to review your website. Check links, both the web address and the web titles, add new services, remove outdated services and information, and check e-mail addresses and phone numbers. Re-evaluate the site periodically to ensure that it still meets its goals and effectively communicates its content and services.

Our DEAL website has been well received by students and faculty, and we feel that it helps us to create a sense of community for distance learners. It is often the first point of contact with distance students and it has become the centerpiece of our instruction sessions as well, whether presented in person at off-campus sites or taught via interactive cable television.

Teaching library research via interactive television
Lessons from the literature

The literature on teaching through interactive television (ITV) is most often focused on classroom faculty who have sufficient preparation time to redesign their courses and to fine-tune teaching strategies throughout the term. Nevertheless, there is a good deal of information which can be adapted by librarians teaching a single session of a televised course. Articles on effective teaching methods for adults and re-entry students are also useful. 'Adult students are self-directed learners in pursuit of solutions to real-world problems. Teaching should be problem-based and format should accommodate a variety of learning styles. The librarian's role should be that of facilitator, whether guiding students through institutional bureaucracy' (Holmes, 2000) . . . or demonstrating the library proxy server .

The general consensus is that traditional classroom material must be reconfigured for the ITV environment. Sufficient lead-time for planning and practising is crucial if the new technology is to be used to full advantage (Bean, 1998).

Real-world experience

In each semester for the past three years we have taught a three-hour live cablecast session on library research methods as part of a required course for graduate students in the College of Education. Traditionally this session is taught in the library instruction lab, where students get hands-on experience at computer workstations.

In the televised version we are dealing with a passive studio environment. Between 12 and 20 students are seated at long tables equipped with stationary microphones, facing a large, front-mounted monitor. For the instructors a lavaliere microphone, lectern, Pentium computer and rear-mounted feedback monitors are provided. The control room technician monitors and announces incoming calls from 30 to 50 students viewing at home or on other off-campus sites with call-in capability. The challenge is to engage the students in a dynamic discourse and interactive learning.

Teaching methods and presentation style evolved as we became more comfortable in front of the camera. Advice from the literature, plus the trial and error of experience, have validated some of our techniques and caused us to discard less successful methods. Surprisingly, the most traditional component of our lecture proved popular and effective for ITV. The conceptual framework of a five-step search strategy, using a relevant topic to demonstrate resources and techniques, remains a significant part of our instruction arsenal. For ITV we tried presenting the search strategy in PowerPoint but the material and examples proved too detailed for slides. The instructor as well as students insisted on hard copy, which they said increases their comfort level – analogous perhaps to a professor's course notes. We provide hard copies in advance to students at remote sites, mailed by the College of Education.

The familiar search strategy model is an important element of the bibliographic instruction method popularized by Evan Farber (1999a, 199b) at Earlham College in the 1970s. Dr Farber trained and inspired several generations of librarians and classroom faculty to work together towards the goal of integrating course-related library instruction into the curriculum. Search strategy endures as a conceptual framework because it is a well-organized, flexible, problem-based approach to illustrating how knowledge is structured within a discipline, using an assignment-related research topic as an example. It integrates process and content, demonstrating how to use appropriate finding tools to access various levels of information in a logical sequence, which includes critical analysis at each step. For these reasons it lends itself, unreconstructed, to the interactive television environment.

We allow a generous block of time following, or concurrent with, our demonstration topic to search databases for material on students' research topics, brainstorming to generate appropriate search terminology. Since the searches are unrehearsed, the students can observe and participate in the cognitive process of formulating, testing and revising search strategies. The studio is not equipped with a printer, but relevant articles and citations can be e-mailed to students, filling an immediate research need and starting them on a path to myriad other resources.

Over time we have become more comfortable with ITV technology, but surprises still occur. We use mishaps as an opportunity to empathize, and acknowledge that research can sometimes be frustrating. We have not yet found time to prepare a detailed script with an extra copy for the control room technician, as suggested by practitioner and consultant Tom Cyrs (2000).

Our advice: team teaching

As we critiqued the videotape of our first ITV experience, it became clear that we had failed to use our best advantage – team teaching. We both taught the session but we did it serially, one at a time on camera, each taking half of the class period. The result was a ponderous pace, limited eye contact, very little interaction and too much 'talking head' on camera. This was easy to correct. Just having both librarians up front together immediately raised the energy level and created a more dynamic classroom climate. Interaction with students increased and the course instructor joined discussions.

The literature confirms that 'team teaching doubles your resources. It provides a co-discussant, which varies the pace and delivery style. Team teaching models interactive, collaborative learning, facilitates responding to questions and handling technical dilemmas. [And best of all] it encourages risk-taking' (Strohschen and Heaney, 2000).

If the luxury of two librarians is not practical, there are several team teaching models in addition to our shared partnership/equal responsibility dyad. Consider inviting a guest star to speak on a relevant area of expertise. We sometimes draft graduate student assistants from University Computing who are happy to make 'cameo' appearances as technical consultants. Involve the course instructor as part of the team. Many faculty participate routinely, asking leading questions or otherwise directing the discourse. And always involve the students in the team effort, those at remote sites as well as those in the studio. Here are more hints from Cyrs (2000) which will help to make televised instruction personalized, engaging, motivational and empathetic:

1 The material must be well organized, presented in logical sequence at a lively, varied pace.
2 Use 'attention grabbers' to start – anecdotes (true or not), overstatements, statistics.
3 Include visual analogies, props and graphics; look directly into the camera to include off-site students.
4 Ask 'how' or 'why' questions every 10 minutes; pause long enough to 'force' interaction.
5 Use movement within camera range to indicate a topic change.
6 Don't expect a lot of eye contact if monitors are in the room.

Finally, here are some practical tips from our real world experience:

1 Always recheck online links and database navigation the day before an ITV session.
2 Don't wear white.
3 Have a back-up plan.
4 Get a copy of the videotape and critique your performance based on the criteria in Appendices A and B.

Conclusion

This chapter has described the implementation of a new programme of library support for distance learners, highlighting collaboration and teamwork as the key elements for success. Beginning with our content-rich DEAL web page and its links to campus services, our goal has been to provide students with practical solutions for real problems. Whether delivered via interactive cable television, face-to-face at off-campus sites, or in a real-time chat-room environment, our library instruction goes beyond course objectives to help students navigate the institutional bureaucracy and cope with new technology. As distance education librarians we promote a winning product: flexible, customized services that anticipate and respond to real and immediate needs.

References

Bean, R. (1998) Lights . . . camera . . . instruction: library instruction via interactive television. In *Eighth Off-Campus Library Services Conference proceedings, held in Providence, Rhode Island, April 1998, Sponsored by Central Michigan University*, ERIC Documents database ED422959, 29–34.

Cyrs, T. E. (2000) Reconfiguring courses for distance learning, *NEA Higher Education Advocate*, **17** (3), 5–7.

Farber, E. (1999a) College libraries and the teaching/learning process: a 25-year reflection, *Journal of Academic Librarianship*, **25** (3), 171–7.

Farber E. (1999b) Faculty–librarian co-operation: a personal retrospective, *Reference Services Review*, **27** (3), 229–34.

Holmes, J. W. (2000) Just in case, just in time, just for you. In Jacobson, T. and Williams, H. (eds), *Teaching the new library to today's users*, Neal-Schuman, 127–44.

Strohschen, G. and Heaney, T. (2000) This isn't Kansas anymore, Toto: team teaching online. In Eisen, M. and Tisdell, E. (eds), *Team teaching and learning in adult education*, Jossey-Bass.

Tittel, E. and James, S. (1998) *HTML 4 dummies*, IDG Books Worldwide, 326.

Bibliography

Buckenmyer, J. A., Kunz, D. A. and Sterrett, J. L. (2000) Interactive television pointers from three first time presenters, *Mid-South Instructional Technology Conference*, available from ERIC/US Department of Education/ED446753, available at
www.mtsu.edu/~itconf/proceed00/buckenmyer.html

Chepesiuk, R. (1998) Learning without walls: training professionals for the 21st century by modem and monitor, *American Libraries*, **29** (9), 62–5.

Cyrs, T. *Tips for presentations on interactive television*, available at **www.zianet.com/edacyrs/tvtips.htm**

Dewald, N. H. (1999) Web-based library instruction: what is good pedagogy?, *Information Technology and Libraries*, (March), 26–31.

Herrington, V. J. (1998) Way beyond BI: a look to the future, *Journal of Academic Librarianship*, **24** (5), 381–5.

Nipp, D. (1998) Innovative use of the home page for library instruction, *Research Strategies*, **16** (2), 93–102.

Wynia, L. (2000) How do students really feel about interactive television?, *TechTrends*, **44** (4), 39–41.

Appendix A
Towards improved classroom ITV

Two areas which, if not handled correctly, most commonly diminish the effectiveness of television teaching are:

- organization of the lecture
- on-camera television presentation.

Organizing a lecture

- State objectives.
- Provide context.
- Highlight important facts.
- Summarize.

TV presentation tips

1 Involve students; invite discussion.
2 Maximize clear visuals; close-ups of illustrations, diagrams, models:
   - avoid visuals with crowded illustrations and fine lines
   - watch image on your monitor
   - on the board, stay within the area that TV can cover legibly; long lines are difficult to frame; good TV writing is approximately 35 characters per line with block letters about 0.375 in. high
   - for the overhead document camera (Elmo) blue paper is better than white
   - blue shirts are better than white.
3 Maximize sound quality:
   - instructor should *wear* microphone
   - remind students to use their microphones or instructor should repeat question before answering it.
4 Plan picture sequences ahead of time and communicate it to the control room technician:
   - move slowly in front of camera
   - request superimposed image of your face while demonstrating or explaining; this improves eye contact.
   - watch monitor and if necessary tell technician which shots you want
   - review videotape of your presentation to see what needs to be done differently.

Appendix B
Video evaluation

Comment specifically on areas that need improvement, for example:

Vocal factors

Consider:

* pitch
* loudness
* quality
* rate
* pause
* articulation
* pronunciation.

Visual factors

Consider:

* posture
* stance
* gestures
* facial expression
* eye contact
* overall bearing
* congruence of vocal/verbal message.

General factors

* Was delivery varied and appropriate?
* Identify any distracting mannerisms.
* To what extent did the presentation sound read or recited?
* How would you describe the speaking attitude or personality presented?

18

ACTIVE INTEGRATION OF INFORMATION SEARCHING SKILLS INTO THE UNIVERSITY CURRICULUM

Virpi Palmgren and Kirsi Heino

Introduction

The new information and communication technologies are rapidly changing the information environment. Users have access to a wide range of information sources. Finding and selecting relevant information is difficult, as vast quantities of information are available via different delivery forms. That is why users today need support, guidance and skills in information searching.

The information support services in the modern organization face many challenges in their attempt to bring quality information to the desktop of their users. In this respect the questions regarding the promotion of new networked services and licensed products, as well as the teaching and learning of required information skills, come into focus. Distance learning adds yet another dimension to these questions.

National strategy for training in the Finnish information society

Finland is progressing towards being a knowledge-based society. In the information society, knowledge forms the foundation for education and culture, and constitutes the single most important production factor. Information and communications technology significantly promotes interaction and exchange between individuals, business enterprises and other organizations. Furthermore, it promotes the utilization of information, provision of services and access to them (Ministry of Education, 1999).

In 1997 the Finnish Committee on the National Electronic Library published its report outlining both the national information provision as well as the organizational structure of the Finnish electronic library for science and research. The national electronic library was not to become a physical entity but a plan for integrated networked resource and service arrangements. The Ministry of Education has been responsible for the funding of the annual budget (approximately £200,000). The National Electronic Library, FinELib, started as a three-year project and in 2001 it became a permanent function of the national library (*Kansallinen elektroninen kirjasto*, 1997).

Today the National Electronic Library programme, FinELib, acquires Finnish and foreign electronic material for Finland, such as scientific journals and reference databases for specialist fields. The goal is to provide material serving as many scientific disciplines as possible. It is also the intention to offer a more effective way of finding material from the internet and to provide common access to information using the data network.

Helsinki University of Technology

Helsinki University of Technology (HUT, **www.hut.fi/English/**) is the leading university of technology in Finland. HUT offers 14 degree programmes in engineering and technology, and also in architecture and landscape architecture. Currently HUT has more than 10,000 undergraduates and some 2500 postgraduates. Almost 20% of the students are women. Studies at HUT are structured to simulate real life as much as possible. Therefore co-operation with industry as well as with other universities is close. The degree structure is flexible and allows considerable academic freedom. HUT is a versatile and broad-ranging technological and engineering university, which has Finland's best research and teaching results. Research findings are used in teaching. The Neural Networks Research Centre and especially the Low Temperature Laboratory are world famous.

The HUT Library (**http://lib.hut.fi/index-en.html**) is the largest library specializing in technology and allied sciences in Finland. The library serves the university as well as Finnish industry and the general public in their need for scientific literature and technical information.

Teaching information searching in Finland

Electronic publishing has multiplied in recent years. More and more learning material, research results, etc. are published on the internet. People increasingly study on the internet, so libraries have to reorganize their activities in that space.

There are 20 universities in Finland, all of which have a functional library. Suikkanen (2001) has mapped current networked teaching methods provided by Finnish university libraries. About 70% of them market courses on their website and out of these 40% have actual networked courses.

Four basic fields

Many libraries provide training for information skills on the internet, but the supply can vary widely. One way to classify these possibilities is to use a 'four basic fields' model (see Figure 18.1) created by Hein (1999, 81). That model divides e-learning into four categories depending on how the network is used. On the left-hand side of the chart the network supports the teacher – it is a distributing channel for the course material: the product. On the right-hand side we have the process; this is the environment where learning and teaching take place. In the lower part of the chart there are totally new elements only possible in the networked environment (e.g. hypertext books or learning solutions), whereas in the upper part there are elements which have existed earlier but have now been moved to the networked environment.

Suikkanen (2001, 72) divided the present supply of information skills courses in Finnish universities into these four basic fields. She classified six courses into 'the interactive networked courses' category (part 4 in Figure 18.1) and these included the course 'Searching for scientific information' organized by HUT library.

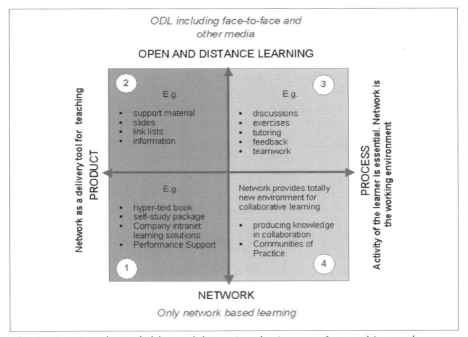

Fig. 18.1   *Four basic fields model in using the internet for teaching and learning (adapted from Irene Hein)*
Reproduced with the permission of Irene Hein.

Thirty years of library user education at HUT

HUT Library has organized courses in information searching for some 30 years. The courses were considered necessary in 1970, when the library moved into new premises on Otaniemi campus. The course was then added to the university curriculum with 0.5 credit points. In addition to this, almost all first-year students have taken an introductory course, including a two-hour lecture on basic skills in library use, and conducted an easy exercise in the library catalogue. This means that the library has educated 30,000 students in 30 years!

During the first 18 years, the programme of the information searching course was almost the same: six lectures on essential aspects about the theory of searching for information, classification, the use of references, etc. Library information specialists gave the lectures. A student passed the course by doing the given exercises under the guidance of a course assistant. The model was very traditional: the teachers told the students what they knew.

The course was totally modified to the 'learning by doing' method in 1988. Brainstorming sessions were held by library information specialists in order to devise suitable parts for the course (Puhakka, 1989). The lectures were reduced to two, each lasting two hours, and the students learned information skills by means of four exercises led by information specialists. Every student undertook a small online search as part of the exercise. This model provided good results, but as the number of students grew it became too costly and demanding on staff time.

In 1994 a new era began: the network enabled course schedules, guidelines and exercises to be accessed from the user's desktop. HUT was the first university library in Finland to create a networked information-searching course. It was the time of Gopher! Students sent in their exercises via e-mail. However, after some years the exercises (adapted to the web after Gopher) became routine and no longer supported individual studies sufficiently.

In 1999 we were able to introduce another completely new course model. At the same time the credit points were raised to 1.0. Throughout this 30-year period, the models of information courses have effectively served the needs of the time.

The Searching for Scientific Information Course
Principles

The present course model has been motivating for both the students and the library information specialists who teach the course. The course material is available via our home page, the address of the English pages being **www.lib.hut.fi/Informatiikkakurssit/#in%20English**.

The course is delivered in a short period of just five weeks. Earlier experience showed that the students fail to meet the deadlines of a more liberal time schedule. In the model prior to 1999, a whole year was allowed to complete the course. The course can be taken four times in an academic year. In Finland students often work part-time and they are also busy with their actual studies. That is why these distance education courses meet the needs of the students.

The ideal situation is to take the course simultaneously with another course where information searching is needed, such as a term paper, a literature survey or even a masters' thesis. Because of this the course is recommended in the latter phase of a student's studies.

The course begins with an introductory two-hour lecture, which is not compulsory. The lecture slides are available on the course website. E-mail is the communication tool for students to return assignments and to ask questions, and for the tutor to give instructions, feedback and support. A learning environment has been tested, but e-mail is a superior medium because of its accessibility and ease of use.

The library's seven information specialists act as tutors for the course. All these tutors have their own area of subject expertise. The average size of a group tutored by one information specialist is about 20 students. The tutoring languages are Finnish, Swedish and English. The students do not get marks for the course – they either pass or fail. More than 80% of the course participants have passed the course. The rest of them have dropped out despite the tutors' efforts.

The main textbook used within the course is the *IntoInfo* study package (**www.educate.lib.chalmers.se/index.html**). After the course the students:

- know the services of HUT library
- know the important libraries in their own field of study, both in Finland and abroad
- know the most important information producers
- know the special features of different networked information services
- know the principles of scientific communication and the new trends in scientific publishing
- should be able to master the basic principles of systematic searching and will have an idea about the content of the important information sources in their own field
- know how to refer to publications (including electronic publications) and how to compile a list of references.

The course in English

The number of international students has grown annually at HUT, and currently constitutes about 5% of the student body. Therefore the need for an English course has become acute. An independent English course started at the beginning of 2000. So far more than 30 students have passed the English course. International students have a particular need for this kind of tutored course because of the cultural shock as they come to a strange, foreign country. Sometimes they also expect more guidance from the teacher (Heino, 2001). The English course has been granted extra course development support from HUT Teaching and Learning Development unit. It has also become an exchange course in the international co-operation programmes organized by HUT.

Structure

The course following the lecture has been divided into three parts. In the first one-week part, students introduce themselves to the tutor and familiarize themselves with the course material. During the second two-week part, students compile a list of the most useful information sources in their own field of study. This list is the most important outcome for the student. In an ideal situation, the student updates the list continuously after the course. For this purpose, on the course website there is a template which the student can fill in systematically. The simplified list of where to start searching for information includes:

- library catalogues
- reviews
- journals
- conferences
- reports
- theses
- patents and standards
- scientific associations
- other databases and reference publications
- internet subject gateways and link collections.

In this part the student also writes an essay about a current topic based on a reading list of selected articles. So far the topics have been 'Recent developments concerning scientific communication' and 'Reliability of information'.

In the third part, the students carry out a search on their topics using the information sources identified in the previous part. It is necessary for their motivation that students use their own topics and have a real need for the information. The search results must then be processed into the form of a bibliography.

Feedback

Filling in the feedback form is an important compulsory assignment in this course. The feedback results give valuable signals as to when it is necessary to make changes to the course content. The feedback from about 400 students has now been analysed. The majority of the course participants have been from the departments of Computer Science and Engineering, and Control and Systems Engineering, because the course is compulsory for them. In the future we are planning to enhance our efforts in marketing the course.

Students' opinions concerning the general usefulness of the course in the near future can be seen in Figure 18.2 – a total of 99% consider the course useful for their needs. The grades given by the students, divided according to their year, can be seen in Figure 18.3. It is clear that the older students have given the highest grades (3–5).

The usefulness of the course in the near future
(n=400) feedback from academic years
1999–2000, 2000–01

Fig. 18.2   *Feedback from the Searching for Scientific Information course, academic years 1999–2000 and 2000–2001*

Year/grade (n=400) feedback from academic years 1999–2000, 2000–01

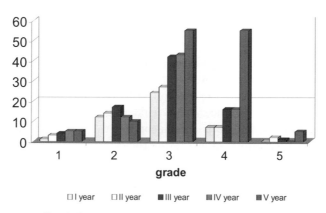

grade

□ I year   □ II year   ■ III year   ■ IV year   ■ V year

Fig. 18.3   *Feedback from the Searching for Scientific Information course, academic years 1999–2000 and 2000–2001 (Grade 1=poor, 2=satisfactory, 3=good, 4=very good, 5=excellent)*

Part of the problem-based learning course

A new degree programme at HUT called Information Networks started in autumn 1999. This interdisciplinary programme trains professionals for the changing world. Searching information effectively and evaluating it reliably is especially necessary. The problem-based learning method (PBL) was introduced at the beginning of this degree programme (Nuutila, Malmi and Törmä, 2000). Using this method, students solve a new case every week. They have group sessions but also study independently, and everybody finds their own solution to the problem.

In spring 2000 and 2001 the Searching for Scientific Information course was combined with a course on Information Networks implemented by PBL, in which information searching was carried out. Fifteen students took the course. They wrote an analysis on how the search had succeeded. The results were positive and we are going to continue the co-operation between these two courses.

In general the new generation of teachers has realized that traditional methods of teaching do not work any more. Passive listening to lectures and cramming for an exam leads students to learn the facts, which are then all forgotten the next day.

In response to the changing higher education environment, HUT Lifelong Learning Centre has in recent years organized a course called Programme on

Higher Education Pedagogy (15 credits). The teachers have been motivated to participate in this training. Today these new teaching skills count when applying for a job.

From information specialist to teacher

In Finland, library and information specialists have an academic training. At HUT, for example, they are usually Masters of Science in Technology. In addition to this, they have taken a postgraduate course and earned a certificate in information management and services. This training has not included much about pedagogical studies, although teaching has been a part of the work. The learning of teaching methods has therefore been intuitive. The work of information specialists has also changed: in the early 1990s online searches were carried out for clients on request, but nowadays clients are trained to search the networked databases themselves.

What then is needed to be a good teacher of information skills? It is always a challenge to work with young people who have started to use the internet. A new perspective should be accepted, namely that the information specialist does not know all the answers. Good pedagogical and psychological abilities emphasize support rather than ready-made answers. This does not exclude the fact that an information specialist must still carry out all kinds of literature and information-seeking tasks. At the same time, one should have knowledge of new teaching methods and how these affect library work.

It is important that students learn the process of searching for information. Teachers have achieved their goal if students become interested in information skills – i.e. lifelong learning has begun (Kühne, 2001, 9).

How a student can grow up to be an expert

Students are often busy with their studies and interests. Even if they concede that developing information skills is important, there never seems to be enough time for it. However, learning to search effectively for information is the 'magic word' in all studying and working life.

What are the abilities needed to be a good information searcher? Bainton (2001, 5) has a comprehensive list – the seven headline areas – which describes the situation (see Figure 18.4 overleaf). The diagram represents an iterative process whereby information users progress through competency to expertise by practising the skills. Only those at the higher end will be practising the highest skill level, to synthesize and build upon existing information, contributing to the creation of new knowledge.

Information skills model

Basic
Library
Skills

IT
skills

1. Recognise information needs
2. Distinguish ways of addressing gap
3. Construct strategies for locating
4. Locate and access
5. Compare and evaluate
6. Organise, apply and communicate
7. Synthesise and create

Information literacy

Novice   Advanced beginner   Competent   Proficient   Expert

Fig. 18.4   *Information skills model (Bainton, 2001, 7)*
Reproduced with the permission of Toby Bainton.

Conclusions

All over the academic world, plans are being made to encourage network co-operation and e-learning activities. In libraries the challenge is to meet the demands of this rapidly changing environment. Being up-to-date calls for constant re-evaluation and revision of courses. Library and information specialists are motivated by the continuous monitoring of the information environment applicable in the course re-evaluation. From the students' point of view it is important that they have state-of-the-art support from their library, and graduate with appropriate information technology skills. After all, the decision-makers of the future are made from the students of today.

Here is a sample of feedback from students about the HUT library course on searching for scientific information:

> It really helped; my searching for information was maybe a bit chaotic earlier. Now it's got some clear sense and order.

> To learn to know the library and its services, the course was quite OK, when one has to work with it for real. The course was nicely compact and light. How-to-use settings which are on the web are useful. Small tutor groups also work well and give the feeling of a small team even though the team never meets. On the other hand it would be nice to meet the tutor, for instance, at the lecture.

The course is quite useful if one is working with literature tasks etc. One gets a good feeling of the world of scientific publications, they don't seem to be such bad bogeys anymore.

References

Bainton, T. (2001) Information literacy and academic libraries: the SCONUL approach (UK/Ireland). In *67th IFLA Council and General Conference*, available at **www.ifla.org/IV/ifla67/papers/016-126e.pdf** [23.8.2001]

Hein, I. (1999) Muurari, maalari ja hanslankari: opettajana oppimisympäristössä [in Finnish: As a teacher in a learning environment]. In Jääskeläinen, M. (ed.) *Open uni: avointa keskustelua oppimisesta*, Jyväskylän yliopisto, avoin yliopisto, University of Jyväskylä, Open University division, 73–83.

Heino, K. (2001) How to ease user access to networked resources. In *Nordic Conference on Information and Documentation*, available at **www.bokis.is/iod2001/papers/Heino_paper.doc** [29.8.2001]

Kansallinen elektroninen kirjasto (1997) [in Finnish: *Electronic National Library*] Opetusministeriön muistioita, 19, Helsinki.

Kühne, B. (2001) Distance education in rural areas via libraries. In *Nordic Conference on Information and Documentation*, available at **www.bokis.is/iod2001/papers.html**

Ministry of Education (1999) Education, training and research in the information society: a national strategy for 2000–2004, available at **www.minedu.fi/julkaisut/information/englishU/index.html** [30.8.2001]

Nuutila, E., Malmi, L. and Törmä, S. (2000) Using PBL in teaching basic-level programming. In *Innovations in Higher Education 2000*, University of Helsinki, 112.

Puhakka, K. (1989) Teknillisen korkeakoulun kirjaston informatiikkakurssin kehittäminen [in Finnish: Developing the Helsinki University of Technology Library course for information sources and systems], Teknillinen korkeakoulu, täydennyskoulutuskeskus, tietopalvelukurssi, 9, Espoo.

Suikkanen, E. (2001) Tiedonhallintataidot, verkko-opetus ja yliopistokirjastot [in Finnish: Information management skills, web-based education and university libraries], *Signum*, **34** (4), 71–3.

19

Remote users in the virtual library: a need for diversification?

Katerina Toraki

Introduction

Remote users of a library are the ones who do not visit it physically but use its services from a distance. They use remote services when they cannot visit the physical library, either because they live in another geographical place or simply because they do not want to move from their desk.

Remote services have been in use for a long time, mainly, in the beginning, as home delivery services. The British Library started its lending activities in 1740, while in 1765 the first American lending library was created in Boston. Subscription libraries appeared in the 19th century, books being lent and sent home under special subscription terms. Remote delivery services in Holland started in 1918, while in the USA 37 out of 44 university libraries provided similar services by 1926. In Russia, in 1937, users were encouraged to borrow books by sending their request by phone or by post – the librarians were called post librarians. All the above data was extracted from Jordan (1970), where the author makes interesting calculations to compare remote delivery services with (physical) visits in the library:

> I assumed that my free time is worth at least as much per hour as my rate of pay on my job. Any time subtracted from optional free time should be worth time and a half. Assuming that my time is worth $10 an hour, my attempt to obtain the 100 books that I wanted was worth $300 to me (30h x $10/h), plus the cost of transportation, telephone calls and book reservation costs. Thus, I conclude that I should be willing to pay up to $3/book to obtain in a more effortless manner, from the convenience of my desk or home phone rather than by 34 exhausting and often annoying trips to a library . . . (Jordan, 1970)

More services were developed for remote users – existing or potential – like sending catalogues, selective dissemination of information and current awareness services, online services, sending photocopies of articles, interlibrary loan facilities and virtual libraries.

Our concern now is how libraries will serve the users better. Systems have already been implemented or are under development, but the issue is how patrons communicate with all these systems (Broughton, 2001). Library systems are being implemented so that remote services are available, but this readiness is mainly on a technical level. Users may not know of their existence or they may not know how to access them or how to use them effectively. This happens because of:

- a lack of publicizing/advertising the services on the part of the library
- a lack of dedicated (well-trained) staff in the library
- a lack of assistance to the users by the library
- a lack of adequate knowledge of how to use the systems on the part of the users
- a conservative (traditional) thinking about technology on the part of the users.

A challenging view for library staff is expressed in a report on remote patrons which claims that 'if we made our work more visible, we would be chosen over search engines' (University of Toronto Library Council, 2000).

Engineers as library users

In an interesting survey that was carried out in the USA in 1995, Mosley (1995) investigated the characteristics of engineers as library users, and the interpersonal skills aspects of communications between them and the librarians. It was found that most librarians use reference interview techniques to optimize understanding and satisfaction of the expressed information need, whilst a great majority (almost 91%) pursue further definition of the terms or subject matter, and almost all of them seek further understanding from a reference source or colleague. Other results were expressed concerning the gender and the age of engineers.

In a review article a few years ago, surveys on the information-seeking habits of engineers and the corresponding results were presented (Pinelli, 1991). As is found in most surveys, engineers have different information-seeking behaviour from other scientists. They have to solve a particular problem, so they have a specific question and they need a specific answer – brief, if possible. They usually work within time constraints. They do not consult the library first for information, but only after they have not been satisfied from their personal collection or from the assistance of colleagues. They use standards, specifications, legislation, reports, handbooks, plans, drawings and maps. Accessibility is the first factor they take into account, so proximity to information is a crucial aspect – that means that they approach the library when other means (like personal collections and colleagues) cannot help, or when the library approaches them first. They follow the law of least effort in order to keep up with the kind of job they do.

The Technical Chamber of Greece Library

The Technical Chamber is the professional organization of engineers, the mission of which is to advance issues concerning engineering and related aspects. Its central responsibility is to meet the needs of its members – the engineers – and to provide technical advice to the government and other official authorities. Its goals are achieved through organizing technical conferences, meetings and continuing education courses for its members, and publishing scientific periodicals, technical reports and books.

The Technical Chamber consists of the main authority located in Athens, and 16 regional sections located in 16 cities around the country. Almost all of the regional sections have small libraries, about 10 of which are staffed with librarians and operate more or less satisfactorily. The Documentation and Information Unit is the central, co-ordinating information and library service in Athens. An integrated networked library system was established six years ago with the aim of providing remote services to all engineers in the country.

The situation described above regarding the information-seeking behaviour of engineers and their relationship to the library is also demonstrated in our case. The Athens library is very old, founded in the 1930s, and engineers appreciate its usefulness for their professional awareness. In a survey conducted some years ago asking engineers to say which of the Technical Chamber services were most useful to them, the majority said that it was the library.

In an attempt to investigate the behaviour of our remote users, and to extract results that will help us to make decisions for the improvement of the system and the implementation of appropriate services for their particular needs and level of response, data was analysed on various aspects of the system.

Library users are defined as visitors (of any physical library) and as remote users (of any physical library or of the virtual library system) (Toraki, 1999). Remote users may either use the system directly (online) and get all the information and data they need immediately, or they may communicate by more or less conventional ways, like e-mail, web forms, surface post, telephone, fax etc. The first option is the more 'innovative' alternative, whereby a really virtual library system operates and all communication between the user and the library takes place online. The second option is, at least at the moment, the most familiar.

Here, the second option is under consideration, taking into account that remote library services were only developed during recent years, that they are not yet well implemented, and that users (as well as staff) are not yet prepared to use (or even to accept) these innovations. The aim was to find which methods remote users use to approach the library, if they have diverse attitudes related to some particular criteria, and if there is a gradual change in their attitude as the library system becomes more automated.

An important issue is that services provided to remote users should not only be simple transaction services like document delivery, loans and access to the catalogue, but also that the specialized staff of the library (engineers) should provide specialized reference services.

In a previous questionnaire sent to a number of engineers, asking them to respond as to how they see the internet library services, it was found that the majority wanted to use the internet to access the library, given that they needed to save time and that they needed to use library services, especially when they lived in a place where there was no library to serve them.

The survey

For this survey only data from Athens Library was used. The requests made to the library during 2000 and 2001 were separated according to how they had been sent, i.e. by fax or e-mail. It should be noted that there were no recorded data for telephone requests, that letters were excluded because they were too few, and that requests (especially the fax messages) were mainly coming from outside Athens, because until recently the library did not provide remote services to users from Athens (for organizational reasons). Remote users were considered to be the ones who did not live in the same geographical place as the physical library, i.e. those who could not contact the library easily and quickly. The location of the library and that of the user may or may not be the same – the network does not recognize or differentiate geographic locations.

E-mail has been selected for comparison with other conventional ways of communication, given that it is the easiest way for the user and the library to communicate remotely (Twidale and Nichols, 1998). Library systems have not yet implemented other efficient forms of interaction between staff and users or, if they have, the users are not well informed how to use them. The main disadvantage of using e-mail is that interaction does not take place synchronously and that the delay which may occur will delay the user being satisfied. According to user studies concerning user–staff interactions, it was found that end-users usually need to return after their first contact with the staff in order to clarify their request, or even to change the initial request, after the response received from the librarian. This was also found in the case of the Athens Library.

On the other hand, e-mail provides a technically easy way to communicate at any time with anyone anywhere, so it is the best way perhaps for remote users to approach the library staff wherever they are located. Also, e-mail provides the means to send remotely, and/or receive from remote places, long text or any other documents.

In general, the requests were of the following types:

- requesting a particular book or report which the user knows is held by the library
- asking whether a particular title is held by the library and, if so, requesting that title
- requesting photocopies of articles from periodicals that are held by the library
- requesting photocopies of articles from periodicals, without knowing whether they are held by the library
- asking for a bibliography on a particular topic from the library catalogue
- asking for a bibliography on a particular topic from foreign databases
- asking for legislation or standards.

Although engineers use internet services and e-mail quite a lot for their jobs, it seems that they do not use them for library services yet. Additionally, although the library web page has existed for years, and the web catalogue since June 2000, it seems that the number of e-mail requests has not increased much. The engineers prefer other forms of communication – the telephone is the most heavily used, but as its use is not recorded, we cannot present comparative quantitative data.

Log analysis of the web catalogue has been recorded for the last three months and the corresponding data has also been collected. Although it is still too early to draw reliable conclusions from present data, it seems that usage of the internet service – at least access to the catalogue – is high. Sometimes, the number of daily physical visits to the library is less than the number of internet visits.

It should be noted that the use of web access logs (as well as loan data) may have an impact on the privacy of library users if used in an unfair (and illegal) way. This was always the case, but the extended use of computer and networked systems can increase the likelihood of this if no care is taken to protect the individual. The very least we have to guarantee as personal data keepers is that this data should not be publicized or disseminated.

Data collected from e-mail and fax messages throughout the last two years (2000–2001) was assigned to one of the following categories:

a)   general enquiries
b)   requests for a bibliographic search on a specific topic

c)   requests to borrow particular documents stored in the library or to receive photocopies from periodicals
d)   requests for legislation or standards.

The number of mail messages was almost one third the number of fax messages. Half of the e-mail messages belonged to category 'b', while the rest belonged equally to the other three. On the other hand, 65% of fax messages belonged to category 'c', while there was only one fax message in category 'a'. It should be noted that most of the loan requests were from places where there is no regional library. Also, for both fax and e-mail, legislation and standards have the same percentage (almost 18%) – although the rate of standards requests would have been much higher if data had been recorded for the requests made straight to the Standards Office, which keeps separate usage records.

Additionally, the fax messages from the regional libraries were twice the number of fax messages from users, and 98% belonged to categories 'b' and 'c' ('c' being the majority again).

The following variables were used to differentiate the users:

• location
• type of professional involvement
• years of professional experience.

The number of years of experience did not seem to make much difference to the results pertaining to remote use. As to their professional involvement, most of them are civil or mechanical engineers or architects, usually involved in construction and building works.

A questionnaire was sent to a random sample of engineers of whom:

• 50% work as freelancers
• 10% come from the private sector
• 25% come from the public sector
• 15% come from the academic/research sector.

The majority of the respondents had a computer and had access to the internet irrespective of their years of professional experience, with just a slight increase among the young members.

Concerning the usefulness of virtual library services, the majority considered it most useful for providing bibliographic search and circulation facilities, followed by document delivery and current awareness in scientific and professional topics. When they were asked to give a more detailed description of the services they expect from the virtual library, those surveyed ranked them as:

1   legislation/standards
2   economic data (prices of materials and services)
3   electronic journals
4   full text of documents
5   general information on engineering topics
6   library catalogues
7   company data
8   access to bibliographic databases
9   document delivery
10   links to engineers' societies' web pages
11   links to other professional and scientific societies' web pages
12   general information about libraries
13   links to other web pages of general interest.

When those surveyed were asked if they would agree to pay for the above services, in general they were not willing to do so. It is noteworthy that for the first and the second options above, half of them might pay if the price was reasonable, but only 18% for the first and 9% for the second option would pay at any price. Even for access to electronic journals or full-text documents, those surveyed did not consider that they should pay at all, and 25% responded that they would not use these services if they had to pay.

Conclusions

The results from the data collected seem to comply with the characteristics described for engineers as information and library users.

Age and years of professional experience may have an impact on computer and information literacy. However, while computer literacy may be higher among younger engineers, information literacy may be the same or even higher among more experienced members, given the information habits and behaviour of engineers as already presented. In the present survey, remote users belong to all age groups, although those using e-mail mostly have less than 15 years' professional experience.

Location has an impact in that the number of remote users who live in a place without a regional library is higher, given that the others prefer to approach the physical library and make their requests through that. It means perhaps that in a time of electronic communication, people still prefer to make more direct, personal contacts.

Fax messages from users outside Athens are twice the number of e-mail messages. This suggests that:

- users are not yet familiar with e-mail as a means of communication
- as the majority of the sample are freelancers, they need to establish dial-up access to send an e-mail and perhaps find this slower
- they usually use fax when they have a particular request, e.g. to borrow a specific book or to ask for a specific piece of law or a standard
- they use e-mail for requests such as bibliographic references, or full-text articles and standards they want to receive by e-mail.

A problem for remote users is that of aquiring primary sources. The Digital Library implemented by the unit provides a way to get the full text of Technical Chamber publications through the internet, although it should include all of them in order to be reliable and more useful. This could only be achieved if authors were persuaded to submit their text electronically. The information sources that engineers mostly prefer are standards, laws, handbooks, etc., and this is material which is usually classified as 'not to be removed from the library'. This is a difficult situation because the library cannot lend such material, which is in printed format, and is not allowed (or cannot afford) to send photocopies for free. In addition, architects, who are also interested in journals with drawings and photos, cannot be served effectively under the present conditions. A solution for access to non-Technical Chamber electronic documents would be to examine a payment system on a pay-per-use basis, but taking into consideration the unwillingness of users to pay, it should be applied only after an analysis of all the parameters.

In an attempt to answer the title question, the general conclusion drawn is that remote users have the same interests and the same habits as other users, but that they do not enjoy the same rights yet, although the library system is defined as 'virtual'. This applies especially to those located in places without a regional physical library, who are more isolated and need even more care from the information service providers. Nowadays, all users are 'remote users' in the sense that the library should be able to provide remote services to anybody (and at any time, if possible).

Thus, for the present system, some measures to improve the situation would include:

- publicizing the electronic services of the library through a variety of means
- providing primary sources online
- having dedicated, well-trained, visionary staff involved with (remote) user services
- developing more user-friendly electronic services.

References

Broughton, K. (2001) Our experiment in online, real-time reference, *Computers in Libraries*, **21** (4)(cited 7 August 2001), available at
www.infotoday.com/cilmag/apr01/broughton.htm

Jordan, R. T. (1970) *Tomorrow's library: direct access and delivery*, Bowker.

Mosley, P. A. (1995) Engineers and librarians: how do they interact?, *Science & Technology Libraries*, **15** (1), 51–61.

Pinelli, T. (1991) The information-seeking habits and practices of engineers, *Science & Technology Libraries*, **11** (3), 5–25.

Toraki, K. (1999) Greek engineers and libraries in the coming years: a human communication model. In *The future of libraries in human communication, 1999 IATUL Conference, Technical University of Crete, Chania, Greece, 17th –21st May, 1999* (cited 24 August 2001), available at
www.educate.lib.chalmers.se/IATUL/proceedcontents/chanpap/toraki.html

Twidale, M. and Nichols, D. M. (1998) *A survey of applications of CSCW for digital libraries*, (ARIADNE Project on Digital Libraries. Technical Report CSEG/4/98), Computing Department, Lancaster University (cited 16 August 2001), available at
www.comp.lancs.ac.uk/computing/research/cseg/projects/ariadne/docs/survey.htm

University of Toronto Library Council (2000) *So near and yet so far: reaching out to the patron at a distance*, Report of the Task Force on Services at a Distance submitted to University of Toronto Library Council, March 2000 (cited 7 August 2001), available at
www.library.utoronto.ca/news/librarycouncil/distance/index.htm

THEME 5
THE PUBLIC LIBRARY'S ROLE IN SERVING DISTANT USERS

20

PUBLIC LIBRARIES MATTER

Clare Nankivell and Juliet Eve

Introduction

The last few years have seen an unprecedented investment in the UK public library sector, focused on developing a 'people's network' – an ICT (information and communications technology) infrastructure, delivering digitized content and access to services, and supported by trained library staff. This paper focuses on this latter area of staff training in ICT skills and the new kinds of roles which may be developing as a result of offering ICT-based services. The authors bring together the results of two research projects which considered these issues from the perspective of library staff themselves (the Training the Future project) and matching these against user needs and expectations arising from end-user experience of using ICTs, particularly in the area of learning support (the VITAL project).

Whilst this paper discusses staff training in the context of recent developments within the public library sector (notably the injection of public money), the authors would like to stress the fact that public libraries support all learners, both formal and informal, and are therefore part of the distributed resource which is the focus of this fourth *Libraries Without Walls* conference. This role can often go unrecognized by institutions of further and higher education, whose students, however, may rely on public library services as part of their learning support.

Background context: UK government support for public libraries

The UK government has taken a number of steps to improve the support for learning provided by libraries. Many of these initiatives are in the academic library sector, where large amounts of funding is going towards digital library projects, such as those discussed at this conference.

Within the public library sector, the government has responded to the key elements of the vision for a network as set out in the document *New library: the people's network* (Library and Information Commission, 1997). This influential document highlighted three specific areas where focus needed to be directed: infrastructure, content development and staff training. Task groups established to consider these three issues published their findings as a companion document, *Building the new library network* (Library and Information Commission, 1998). Government support, via the New Opportunities Fund (NOF), which distributes monies raised by the UK's lottery, has directed £50 million towards the creation of digitized content, and £100 million for infrastructure development, distributed via the People's Network Team, set up as part of Resource, which also provides strategic focus and support for public library authorities across the UK. Resource is the body which oversees developments within the library, museums and archives sectors. The Library and Information Commission, established in 1995, became part of Resource when it was established in 2000.

Twenty million pounds has also been allocated for the training of all public library staff in basic ICT skills. The impetus behind such support comes from the government's belief that public libraries have a key role to play in delivering parts of its social policy agenda, as set out in the policy document *Our information age* (Central Office of Information, 1998). The key areas of this policy are the tackling of social exclusion, in part by the development of lifelong learning opportunities, particularly via the uptake and exploitation of new technologies (Eve, 2000).

Developing public library staff skills

As highlighted by *New library: the people's network*, one impact of the proposed network is the necessity for reskilling staff 'so that they can continue to fulfil their widely valued role as intermediary, guide, interpreter and referral point'. The report further developed the emphasis on the public library network's role by outlining five new roles for public librarians in the 21st century as:

1 net navigator: exploiting the potential of the internet
2 IT gatekeeper: managing ICTs for development of services and in supporting user access
3 information consultant: advising users on sources appropriate to their needs
4 information manager: organizing and exploiting a library's information resources
5 educator: training both staff and users and application of ICTs to support lifelong learning (Library and Information Commission, 1997, 32).

The task group focusing on training established skills specifications which were set out as *basic competencies*, which all library staff should have, supported by a *set of more advanced skills*, which would enable staff as a whole to successfully fulfil the five new roles described above. The recommendation was for the European Computer Driving Licence (ECDL) (now International CDL) to be used for training to ensure that all staff have the basic competencies in order to fulfil four key roles: supporting learning; providing access to information; promoting reader development; and providing remote access to public services.

The UK government has given a great deal of both moral and financial support to the implementation of the people's network. The authors of this paper are concerned, however, that all the funding is project-based and short-term, with no clear indication of how libraries are to support learners in the longer term in relation to ICTs and other developments in learning. They are also concerned that the initiatives will not go all the way to meet the aims set out in *New library: the people's network*, such as equipping public library staff to become e-tutors, which will require more learning for staff both in the area of ICTs and also in learning methods. There is also concern that these developments are taking place in isolation from initiatives in other sectors, particularly further and higher education.

User expectations: the VITAL project

Inevitably, large injections of capital funding for a publicly accessible ICT network generate the need for evaluation, and an assessment of value and worth, both for individual users and for considering the extent to which it may fulfil government objectives. The VITAL (Value and Impact of IT Access in Libraries) project has made a significant contribution in this area by developing a set of methods suitable for use across UK public libraries to assess the impact of providing ICT services, focusing on qualitative indicators of *value*.

VITAL was managed by CERLIM (the Centre for Research in Library and Information Management) based at Manchester Metropolitan University. The project was conducted in liaison with three UK library authorities (Birmingham, Cheshire and Cumbria), which piloted the methods over a six-month period. The methods developed included:

- a questionnaire to library users (including users and non-users of ICT services) to assess general levels of use, and support for ICT services, as well as indications of how these facilities were used
- a series of semi-structured interviews with ICT users in the library, enabling richer pictures of use and value to be built up
- a survey of non-library users, to ascertain levels of awareness of services provided by public libraries, and if non-users might become library users if such facilities, and support in their use, were available.

This paper draws on the results from the library user surveys and the interviews with ICT users, drawing out the data which relates to expectations of staff skills. For a more detailed analysis of the data from the project, the final report is available from the CERLIM website (**www.cerlim.ac.uk/projects/vital.htm**).

The questionnaire survey

The questionnaire focused on the expectations and use made of ICT services (e.g. for work, study or independent learning) as well as use made of staff assistance.

Across the three authorities, 1041 questionnaires were returned, and 231 (20%) library users indicated they used ICT facilities. Online Public Access Catalogues – OPACs – were not considered as part of the ICT facilities for the purposes of this survey. ICT users were asked to indicate whether their *main* use of the facilities was:

- to support a course of study
- for leisure/general enjoyment
- for independent learning/research.

On reflection, these categories may have made false distinctions between activities users themselves either did not regard as different, or it may have been difficult to identify one main use, as evidenced by the instances of users who ticked more than one option. The figures for those following a course of study were similar across all three authorities, averaging 20% of users. The instances of leisure use increased in proportion to the rural nature of the authority, from 19% in Birmingham, to 26% in Cheshire and 41% in Cumbria. The figures for independent study were more similar: around a quarter in Birmingham and Cumbria, and 30% in Cheshire.

Users were also asked how the withdrawal of facilities would affect them – some indicated this would be inconvenient, in that they would have to find other facilities, but others gave more emotional responses, such as:

> This is UNTHINKABLE!!

> I would feel isolated and I would no longer be able to communicate with friends easily.

> I would have to give up my course and be devastated.

Other users, despite having ICT access elsewhere, preferred to use services within a library setting because of the availability of other support and resources (including staff). The survey of non-users further indicated that people might be attracted to using ICTs in the library if they could also access training there, suggesting that the educator role discussed above will be one of the most important for public librarians.

Interviews with ICT users
Use of facilities

Many of the findings from the questionnaire results were reinforced by the more detailed data gathered from transcripts of 96 interviews conducted with users across the three authorities. Forty of these identified some kind of study (formal or otherwise) as being a major part of their use of public library ICT facilities. Purely leisure purposes appeared to account for relatively infrequent use – it was more likely to be combined with research, or job-seeking related activities, the latter being particularly frequent in Cheshire, where 19 of the 40 interviewees indicated this use. Although practical reasons for using the facilities (no other access, free access) account for the majority of reasons for using ICT in a public library, those who did have access elsewhere were still keen to use library facilities, as:

> The library is a comfortable place to go . . .

As outlined above, public libraries are valued not only as a physical space but also because of what else they offer in terms of additional support for learning:

> Because you have a greater variety of information that I can get in one place . . . it's ideal being in one place.

> You can cross-reference things using the books etc.

This indicates that, although access to electronic resources of the kind described at the conference is an important aspect of learner support, the 'hybrid' approach to learning is most certainly still a dominant model.

Staff support

Users were asked if they approached staff for assistance and, if so, whether the staff were able to help. The vast majority indicated that they would ask staff for assistance and, when they did so, problems were resolved. Many comments revealed, however, that users would like more training, yet despite this, were in some instances more knowledgeable than staff themselves. One Birmingham user, for example, found that staff were not able to help

> . . . due to a lack of training the library staff have had themselves.

A user from Cumbria felt that

> . . . one or two could do with training, they know how to switch the computer on and that's it!

However, users seemed overwhelmingly sympathetic to and supportive of staff, even when recognizing that their needs as users were not being met. Users in Cheshire, for example, using facilities in the dedicated IT Suite, articulated the problem but showed awareness of the pressures on staff due to lack of resources:

> . . . you get really snowed under, if more than one has a problem... sometimes it looks like you could do with help.

> I know you can be quite busy at times. Ideally perhaps I would like a bit more help but I appreciate there are a lot of people around and there is only one member of staff . . . ideally I could do with someone sitting next to me.

Interestingly, many comments reflected the fact that this is an area where staff were at varying levels of skill themselves, that technical knowledge was limited, and that staff were only just beginning to adapt to the impact of the new technologies on their roles:

> They are not quite experienced and are not sure what exactly has gone wrong. Usually they shut it down and then open it up again. It would be useful if they had someone who was well up on the system.

> I'm not being critical here . . . because I think they're great staff, but I don't think they feel very confident about it. There will always be just about one person that knows about it . . . if they happen to be dealing with something else I usually have to wait.

Comments such as the one below could indicate either that (this) user('s) expectations have not yet reached the point of expecting assistance with ICT or, more worryingly, that staff attitudes (highlighted as a potential problem area in research referred to in *Building the new library network*) are off-putting:

> I would ask staff who are usually helpful, but you feel that you are disturbing them and that they are not really there to help you with computers.

Overall, it appears that those users with limited skills themselves find staff more helpful, but users requiring more specialized knowledge are less well served. This would imply that advanced roles, such as net navigator, will become increasingly important:

> I will get something like 2 million references. So you have to know how to use it, how to narrow the search down . . . it would be nice if the library would consider it their duty to show me how.

Staff expectations: the Training the Future project

The VITAL project established that users increasingly expect the public library to provide support for learning via ICT resources developed and managed by knowledgeable and helpful staff. The Training the Future project examined how staff themselves felt about their changing roles in the networked library environment, the reskilling they would need to fulfil those roles and the opportunities for training provided by flexible, technology-based methods. The research was conducted by a team based in Birmingham Public Libraries working in partnership with Shropshire County Libraries and the Centre for Information Research (CIRT) at the University of Central England. Findings from the research fed into the *Building the new library network* report discussed above, clarifying not only the skills needed, but the development of realistic ways for staff to acquire them. (For a more detailed discussion of the findings from the Training the Future project, the final report can be ordered from Marje Westley, Bookings and Sales, Floor 2, Central Library, Chamberlain Square, Birmingham, B3 3HQ.)

Staff perceptions

The project began by exploring the views of staff at all levels on the impact of recent and current changes to their roles. Staff views were gained through a series of group interviews which explored a variety of interlinked issues:

* current and future roles, and the impact on these of developments in new technology
* shifts in user expectations
* skills and knowledge necessary to fulfil new roles

- consequent training needs, including preferred training styles
- how staff felt about the changes.

The findings from these interviews were used in conjunction with the findings of a literature review and a Skills Task Group to develop three tables, mapping the 'old' (or traditional) and 'new' (or enhanced) public library service roles. Included were:

- the role of the public library
- the role of public library staff
- the skills required to fulfil the roles.

One of the key roles defined was *A place for learning*. Although other roles also relate to learning (e.g. *the library as equal access provider* and *the information provider*), it is on this core role which this paper focuses. Within this role the 'new' roles for the public librarian included:

- providing open and flexible learning resources
- advising learners on selection and use of technology-based training
- assisting learners with using ICT facilities
- encouraging and supporting people with computer literacy needs
- providing information on ICT-based learning opportunities
- maintaining and developing homework clubs and learning centres.

Many staff felt that supporting learners was a crucial part of their work and voiced concerns about their ability to remain effective supporters of learning within the community as customers' needs moved from a print to a multimedia base. These concerns were expressed by staff at all levels. There appeared to be no correlation between staff experience and knowledge of ICTs – staff at all levels might equally be 'a whiz' or a complete beginner.

All staff accepted that ICT would play a growing part in the services and resources which they provided through their libraries. However, the group interviews showed that many staff were concerned not just with specific ICT-related issues but with a much broader problem of defining exactly what their roles might be in the future. These concerns related to uncertainty about the services the library might provide and the consequent status of different staff – for example, library assistants were often seen to be better equipped to support customers' ICT-related needs, as *IT is a great leveller*. There were also concerns about staffing levels required to support new services, as well as the skills required.

Staff expressed a desire to be confident with the technology and ICT-based services and many identified a need for very basic-level 'awareness' training in ICTs and new services available via these means. Confidence in using ICTs was a key need identified by staff at all levels and with a variety of experience. For example, some staff with a solid basic understanding of computers, and of some new library services delivered via ICT, still felt unsure about their skills when it came to supporting customers in their use of these services. Staff were also concerned that ICT had changed their relationships with their customers:

> They expect you to be an expert.

And this is no longer possible, leading to a lack of confidence and a diminishment in job satisfaction. As one member of staff interviewed said:

> We all have the skills – we just get a blockage because we're not confident with the technology.

Staff training

Key priority areas of training were defined by the staff interviewed. An awareness of ICT-related services, resources and facilities and how these can be used to develop and enhance existing services, as well as basic ICT and trouble-shooting skills were seen as essential. In addition, staff were keen to explore the application of their existing customer care skills in relation to ICT services. Awareness of new electronic information sources, particularly the internet, was also identified as important, along with how to search them effectively. These areas map closely onto the needs explored in the VITAL research, and clearly match the problems highlighted by users.

The staff interviews also explored training styles and methods, and identified good examples as well as barriers to learning. Most staff were willing to develop new skills to support their ability to provide high quality services to the public. However, a number of barriers to learning and developing these skills were identified as:

- time for initial training and, importantly, to consolidate skills – ICT skills were felt to be best developed through practice
- appropriate places for learning – public spaces within the library are not effective places for library staff to learn new skills
- organizational structural and cultural barriers – staff not wanting to learn from their juniors, staff afraid of 'looking foolish', inconsistent management support for ICT training or for staff development more generally.

The data from the staff interviews were used to develop pilot training packages for a sample of staff from both authorities, selected as case study volunteers. All learning was conducted at a distance, using a mixture of CD-ROM and disk-based learning packages. The training priorities for the case study staff were identified using a questionnaire and log sheet. Staff were interviewed to explore their preferred learning styles and appropriate training programmes were then selected. All staff involved in the case studies were monitored and supported by the project team throughout their training and had support from their line managers. The case studies were evaluated through interviews at the outset and close of the training, and through two group de-briefing sessions (one in each authority).

The training case studies demonstrated that useful training packages already exist which can be effective in developing ICT skills for public librarians. They also showed the value of tailoring the training package to the individual, both in terms of content and in terms of learning style. Those case study staff who had previous experience of distance learning found the exercise easier to manage than those who had no prior experience; however, nearly all participants enjoyed learning in this way. The case studies indicate that library staff with a broad variety of learning styles can learn ICT skills effectively via technology-based training packages and materials. These findings may be useful in future when considering ways of supporting learners or providing training in ICTs for both public library users and staff.

Conclusions

Both research projects have confirmed the value of the public library in supporting learning within local communities. Public library users and non-users, and public library staff, all see support for learning as an integral and crucial aspect of the public library service. Users and staff are concerned about the effectiveness of staff to continue to provide this role in the rapidly changing environment of learning via ICTs. Public library users have a mixed view of the current effectiveness of staff in supporting their ICT services, with those users with minimal ICT experience reporting higher levels of satisfaction with staff than those users who have more advanced ICT skills and needs. Library staff want to be able to support users in exploiting these new services and resources, but often lack the skills or the confidence to do so.

Government initiatives have put public libraries at the centre of lifelong learning and social exclusion initiatives, and the funding for public library staff has gone some way to fill the need to equip library staff to support learners. Basic training provided through this funding should enable all public library staff to feel more confident in dealing with their customers' ICT needs and the advanced modules should allow public libraries to develop 'expert' staff to support specific areas of need, such as expertise in online searching. Technologically based, tailored training may provide a longer-term addition to this training as it will allow public library staff to develop and maintain skills at their own pace and to become proactive in developing and supporting services to learners within their communities.

National initiatives which address support for learning across all library sectors are now necessary to ensure that the vast experience and the enormous network of learner support that is the UK public library network can move into the future learning framework which teachers and academic libraries are now developing. If public libraries lag further behind, the consequences will be felt not only by individual learners but by teachers, course administrators and university managers nationwide.

References

Central Office of Information (1998) *Our information age*, Central Office of Information.

Eve, J. (2000) The evaluation of IT facilities for lifelong learning in UK public libraries: the VITAL project. In Brophy, P., Fisher, S. and Clarke, Z. (eds) *Libraries without walls 3: the delivery of library services to distant users*, London, Library Association Publishing, 191–204.

Library and Information Commission (1997) *New library: the people's network*, LIC, available at
www.lic.gov.uk/publications/policyreports/building/index.html

Library and Information Commission (1998) *Building the new library network*, LIC, available at
www.ukoln.ac.uk/services/lic/newlibrary/

Bibliography

Brophy, P., Fisher, S. and Clarke, Z. (eds) (2000) *Libraries without walls 3: the delivery of library services to distant users*, London, Library Association Publishing.

Department for Culture, Media and Sport (1998) *'New library: the people's network': the government's response*, DCMS, available at
www.culture.gov.uk/heritage/new_library.html

Eve, J. and Brophy, P. (2000) VITAL issues: the perception, and use, of ICT services in UK public libraries, *LIBRES: Library and Information Science Research*, **10** (2), available at

www.curtin.edu.au/curtin/dept/sils/libres/

Eve, J. and Brophy, P. (2001) *The value and impact of end-user IT services in public libraries*, Library and Information Commission Research Report 102, Resource.

Jones, B. et al. (1999) *Staff in the new library: skills needs and learning choices*, British Library Research and Innovation Report 152, The British Library Board.

21

PULMAN: Europe's Network of Excellence for public libraries, museums and archives at local level

Rob Davies

Introduction

The PULMAN Network of Excellence (**www.pulmanweb.org**) was launched on 1 May 2001 under the European Commission's research programme for a User-Friendly Information Society (DG Information Society).

Europe's public libraries have an increasingly important part to play in the implementation of the relevant key policies and initiatives which are central to the future of e-Europe. However, although public libraries have made significant strides in recent years, there is a pressing need to spread the type of strategic initiatives adopted in some countries across the whole of Europe and to support their implementation in the form of innovative and appropriate new services.

Much work remains to be done to provide infrastructure, to ensure that access is available to all, including people with disabilities, to develop necessary skills, to integrate new technologies and to adopt appropriate standards.

Public libraries also need to work with their sibling institutions, museums and archives, in the digital cultural sector in order to provide widespread local access to rich content for education, commerce and leisure etc. The terrain for this co-operation is only beginning to be mapped out. It is not yet clearly understood by all stakeholders how local public institutions can best contribute and what work they need to do.

It is therefore important that there should be an action such as PULMAN which focuses upon cultural institutions operating at local level: their interests and importance are too frequently overshadowed by those of national institutions.

The PULMAN network will stimulate and promote sharing of policies and practices for the digital era, in public libraries and cultural organizations which operate at local and regional level. It is hoped that PULMAN will do much to quicken the pace of exchange of knowledge and experience and the extension of good practice.

Objectives and scope

The broad objectives of PULMAN are:

- to strengthen the performance and help achieve the potential of public libraries in new economic, social and cultural roles
- to help spread strategic initiatives across the whole of Europe through knowledge sharing, exchange of experience and the extension of good practice involving both policy-makers and practitioners
- to provide support for innovative and appropriate new services
- to enhance cross-sectoral links between all cultural institutions working at local level
- to contribute to the future research and development agenda for public libraries and other local cultural institutions
- to establish the feasibility of a sustainable European agency or mechanism to promote the interests and development of public libraries.

Specifically, by the time of its completion in April 2003, it is planned that PULMAN will have:

- created a human network of excellence involving public libraries, local public cultural organizations, policy-makers, technical partners, associations – across all EU member and candidate countries
- encouraged Europe-wide awareness, collaboration and dialogue on digital initiatives and best practice by identifying key national players, lobbying and communication activities
- organized high-impact events to build consensus and promote collaboration at national and European level – these will include national workshops in every participating country and a European Policy Conference early in 2003 targeted at senior policy-makers, practitioners and national representatives of public libraries, museums and archives
- promoted stronger links between public libraries, museums and archives and established an agenda for co-operation
- issued a policy manifesto or declaration 'forecasting the role, research and development needs of local public cultural institutions' – this will be designed to drive forward future phases of collaboration and innovation in the work of local public cultural organizations
- developed an international co-operation agenda intended to disseminate the work of the PULMAN network internationally and to extend interaction to other parts of the world
- compiled and published Digital Guidelines Manuals (DGMs) – 'state of the

art embodiments of good practice in innovative public library services' – translated into major European languages, promoted to policy-makers and practitioners, and supported by a Technology Watch, which will help to keep them up to date
- provided an access point and reference tool for professionals and policy-makers: a PULMANWeb gateway and dissemination service and the *PULMAN Express* e-newsletter
- organized in-service training workshops on innovative practice for public library managers, to be held in centres of excellence across Europe
- provided structured access to professional distance-learning materials by publishing and maintaining a web-based distance-learning registry, to offer improved access to high-quality distance learning materials for professionals working in local public libraries, museums and archives.

Membership of the PULMAN network

Initial membership of the PULMAN network includes representatives of 26 European countries (**www.pulmanweb.org/**). The PULMAN approach is inclusive and participation will be extended, in the first instance, by the establishment of wider 'support groups' of activists in each country, but eventually to a very wide group of managers and policy-makers.

The structure of project participation is relatively complex, involving:

- 18 full partner organizations
- 5 work package leaders
- 9 management board members
- 16 topic co-ordinators for the digital guidelines manuals
- 26 country co-ordinators (including 13 partners)
- a project co-ordination team
- country support groups in each country
- a virtual advisory board, comprised of an invited list of experienced and influential people in the sector acting as a sounding board and quality assurance mechanism.

Several organizations fulfil more than one of these roles. The role of the country co-ordinators is actively to involve the whole professional community concerned with public libraries and local cultural institutions in the activities of the PULMAN Network of Excellence, first of all by establishing a 'core group' of active workers. The co-ordinators will have a specific set of tasks, including:

- disseminating information and the results of PULMAN as widely as possible
- feeding back on draft guidelines and organizing their translation
- survey implementation
- organizing a national workshop
- making appropriate policy and cross-sectoral contacts
- ensuring appropriate national participation in project-level and training/awareness-raising workshops and the policy conference
- stimulating and co-coordinating contributions to PULMAN-net.

The PULMAN workplan

The work of PULMAN is organized in several work packages, which are presented below.

Work packages 1 and 2 – Digital Guidelines Manuals (DGM)

These activities focus on the compilation, agreement and packaging of Digital Guidelines Manuals (DGMs) – social and technical, respectively (see Tables 21.1 and 21.2). This process requires the identification of best practice right across Europe through a survey conducted by country co-ordinators of existing best practice, innovation and existing guidelines, in addition to extensive desk research.

Table 21.1 *Social guidelines*

Topic co-ordinator	DGM
1.1 Amitié	Digital literacy
1.2 Ljubljana	Social inclusion
1.3 Bremen	Lifelong learning
1.4 Oeiras	Support for formal education, distance learning
1.5 Aquitaine	Support for business and the economy
1.6 Dublin	Citizen participation in new civic governance
1.7 Olsztyn	Access to diverse cultural content
1.8 FORCE Foundation	Access and services for people with physical and visual impairments
1.9 IAML	Access to music and non-print material
1.10 Helsinki	Management: models for co-operation/partnership in service delivery
1.11 Antwerp	Funding and financing opportunities
1.12 Eblida	Access to copyright-protected materials/licensing/ rights

Table 21.2 *Technical guidelines*

Topic co-ordinator	DGM
2.1 Essex	Resource description, discovery and retrieval
2.2 CERLIM	Digitization
2.3 MDR	Multimedia digital service delivery
2.4 MDR	Applications of newly developing technologies
2.5 Cluj/Essex	Developments in integrated library systems
2.6 CERLIM/MDR	Performance measures and evaluative tools
2.7 Essex/Aquitaine	Tailoring of services; citizen interaction and participation
2.8 Eblida	Handling of legal issues (privacy, data protection, IPR)
2.9 Essex	Technical responses to multilingual issues

The DGMs will then be edited and validated through a series of evaluation workshops before finalization and translation.

The DGMs are intended to provide important and adaptable reference tools for public library policy-makers and practitioners in designing and delivering new services and to support argumentation and case-building with decision-makers. They will incorporate live links to sources and demonstrators and will be living documents, to be updated over time as circumstances change.

Individual PULMAN partners will be responsible for the compilation of at least one set of DGMs in their area of expertise.

Work package 3 – policy and cross-sectoral development

The focus of this work is to stimulate a process of interaction at the policy level between:

• public library practitioners and policy-makers
• those involved with public libraries and other cultural institutions which deliver services at the local level, i.e. museums and archives.

The work package is led by Eblida (the European Bureau of Library, Information and Documentation Associations).

The policy-makers to be targeted will include national ministries and agencies responsible for public libraries, culture, education, business and industry, and other sectors upon which public libraries have an impact, and European and supra-national bodies which have an impact on policies affecting public libraries and cultural institutions at local level (e.g. European Parliament, Council of Europe).

The main effort of PULMAN will be focused upon those parts of Europe where such innovative and cross-sectoral policies involving public libraries are not yet established, and where policy-makers may as yet be insufficiently aware of the potential of public libraries to deliver new services. Interaction with policy-makers will draw upon experience in those parts of Europe where such developments have begun or successes have been achieved.

At European level, Eblida will also develop interaction on behalf of public library practitioners with equivalent bodies from the museums and archives sector (e.g. ICOM, ICA, EMII) and with bodies representing groups of national public library authorities, such as NAPLE, which is currently a forum for such authorities from several member states. This process will culminate in a high-level conference intended to build scenarios and help resolve future cross-sectoral strategies and actions.

Work package 4 – dissemination

Work package 4, co-ordinated by Oeiras (Portugal), provides a multi-stranded approach to disseminating good practice through the work of PULMAN. It will support the widespread availability of the Digital Guidelines Manuals through a PULMAN-net website and will provide linkage to innovative demonstrators and services through a gateway site.

Training and awareness-raising workshops held in centres of excellence will target individual public library managers with a capacity to conduct specified 'multiplier' activities in their own countries (e.g. set up discussion lists, publish or organize meetings and workshops). The centres of excellence involved will be Aarhus, Helsinki, Ljubljana and Veria, each offering a different set of achievements in a variety of political, social and economic environments. The training and awareness-raising will be mainly directed toward senior professionals and policy-makers in South, Central and Eastern Europe.

Access to relevant distance-learning facilities relevant to public library practitioners in the information society will also be made easier through the compilation of a registry and their availability through the PULMAN gateway.

Management of the network

The various strands of work will need careful co-ordination and consolidation. This will be provided by the co-ordinator, Antwerp City Library, and MDR Partners, the project manager responsible for conducting the day-to-day work.

Finally, some of the key milestone dates and events during the lifetime of PULMAN are:

31 December 2001	Draft DGMs ready
February 2002	Consensus-building conferences on DGMs
October 2002	Translated DGMs published
September–November 2002	National workshops in each country
February 2003	Policy conference
April 2003	Training workshops completed

PULMAN Network Co-ordinator
Jan van Vaerenbergh, Antwerp City Library, Belgium
jan.vanvaerenbergh@cs.antwerpen.be

PULMAN Network Project Manager
Rob Davies, MDR Partners, UK
rob.davies@mdrpartners.com

PULMAN Network Administrator
Mary Gianoli, MDR Partners, UK
mary.gianoli@mdrpartners.com

THEME 6
CONTENT DEVELOPMENT FOR THE VIRTUAL ENVIRONMENT

22

OMMAT: DEALING WITH ELECTRONIC SCIENTIFIC INFORMATION

Jan Kooistra and Kees Hopstaken

Introduction

Ommat (**www.fss.uu.nl/ommat**) was developed in 1998 as an educational program/university training on the internet giving students insight into how science *works* using ICT, and pursuing this aim by means of ICT. This program is written in Dutch but would work in any language that is used by scientists. (Kooistra and Hopstaken, 2000). The name of the program is an abbreviation which in Dutch refers to the *daily practice of dealing with scientific sources*.

The program connects ideas put forward in other work which states that:

> . . . we are in need of an outward oriented ICT-methodology which could handle the situation of being connected the digital way, a methodology which has its own pragmatics which will process people into a new system. (Kooistra et al., 2001)

We presumed that the consequence of the ICT methodology will be that an individual is persistent at an address in a process of growing intelligence. We called this 'being@'. An individual is part of a growing intelligent agent, a 'gi@'. The gi@ in its turn functions like a *virtual deputy*. The gi@ guarantees the quality and is a safeguard. A deputy refers to a complex system which acts like a moderator, and is empowered to manage the parameters of a site which are set by the community of site users. Ommat covers these ideas.

We report on the different elements of Ommat in more detail below. We also discuss the next generation of the Ommat program. The development of this later program, called DELFTSpecial, is initiated by the library of the Delft University of Technology (**www.tudelft.nl/delftspecial**). This programme is part of a broader strategy: to change the position of the library itself from a modern library into a (more) interactive one. That means a library using agent technology and server-based information to speed up the processes of knowledge exchange and academic correspondence.

Ommat: knowledge exchange

In practice Ommat is an interactive program for the search and exchange of data, information and knowledge on an internet site in use at the Faculty of Social Sciences, Utrecht University, in the Netherlands. At first sight Ommat looks like a virtual library manual, but at the point where other manuals end, Ommat makes a move forward. Ommat leads the student from the area of skills into the area of strategic searching.

To initiate the process of strategic searching, the program is linked to the student curriculum. This strategic searching cannot be successful if the student does not obtain understanding about the laws that rule the scientific area being searched at that moment. What is the value of the data, information, etc.? Where *is* the student in fact? Who is the deputy in the area? Here the program goes into the next phase. The student learns to look for the sources the teachers are using themselves. What has the teacher published and to which references is the teacher referring? In this way students start searching for the network of scientists that they may join in the future.

Thus students get the idea of how science 'works'. Data, information knowledge, etc. are products that circulate among special groups of people called 'scientists', and there are procedures to change or to maintain these products. So the student learns to acknowledge the power hiding in the structure of the knowledge since it (the knowledge) is linked to the student by means of identity and socialization. At that point Ommat takes another final step: by creating an online newsgroup on the (local) net. Those students who are working on the same theme (searching for the same kind of information) start to communicate in a shared workspace. Thus students meet there and then the challenge of completing an assignment in which being@ is the focus (Kooistra and Hopstaken, 2000).

Ommat: didactic procedures and strategy

There are three didactical procedures hidden in the structure of the Ommat programme. From start to finish the student gets guidance from different sides in the direction of the deputy. This guidance comprises:

1 Following search procedures from closed to strategic solutions. The closed solutions represent the right answers to the questions imposed. Where can I find what information? And why there? The strategic solutions represent the ability to switch between the different solutions and different levels of information. What kind of information do I need to complete my project?
2 Narrowing the search down from interesting themes into the discourse of the discipline (study). Which theme is interesting? What theories lie behind the

themes? Do they belong to my field of study? Which scholars should I refer to? Do my professors refer to these scholars? Why or why not? What is the relation between me and my discipline (study)?

3   From isolation to correspondence. What have I got by finding this information? Is there somebody I can ask about the value of it? Do I know someone I can meet face-to-face to talk about it? Is it possible to ask my questions, to voice my insecurities virtually and anonymously? Is there some place I should be at? (Kooistra and Hopstaken, 2000).

Speaking about *strategy*, the three didactic procedures are not only guiding the student to the position of being@, they are also changing the status of the student. The pragmatic consequence of the use of ICT is that the students are becoming correspondents. They move up to the (former) position of the librarian. Since the position of the librarian was that of selecting, acquiring, ordering, indexing and making available data (information, knowledge), these tasks are split into a number of actions: typifying (identifying) and selecting (using search engines), acquiring, making available (using all kinds of sources and databases) and ordering, opening up and guaranteeing (networking/using virtual correspondence). The use of ICT reduces the gap between staff and student. Students become librarians as they were at the beginning of the era of modern science.

Ommat: the structure of the program

Figure 22.1 overleaf shows the structure of Ommat. The program provides training that includes all kinds of procedures, skills and tools to search for information strategically. Through interaction with fellow students (being@ a workspace) a student is learning simultaneously:

- to find information about a topic
- where/how this information can be acquired
- who represents the scientific network that authorizes that information.

At the Utrecht University Ommat has been installed as a part of an e-education program (Blackboard). In the case of an e-education platform, a log-in provides identification, the start of a support system, access to all kinds of domains and the opening of a virtual workspace. Blackboard does not make a difference to the structure of the Ommat programme but makes its use easier.

By starting the programme students enter the digital workspace, where they will find their assignment (link to the curriculum), group members (names and e-mail addresses) and a start document (article/paper/chapter). The start document is used to facilitate the learning process. Together with group members students have to *typify*, *find* and *validate* the information which is incorporated in the start document.

By this process students learn that a solid search strategy is always necessary for these three stages (typifying, finding and validating) and that each stage contains different steps. Most of these steps involve the use of specific skills and tools. In Ommat all the tools can be consulted (digitally) by clicking on the text/icons in the training schedule. So by following the scenario in the training, students not only get a lot of practice (including examples, exercises and tests)

1. Network training: search and find the scientific network	
Start: Log in (identification / start support system / access to domains, opening virtual workspace)	
Assignment: (by teacher or by own authority))	
Group members: (names and e-mail addresses)	
Start document: (article / paper / chapter)	
Typifying	Which are the central concepts and/or theories?
Identifying	Which literature is used? Selection of relevant references.
Clarifying	What kinds of documents are referred to? Dissemination of information
	How old are the sources / documents?
Searching and Finding	Which publications are listed/available at the library of your university?
Acquiring	Are others publications of the same author listed/available at the library of your university?
Getting (more) information	Are publications listed/available elsewhere?
	Can you find descriptions of the articles? Are the articles indexed?
	Articles full text available? (Digital)
	How to acquire the non-digital documents?
Validating	Who are the experts on your topic? Which are the expert organisations? Are there special libraries or documentation centres on your topic.
Evaluating Resources	
Networking	Are your authors cited / quoted by others?
	How prominent/leading are the journals?
	Which information is available on the Internet?
	Which discussion groups you can find on your topic?
	Are there news groups on you topic?
2. Strategic searching (searching for information by applying the network training)	
Start: Log in (identification / start support system / access to domains, opening virtual workspace)	
Assignment: (by teacher or by own authority))	
Group members: (names and e-mail addresses)	
Search procedure form: (form gives all steps systematically	

Fig. 22.1   *Structure of the Ommat site*
Reproduced with the permission of Jan Kooistra.

but also learn to correspond with fellow students about findings – and thereby build their own (virtual) network. Or, from the point of view of the whole group, the group is learning to search for a scientific network by becoming a network itself.

When students have passed through every stage, they are equipped to do their own strategic searching. At this point the actual assignment (link to the curriculum) becomes visible: strategic searching. The student has to write a paper, prepare a presentation etc., using Ommat as a vehicle to get better results.

Ommat: theoretical notions

We constructed Ommat using theoretical notions/ideas about human systems as contributed by cybernetics and systems theory. Specifically we have looked for systems that cover the *social activities* that people develop when they are looking for knowledge. Ommat is not so much a program for finding information as a program that offers students *the best opportunity* to get and to contribute to the kind of knowledge they need (to survive socially as a scientist).

The following reports briefly on our notions of the ice-canoe, the gi@, being@ and defrosting and speeding up knowledge.

Ice-canoe

Systems that are based on how people deal with knowledge refer to special kinds of systems. The structure of these systems is simultaneously the means *and* the outcome of social practices of system elements (economies, technologies, social security practices, etc.). This means/outcome mechanism is what we call an ice-canoe. The story of the ice-canoe is as elementary as it is illustrative: once an artist built a canoe out of ice, he launched it on a pond and paddled around until his boat melted and vanished into its original state – water.

One can refer to knowledge as being an ice-canoe. It is made of the same material that people try to sail on:

> Knowledge is frozen ignorance. Only with a lot of energy (social constructions, education and technology) can we succeed in keeping our knowledge frozen. (Kooistra et al., 2001)

Ommat is like an ice-canoe (see Figure 22.2). The program shows the structure of science at the end of the last millennium. Science as the art of framing perishable data/information/knowledge into an electronic vehicle that is driven by a set of interdependent (formerly) social activities: querying, distributing, communicating and keeping.

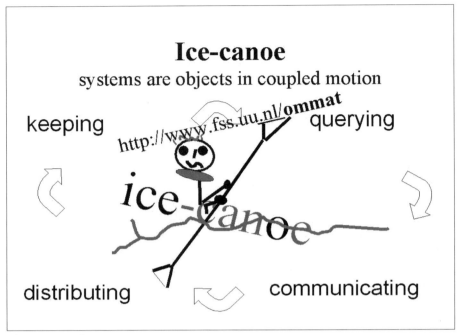

Fig. 22.2   *The ice-canoe*
Reproduced with the permission of Jan Kooistra.

Gi@

The old established duties of librarianship are: selecting, acquiring, ordering, indexing and making available. These duties have been changing rapidly since the introduction of ICT. How can you make a librarian out of a student? In other work we referred to the work of Fred Johansen. He has developed the idea of a *knowledge agent*. The knowledge agent is 'a type of intelligent agent that deals in knowledge, in the way of *keeping, querying, distributing* it or *communicating* it whether as a primary or secondary function' (Johansen, 1997).

We extended Johansen's concept with the idea of the gi@ – growing intelligent agent (Kooistra et al., 2001). The gi@ (see Figure 22.3) conveys the ongoing interweaving of the quickly advancing ICT and classical human qualities like feeling, searching, thinking and (ir)rational decision-making. It is an interactive workspace that is not just a tool used by individuals or groups, e.g. school classes. It is really a deputy: a partly virtual and partly human substitute that has the managing power to deal with collected information, to draw conclusions, to take initiatives based on recursive server-based information.

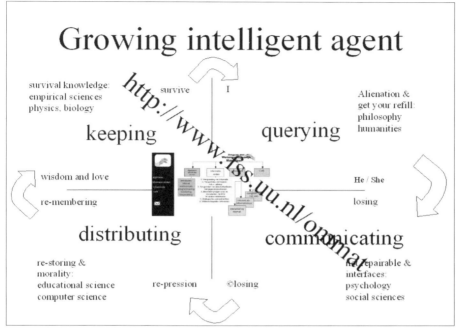

Fig. 22.3   *Gi@ Ommat*
Reproduced with the permission of Jan Kooistra.

We can understand the four activities of Johansen's knowledge agent (keeping, querying, distributing and communicating) as coupling the elements of a system. The system, in this case, is the production of (survival) knowledge by an agent about a subject (theme, topic). The agent can operate at different levels (group, class, staff) and within different areas (neighbourhood, nation, institute, university, etc.). The concept of *survival knowledge* underlines the basic notion of education: in general, parents die sooner than their children. So they have to hurry to teach their kids how to survive. Students have to survive their teacher. Ommat is a gi@ that is processing survival knowledge on behalf of a student at a permanent address on the internet – being@ (Kooistra et al., 2001).

Being@

In every society the production of discourse (formal speech) is at once controlled, selected, organized and redistributed according to a certain number of procedures. The role of these procedures is to avert its (discourse) powers and its dangers, to cope with chance events and to evade its ponderous, awesome materiality. (Foucault, 1971b, 8)

By emphasizing that these procedures are rules of *exclusion*, Foucault creates insight into mechanisms which are responsible for the freezing of ignorance into knowledge. The idea of the ice-canoe shows the interdependence of the subject and the object. The object (knowledge) is communicated by means of the speaker, who has to pay a contribution to survival. Man appears in the ambiguous position of an object of knowledge and as a subject that knows. Survival is in the discourse. We are *at* our knowledge. The way Foucault's anti-subject philosophy evaluates the relation between man and knowledge gives us a notion of the (epistemological) set-up of being@.

Being@ is the discourse as sustained by its virtual members. At any moment it is the direct outcome of an information process. It is a knowledge-recording medium made out of visitors (membership) and search engines (exclusion). It is easy to see that a lot of the sites we could be@ often offer rigid deputies of something (for instance, sex pictures) because the users seem to want to have just that information by which they are already selected (note the recursive energy in it). This represents the idea of Foucault about the exchange of subject and object. Sex pictures are (become) the formal language beyond which these users (log-ins) cannot speak and so they are selected by this (in)capability (Kooistra and Hopstaken, 2000) – man as enslaved ruler, as observed spectator (Foucault, 1971a).

Defrosting and speeding up knowledge

> A supportive post modern weather report means no longer a report on the weather as such, but it signifies and graduates the quality of the relationship we have with the institute itself which collects and distributes the information in question. (Kooistra, 1991)

In this report on the four different qualities of knowledge, we stated that the relationship we have with our knowledge is determined to a large degree by the logistic and technical possibilities we have developed to retain and store it. Until recently we have always committed our knowledge to paper. Following all the procedures that are required by 'what paper is capable of and what not', it is not difficult to realize that by using ICT we will have to devise another kind of methodology to deal with knowledge.

What are the required activities in such a methodology? Our first assumption is that these ICT activities (ICT values) will process again the 'old' academic values. We are just human. Secondly, we assume that the activities will be inextricably bound up with the belief in the benefit of participation. Being connected by ICT means that solving a problem, developing a set of action plans or taking a decision cannot be done in isolation (Kooistra et al., 2001). Whereas the paper methodology meant that you had to sit down, write the knowledge into a paper and send it to a journal, the ICT methodology means that we have to put questions and ideas on the (inter)net and ask for feedback.

The paper sources and the networks of scientists presenting papers as they existed during the 20th century will vanish. Anonymous and unfinished material (data) will circulate like a ball being pushed in a pinball machine. The consequence of the ICT methodology is that the individual is persistent at an address (being@) in a process of growing intelligence. The walls of the library will disappear. What is in books will be speeded up into a better, more open and more interactive relationship between the user and the institute which collected and distributed the information in question.

DELFTSpecial: a correspondence library

How much of gi@ is in a student and how much of a student is in a gi@? Could something like a gi@ be viable? We think so. The principle that students are connected with other students by e-mail (hotmail) is already normal. The introduction of e-education platforms means that the students are connected with the sources at the library, with the (raw) material of their courses and the material that is produced at that very moment in their virtual workspace. In this way it is easy to understand that the library can be seen as one of the centres where users enter into correspondence (and maintain correspondence) with other students/people directly or indirectly. Being@ the library, corresponding with other people indirectly at the library, means searching for the information they left behind, and you can also correspond directly (work together) with them.

Constructing DELFTSpecial, which is the next-generation Ommat, signifies the importance of this direct and indirect correspondence, bringing people closer to each other. At DELFTSpecial we are adding another two functions to the three functions (typifying, finding and validating) which we are already using in Ommat. It concerns the functions of archiving (portfolio, remembering, reminding) and of alerting. It is the idea that the archive function will not only enable systems to store material (and here one could learn a lot from librarians), but will also remember your relationship with the material by storing the names of the people you met, and remind you how you evaluated the course, what was in the news, or even the bad or good mood you were in at that time. We call this 'remembering the membership'.

Remembering the membership opens the relational quality of your knowledge. It is informative the other way around, like searching the network. We think that the different archiving functions together with the function of alerting (using server-based information) could be a realistic basis for a gi@. However, we are still at the start of this new development. By installing DELFTSpecial in the library of the Delft University of Technology, and by making arrangements with two faculties at the University, we are going to develop and try out the idea of gi@.

References

Foucault, M. (1971a) *L'ordre du discours*, Gallimard.

Foucault, M. (1971b) Orders of discourse, *Social Science Information*, **10** (2), (translation of Foucault, 1971a).

Hough R. R. et al. (2001) Growing intelligent agents for the delivery of knowledge, a collaborative form, *Systemica*, 13.

Johansen, F. (1997) *Site knowledge agent*, available at
www.ifi.ntnu.no/grupper/ai/fredj-masters.html

Kooistra, J. (1991) Speeding-up knowledge, *Conference: problems of support, survival and culture*, University of Amsterdam.

Kooistra, J. and Hopstaken, C. W. J. (2000) Being@: keep company with electronic evidence! In Trappl. R. (ed.) *Cybernetics and systems 2000*, University of Vienna/ASCS, 438–43.

Kooistra, J. et al. (2001) Growing intelligent agents for the delivery of knowledge: a structure, *Systemica*, **13**, 349–58.

23

COPYRIGHT MADE INTERESTING

Judy Watkins and Tracy Bentley

Introduction

When developing new services, librarians have to be aware not only of what is desirable and technically possible, but also of what is legal, as most of the information will be protected by copyright. The word 'copyright' can strike terror into the hearts of many librarians. A recent report by JISC claimed:

> Most academics prefer to know as little about copyright as is absolutely necessary. It is almost as if they have erected a mental barrier, the more they know, the more difficult they may find it to carry out their normal teaching duties. (Weedon, 2000)

From our own experience perhaps the most common barrier to finding out more about copyright is that it is thought to be a bit boring. No conference paper could make this subject easy, but it is hoped that this paper will persuade readers that copyright is not as bad as they think and to see it in a more positive light.

History

Throughout the world copyright law has evolved, with new legislation being added as a piecemeal response to new situations. In Europe, some laws grew from the copyright tradition and others from the *'droit d'auteur'* tradition. The copyright tradition developed in England and was enshrined in law in the Statute of Anne 1709. The idea behind the Act was that copyright protection of material would encourage dissemination, thereby benefiting the public at large. The copyright tradition tends to give rights to a wider group than just the authors. Quite often groups such as producers of film and records also receive rights.

The *droit d'auteur* tradition originated in France. It developed from the premise that authors should be rewarded for their work. The public good does not enter into the equation. Under this tradition, rights were normally not given to those other than authors. These associated rights, or *neighbouring rights* as they are often called, became more common after the 1961 Rome Convention for the

Protection of Performers, Producers of Phonograms and Broadcasting Organizations (**www.wipo.org/treaties/ip/rome/**).

Distinctions have become blurred over time, and individual laws have developed in response to international agreements such as the Berne and Rome Conventions.

Basic copyright principles

Copyright is an acknowledgement that the person creating an original work should have control over their creation. This is partly for financial reasons (economic rights) and partly to protect the investment of the creator's 'self' in the work (moral rights). Different categories of original work are protected by copyright, including music, broadcasts, films, videos and, the most common category, 'literary and artistic works'. This latter category tends to be defined very widely and flexibly. Computer programs, for example, are protected as literary works. Copyright protection extends to expressions in a fixed format but not to ideas, procedures, methods of operation or mathematical concepts.

Copyright protection takes the form of restricting certain acts which can only be performed with the work by the copyright holder, or with their express permission. Typically these restrictions include:

- copying the work
- issuing copies to the public
- performing, showing or broadcasting the work
- adapting or translating the work (including converting it to an accessible format)
- lending or renting the work.

These are often referred to as 'economic rights'. In addition creators (whether or not they own the economic rights) enjoy what is often called 'moral rights'. These generally include the following restrictions:

- no one is allowed to change, add or remove anything from the work, if by doing so the reputation of the creator is adversely affected
- the right of the creator to be named as such
- no one else may claim to be the creator
- not having your name attributed to anything you did not create.

The creator of the work is normally the first copyright holder, but they may assign the economic rights to a third party (such as a publisher). Moral rights are generally inalienable. The UK is one of the few countries where the creator may choose to waive them, although there are moves afoot which may change this provision.

Rights of the copyright holders are not absolute – there are some limitations. For example, a work is not protected forever – there is normally a time limit set from the end of the year in which a specific event, such as death or publication, occurred. Copying for specified purposes, provided it does not harm the rights of the copyright holders, is often permitted. It is also generally agreed that copying an 'insubstantial' part (in terms of quantity and quality) of the whole is not an infringement of copyright.

Current situation

Copyright law does vary from country to country, particularly as different countries adopt their own response to new developments. Although international conventions offer a framework in which copyright laws can develop, the subtle differences are causing problems for international document suppliers. They are not competing on a level playing field, as some countries allow certain types of copying to be performed without a copyright fee, whereas others do not. The requesting library must be aware that, while an overseas library is able to supply the copy, it may be an infringement for the requestor to receive it.

EU directive

The European Parliament has recently introduced a directive intended to harmonize certain aspects of copyright and related rights. The directive deals with the electronic environment in order to avoid each member state adopting individual piecemeal responses. It should be incorporated into member states' national laws by the end of 2002.

The Directive covers:

* *reproduction right* – which includes direct and indirect copying, whether temporary or permanent (in effect, this would make all transient copies infringing copies)
* *distribution right* – which is distribution by sale or otherwise of originals and copies
* *communication to the public right* – which is making material available to the public by wire or wireless means (this would include making something available over the internet an infringement)
* *exceptions to the above* – as all the above rights are exclusive rights of the

copyright holder, there is a list of actions that may be allowed with permission (these are discussed in more detail below)
- *technological protection mechanisms* – the directive deals with protection of the mechanisms used to protect the content.

Exceptions

One of the biggest bones of contention with the directive is the exhaustive list of exceptions which, being mainly optional, will potentially limit the level of harmonization. Member states will be allowed to distinguish between paper and digital copies, so some exceptions may be applied differently in the hard copy and the digital environment. In the 'recitals' accompanying the directive in its draft form, there was much emphasis placed on the digital environment being more open to piracy. This notion is one which many commentators reject, particularly as technological protection mechanisms could make the digital environment actually safer. Some of the permitted exceptions could also include 'fair compensation' – a phrase which has caused a great deal of concern. According to the Berne Convention, exceptions are only permitted if there is no loss to the copyright holder. Therefore, if there is no loss, there should be no compensation. After a great deal of lobbying on this point it has been acknowledged that the level of compensation can be set at zero.

The only exception which every member state *has* to adopt is the one relating to the reproduction right, which states that 'temporary or incidental copies which are essential and integral to the technological process and have no independent significance' will not be infringing copies. This means, for example, that copies automatically made by a computer when browsing, booting up or using information will not be viewed as infringements. The other exceptions are all optional, so may or may not be adopted.

One permitted exception is to the reproduction right only, and allows 'specific acts of reproduction by establishments accessible to the public'. The recital accompanying the directive stresses that these should be non-profit-making institutions and would include libraries and archives. If this exception is adopted then existing exceptions for prescribed libraries (such as interlibrary supply, preservation and replacement copying) could continue. A further exception allows copying for 'teaching or scientific research for non-commercial purposes', which would allow the continuation of supply to individuals. At the moment, the UK Copyright Law states that copies can be made for research, the words 'non-commercial' being dropped from drafts of the 1988 Act, leading users to believe that copying for commercial research was acceptable. In earlier drafts of the directive there was much debate about the effect of the words 'non-commercial', particularly as in today's climate many 'non-commercial' institutions – for example universities – undertake sponsored research. The recitals of the directive give some advice on determining what would be considered commercial. This should be judged by the activity itself: organizational structure and means of funding will not be the decisive factors. Therefore this exception may not be as restrictive as was first thought.

The directive provides for exception on the grounds of disability. The UK is one of the EU member states which does not already have an exception allowing disabled people to convert information into an accessible format, although there are trade guidelines issued by rights-holders in association with organizations for visually impaired people. These guidelines only apply to people with a visual impairment that cannot be rectified with glasses. The permitted exception in the directive could widen the guidelines to include all forms of text and hearing disabilities.

Other permitted exceptions are similar to those we already have in the UK, such as for reporting current events, criticism or review, and security, judicial or parliamentary use.

The directive also offers protection for technological protection mechanisms. Once in place, the directive will make it illegal for anyone to circumvent these or to make a device intended to circumvent such mechanisms. This is a requirement of the recent World Intellectual Property Organization (WIPO) treaty, and has already been incorporated into USA law. There is currently a case in America involving a Russian who visited the USA to speak at a conference and was arrested because he made such a device in order for visually impaired people to convert Adobe files into an accessible format (**http://dailynews.yahoo.com/h/ nm/20010727/tc/tech_hacker_dc_5.html**). These devices are an infringement in the USA but not in Russia. The EU directive is slightly more forgiving than The Digital Millennium Copyright Act, as it does allow circumvention to take advantages of exceptions to which the user is entitled if the rights-holder does not provide a means for doing so. There was extensive lobbying to get that stipulation included, but it may prove useless if foreigners can still be prosecuted in America for something which would be lawful in their own country.

Licences

The directive does not state that exceptions cannot be overridden by contracts. This is particularly worrying as electronic information is increasingly controlled by licence. In particular, shrink-wrap and click licences are becoming more prevalent. Although such licences have the advantage of explaining what can be done, often they explicitly exclude actions such as copying or lending which would normally be allowed. As contracts normally require the signature of all parties, the legality of shrink-wrap and click licences is debatable. However, providing the terms are displayed clearly on the outside, and buyers can return the product if they do not agree with the terms, it is considered that there is at least an implied licence. If individual product-specific licences continue to be the norm, then library staff will need to be aware of all the different licence terms and conditions instead of one licensing scheme such as that offered by the Copyright Licensing Agency, which has the same terms for all relevant material.

Should we worry?

At the time of writing there are still around 12 months left to lobby for the changes in national law to ensure that the legislation resulting from the directive is the best possible for information providers under the circumstances. The library lobby has already achieved a great deal by influencing many of the exceptions and recitals included in the directive. Although at times the draft versions have been extremely worrying, the final form has the potential to maintain the current situation, so nothing should be lost. The balance of rights between copyright-holders and users can be maintained. We still need to address the issue of distinction between analogue and digital copying. The WIPO treaty states that exceptions should be extended to include the digital environment, but this will not necessarily happen with the new legislation.

The optional list of exceptions could result in a lack of harmonization between countries. There are already differences between what can be supplied and received between countries. If different exceptions are adopted by different member states, this situation could continue even within the EU. This could have implications for anyone serving overseas customers.

For those in the UK, the need for hand-written signatures on the statutory copying declaration form is a pressing issue. The good news is that the government is addressing this issue, and that the Statutory Instrument (SI) could well be repealed before the other changes are made to copyright law. Of course, repealing the SI is only the first step. There then has to be agreement as to what would be considered acceptable as an electronic signature, but at least a start would have been made.

Conclusion

In Europe, as in the rest of the world, we are at a crossroads. Many factors, including the demands of the library sector, will determine the routes available and the route we end up taking. But one thing is certain: we are nowhere near the end of our journey as there will be more challenges, more possibilities, and more solutions. This is what makes the field of copyright and information provision so interesting – and frustrating!

Reference

Weedon, R. (2000) *Policy approaches to copyright in HEIs*, a study for the JISC Committee on Awareness, Liaison and Training (CALT), University of Strathclyde.

THEME 7
KEY TECHNOLOGY ISSUES IN DELIVERING
SERVICES TO DISTANT USERS

24

WORKING WITH THE BRITISH LIBRARY: THE *zetoc* EXPERIENCE

Ross MacIntyre and Ann Apps

Introduction

A market research report commissioned by the British Library was used as the basis of a detailed list of requirements for the provision of digital services to the UK higher and further education sector. The services stemming from these requirements centred, in the first instance, on the British Library's Electronic Table of Contents data (ETOC), which lists the titles of nearly 15 million journal articles and conference papers. A key approach to the development of these services will be the conformance to accepted standards and open systems, thus enabling greater potential for interoperability with developments elsewhere. As a first step towards this, the British Library contracted Manchester Computing to develop and mount a Z39.50-compliant version of the ETOC database – a service now live and entitled '*zetoc*'. This service is free to UK institutions supported by the Joint Information Systems Committee (JISC) of the UK Higher Education Funding Councils. In addition to this operational service, which is based on existing and well-established proprietary database management applications, a separate pilot version is being developed using a subset of the data in XML format, which will conform with the Dublin Core and exploit 'Cheshire II' software.

As well as a number of Z39.50 interface developments, a current-awareness alerting service based on the ETOC data has been implemented. The ultimate aim is to develop the alerting service to enable it to link seamlessly with document ordering systems and integrate with other current-awareness mechanisms. The document ordering interface will present the user with the option of selecting a source of supply. If the item is contained within an electronic journal to which the user's institution subscribes, the intention is to link the user automatically to the electronically stored journal. If the item is not held 'locally', the user will be presented with an option to request the document either directly from the British Library or via their local library. This functionality will be achieved by integration with other systems, including 'brokering' services, developed within the UK education community as part of the JISC's accurately named 'Join-Up' programme.

This paper describes the development process, the systems themselves and the support services created to provide academic and research communities with a valuable resource both in terms of discovery/location and content provision. The British Library is working in partnership with Manchester Computing at the University of Manchester, with the Universities of Liverpool and California–Berkeley as associate partners.

Background

The British Library (BL) is the UK's national library and has had a close relationship with the UK higher education (HE) community for a long time. It is the prime source for document supply and interlibrary loan (ILL) requests and has been active in many other areas, such as the MODELS series of workshops (**www.ukoln.ac.uk/dlis/models/**).

More recently, the British Library has placed an increasing strategic emphasis on collaboration to deliver its objectives. In particular, the BL has been seeking closer working ties with UK HE. In April 2000, a joint BL/HE task force was announced with the aim of identifying 'specific initiatives for mutual benefit' (**www.jisc.ac.uk/press_releases/000524_blhe.html**).

Prior to the formation of this task force, the BL had already approached MIMAS (**www.mimas.ac.uk**), located at the University of Manchester, to identify and discuss possible collaborations. MIMAS is the UK's largest national academic data centre and receives funding from the Joint Information Systems Committee (JISC), (**www.jisc.ac.uk**) of the Higher and Further Education Funding Councils to provide services to the academic community in the UK and beyond.

The BL had in mind to offer to license its *inside* product free of charge to the UK's HE, FE and research communities. This product was already in use at a number of institutions and these were to be refunded their licence fee.

At the heart of the *inside* product is the ETOC database, containing approximately 16 million records corresponding to journal articles or conference papers. The data go back to 1993 and cover 20,000 journal titles and 16,000 conferences per year. The entries are mostly keyed in, typically within 72 hours of publication, and the database is updated daily with around 10,000 new entries. The database itself does not contain the full text of the articles/papers, nor does it contain many abstracts. However, the presence of a record indicates that the BL has a copy for supply. The journal titles represent those most often requested and, as UK HE generates approximately 50% of these requests, reflect what that community needs.

The BL/MIMAS discussions led to MIMAS signing a formal contract with BL covering:

- assisting with a document supply requirements analysis
- developing a service using the ETOC data by the 2000/2001 academic year
- prototyping a service based on open standards.

The contract period was April 2000 to March 2001, and the BL was to fund all the above, though JISC was to be approached about ongoing funding of the service, which it subsequently agreed to do.

The requirements analysis was to be derived via a market research exercise involving a specialist firm, Orbitel Marketing, during April and May 2000. The results have subsequently been made available to the community and have been adopted by the 'Join-Up' programme, which is mentioned later (**http://edina.ac.uk/ projects/joinup/index.shtml**). The report itself is not considered further in this paper.

The ETOC-based service was to be Z39.50-compliant (which *inside* was not) and include a web interface, for those users without Z-client software. The service was soon referred to as 'ZETOC' and later trademarked by the BL as *zetoc*.

The prototype was to be based on XML and open source application code for indexing, access and Z39.50 compliance. Relevant standards were to be adhered to wherever possible.

Development approach

Counting back from September 2000, it was apparent that the application and service components needed to be developed 'quickly'.

It was decided to reuse existing software and application code where appropriate, and to involve staff already employed within the Manchester Computing department. Similarly, there was a need to minimize any training and support documentation requirements which would be required for the new service. This led to the service being based on a user interface from COPAC, the UK's research libraries online catalogue (**www.copac.ac.uk**), which was familiar to, and well used by, the target audience. A further advantage was that Z39.50 compliance could be offered by reworking the COPAC application code, which utilized CrossNet's ZedKit software (**www.crxnet.com**), developed as part of the ONE project, and a BRS/Search database (**www.opentext.com/dataware/**).

The opportunity was also taken to make use of relevant feedback MIMAS had received regarding other services – for example, that people do not like having limits set on the number of 'hit records' they can have when searching.

The prototype, consisting of a subset of the full ETOC records, was to utilize Cheshire II software (**http://cheshire.lib.berkeley.edu**), which was developed at the University of California–Berkeley School of Information Management and Systems, underwritten by a grant from the Department of Education. Its continued development at the two Universities of Berkeley and Liverpool receives funding from JISC and the US NSF (National Science Foundation). This was chosen because it offered a more flexible and open development path than the BRS version.

zetoc service development

The development began with a data analysis exercise. This covered both the data to be held in the database itself and the daily update files.

The BL actually also used BRS/Search for the *inside* service and this simplified the mapping, though certain changes were to be made, principally stripping out BL's internal processing data. The BL extracted the data into files in six-month 'chunks', and MIMAS converted and loaded the data into a newly created BRS database. The data design and database placement took most of July and the subsequent bulk-loading process took all of August to complete.

The BL supply update files in SGML format. MIMAS developed an SGML DTD for the data and developed code to convert the data into the required BRS load file format. This daily update is now a totally automated process, including the ftp download from the BL.

The web application was developed essentially as a search facility, offering three search options:

1 *General.* This option provides a search of the whole database of journal articles and conference papers by article/paper title, author(s), ISBN/ISSN and year of publication. For example, you might wish to see what articles/papers are available by a particular author, or you might search for the details of a specific document using the author and title.
2 *Journal.* This option supports a search for journal articles by article title, author(s), journal title, volume, issue, part, start page of article and year of publication.
3 *Conference.* This option limits a search to conference proceedings only. You can search by paper title, author(s), keywords and conference details (conference name, sponsor, venue and date held).

As an example, a search in *zetoc* for articles by an author 'apps a', results in a list of brief search results including:

```
Dublin Core Metadata for Electronic Journals / Apps, A;
MacIntyre, R
LECTURE NOTES IN COMPUTER SCIENCE - 2000; ISSU 1923;
Pages: 93-102
```

Following a link beside this brief record displays a more detailed record for the article:

```
Article Title:    Dublin Core Metadata for Electronic
Journals
Author(s): Apps, A; MacIntyre, R
Journal Title:    LECTURE NOTES IN COMPUTER SCIENCE
ISSN:             0302-9743
Volume:    1923
Year:      2000
Jnl Issue Title: Research and Advanced Technology for
Digital Libraries
Page(s):   93-102
Editor(s): Borbinha, J; Baker, T
Publisher: Germany : Springer-Verlag
Language:  English
Dewey Class:      004
LC Class:  TP372.5
BLDSC shelfmark: 5180.185000
ZETOC ID:  RN085008791
```

End-users of the web service may request discovered records to be e-mailed to them.

In addition to the web search interface, *zetoc* also has a Z39.50 interface. It allows for searching via the Z39.50 Bib-1 Attribute Set (**http://lcweb.loc.gov/ z3950/agency/defns/bib1.html**).

The system will return information as SUTRS (Simple Unstructured Test Record Syntax), GRS-1 (Generic Record Syntax, **http://lcweb.loc.gov/z3950/ agency/defns/tag-gm.html**) and a simple tagged reference format. In order to be 'Bath Profile compliant', referring to the specification for library applications and resource discovery (**www.nlc-bnc.ca/bath/bp-current.htm**), *zetoc* also has the option to return simple Dublin Core records encoded according to The Consortium for the Computer Interchange of Museum Information (CIMI) Dublin Core Document Type Definition (**www.nlc-bnc.ca/bath/bp-app-d.htm**) using an XML syntax. The mapping of most of the fields in a *zetoc* record is obvious, but there are issues with returning bibliographic citation information in this format (Apps and MacIntyre, 2001).

The SUTRS format is similar to that displayed as the result of a search using the web interface, but as plain text without the HTML tags. The simple tagged format returns fields of the record preceded by a token, e.g. TI: precedes a title, again in plain text. This format may be used for importing citations into a personal bibliographic database.

Access to the database is via **http://zetoc.mimas.ac.uk** and controlled by IP/domain address filtering and ATHENS authentication – a standard authentication system for UK resources (**www.athens.ac.uk**).

The *zetoc* service was launched on schedule on 26 September 2000 at the British Library, St Pancras, London. As well as being available to British and Irish higher and further education institutions and Research Councils, access has recently been extended to the National Health Service via the NeLH (National Electronic Library for Health). Additionally, the use of the Z39.50 target is currently being trialled by the CIC (Committee on Institutional Cooperation) consortium in the USA.

zetoc alerting service

To supplement the basic search and retrieve functionality of the service, a current-awareness alerting service based on the table of contents data was also developed. The aim was to 'fill the gap' left by the demise of the popular 'Autojournals' service offered until July 2000 by BIDS, another of the UK's national academic data centres. The application had to work with both the operational and prototype versions of the database so as not to prejudice any future decision concerning the service's technical architecture.

The alerting service allows the user to create one or more named lists of journal titles of interest. Users may choose journals in three ways:

1 Select journal names beginning with a letter – a user looking for a specific journal selects the first letter of the title to view an alphabetical list of journals beginning with that letter.

2 Select journal names containing a string – if part of the journal title is known, it can be typed in the box and the search button activated (note that this is *not* a keyword search).

3 Select journals by subject category – the journals in *zetoc* have been grouped into subjects according to the Dewey Decimal subject classification. Selecting one of the subjects gives a list of journal titles in that category.

They are then sent the table of contents of newly loaded issues via e-mail. This process is driven by the daily update of the main database.

An example extract of an Alert e-mail when first released:

```
Subject: ZETOC Alert: NEW SCIENTIST
ZETOC Alert results for list MYSCIENCE

NEW SCIENTIST
ISSU 2255; 15 September 2000
ISSN 0262-4079

24-29
Titanic You may think today's stars are awesome, but
compared with the first suns they're mere whippersnappers
Chown, M.

30-33
Hairy space probes What's purple, furry and sensitive all
over?
Brooks, M.
```

The first version of *zetoc* Alert was released in October 2000. Subsequently each article was linked to its corresponding *zetoc* record via a URL of the form:

```
http://zetoc.mimas.ac.uk/zetoc/wzgw?terms=
RN085008791&field=zid
```

The purpose of this was to allow the user to move directly to the record and from there take advantage of full system functionality without having to duplicate features. The obvious future goal is full article access.

Support facilities

As well as the service application development, documentation was produced to assist the users and library support staff. As the application was specifically designed to be simple and familiar, there has been little need to produce more than an online user guide and workbook.

The BL ran a series of training/familiarization sessions throughout the UK during 2000 and 2001. The services have received promotion via the well-established JIBS user group (JISC (assisted) Bibliographic dataserviceS, **http://hosted.ukoln.ac.uk/jibs/**), which keeps institutions up to date with new JISC services and where they may be useful. JIBS are also a key route for feedback from the community to service and content providers alike.

A range of statistical measures has been generated as part of the service and is accessible via the website (**http://zetoc.mimas.ac.uk/stats/**). For the *zetoc* service there are monthly usage figures broken down by domain and web versus Z39.30 access. For 'ac.uk' domains these are further broken down by individual institution. The figures are available as tables, graphs and as a 'csv' format file for downloading.

Alert statistics are updated each day and show the number of users (6644), lists (9668), journal titles selected (107,435) and e-mails sent (3189) – figures in brackets are as of 9 August 2001. The journal title count shows that there are an average of over 11 journals on each list and that each user has on average 1.5 lists. There is also a monthly 'Top 20' list of journals requested. As of 9 August 2001, the top five were: *Nature, Science, Lancet, British Medical Journal* and *Journal of Academic Librarianship*.

zetoc prototype

MIMAS and the British Library are now working on an enhanced version of *zetoc*, which is currently a prototype. It was decided to investigate a solution based on open standards and using open software. Within this version of *zetoc* the data is stored as Dublin Core records, using an XML syntax, generated by bespoke programs from the supplied British Library SGML. This XML is indexed using the Cheshire open source software. Cheshire II is a next-generation online catalogue and full-text information retrieval system. It was developed using advanced information retrieval techniques and provides customizable web and Z39.50 interfaces.

It is the intention to use this prototype version of *zetoc* to trial enhancements to the service, such as the facility to order, or link to, the full text of discovered articles, and subject-based alert requests. Within an internet cross-referencing paradigm of 'discover – locate – request – deliver' the present *zetoc* current-awareness service provides discovery of research articles in a timely fashion. Early enhancements to *zetoc* will provide 'request and deliver' through document supply from the British Library.

Future enhancements may include 'locate' of the appropriate copy, through an initiative such as SFX Content Sensitive Reference Linking (**www.sfxit.com**) or other resolution services, and 'request' and 'deliver' via internet linking mechanisms – including Digital Object Identifiers (Atkins et al., 2000) and CrossRef (**www.crossref.org**) to freely available articles or those covered by an institutional subscription. It will be simpler to implement these and future enhancements with the data held in open standard formats such as Dublin Core and XML.

Future development

Four areas for future service development are outlined below.

Document ordering

The service will be enhanced during September 2001 to include the facility to request the article/paper from the British Library's Document Supply Centre (BLDSC). Initially this would require the user to pay a copyright fee, as this was technically the simplest way to enable the facility. In early 2002, however, interlibrary loan requests will be supported. The emphasis will be on ISO ILL-formatted requests (ISO 10160/10161), which can already be handled by the BL.

Subject/author alerting

The Alert service will allow users to enter key words/phrases and/or author names. The daily update file will be searched for occurrences and hit records will be sent to the user via e-mail. An example extract is shown below, where 'fish' has been entered as a title keyword:

```
Subject: zetoc Alert: (fish)[ti]
zetoc Alert results for list fishtest belonging to manfish

CANCER CAUSES AND CONTROL VOL 12; PART 4 pp. 375-382
A pooled analysis of case-control studies of thyroid
cancer. VI. Fish and shellfish consumption
Bosetti, C.; Kolonel, L.; Negri, E.; Ron, E.; Franceschi,
S.; Maso, L. D.; Galanti, M. R.; Mark, S. D.; Preston-
Martin, S.; McTiernan, A.
http://zetoc.mimas.ac.uk/zetoc/wzgw?terms=RN097856709&field=
zid
```

Bibliographic data

Within the *zetoc* service the user will be able to request records to be e-mailed in short tagged format, suitable for loading into a personal bibliographic database. For example:

```
AU: Noga, E. J.
AU: Fan, Z.
AU: Silphaduang, U.
```

```
TI: Histone-like proteins from fish are lethal to the
    parasitic dinoflagellate Amyloodinium ocellatum
JT: PARASITOLOGY -CAMBRIDGE-
IS: 0031-1820
PD: 2001
IU: VOL 123; PART 1
PG: 57-66
FQ: Bi-monthly: 5-8 issues per year
PB: CAMBRIDGE UNIVERSITY PRESS
PP: Great Britain
LA: English
DC: 616.96
LC: QL
SM: 6406.000000
ID: RN098262714
```

The 'Join-Up' programme

Subsequent to the May 2000 meeting of the BL/HE Taskforce, the BL was invited to discuss the perceived overlap between some of the projects submitted for JISC funding and the BL's own development plans. The outcome of the meeting was that the respondents were asked to try and present their projects within a more coherent framework, as each specifically addressed one or more of the 'discover – locate – request – deliver' functions. The projects, XGRAIN (a Z39.50 end-user interface to A&I databases), ZBLSA (a locator mechanism based on serials information) and Docusend (a locate and document delivery system based on Fretwell-Downing's VDX system), together with *zetoc*, have since been drawn together formally into the 'Join-Up' programme.

The *zetoc* service can support 'Join-Up' through work that is already underway or planned:

- the development of a Z39.50 target on ETOC, thus enabling it to interface with XGRAIN
- the use of ZBLSA as a serials-based locator for document ordering purposes
- implementation of the ISO/ILL protocol as a way of accepting requests from Docusend
- alerting as an additional facility within the overall system.

Any duplication with Docusend with regard to document ordering functionality can be reconciled in that the prototype implementation with the Cheshire II software is an 'open systems' alternative to the proprietary system of Docusend. The projects have also agreed to work together to identify common deliverables and goals. The area of evaluation is one such obvious candidate.

Conclusions and observations

Overall, the collaboration has been very successful in that a new service was developed and made available in a very short timescale and for a very small cost to the community. The following comments apply to various aspects of the service development.

Content is king

The area of content provision is clearly one of the major strengths which the British Library can bring to benefit the community via initiatives such as the *zetoc* service. In turn, the BL have stated that they view *zetoc* as a key part of the British Library's strategy to open up access to its collections (in this instance its Electronic Table of Contents) through networked services, especially to UK HE. So, simplistically, it seems like a 'win–win' situation.

Application development

The re-use of existing application code supplemented by the use of open standards and a modular design has enabled very rapid and efficient service development. The non-duplication of functionality has been possible by enabling the applications to communicate and interoperate. Looking forward, the number of opportunities enabled by such an approach are also significant.

KISS

The use of a simple and familiar interface reduced drastically the need for user support and training. This is borne out by the end-user enquiries received by the MIMAS help desk, which tend to be about people wanting access either to the service or to the full text of the articles, rather than problems understanding or using the system's features. The old adage of KISS – 'Keep It Simple, Stupid!' – remains valid.

Feedback

It is important to make it easy for people to comment constructively, provided that feedback is then acted upon. Always provide a mechanism to allow people to supply unstructured comments and do not assume all users will have access to an e-mail client at their workstation. It has been noticeable that people will often use these routes to say 'thank you', i.e. to provide positive feedback. Relevant user groups, such as JIBS, should be used to provide expertise in explaining, classifying and prioritizing the requirements.

Service perspectives

It is interesting to note a difference in perception of the service from the perspectives of the BL and the end-user. The BL regards the database as a list of (a very small part of) its holdings and thus view *zetoc* as a document ordering facility, whereas the end-user seems to regard the service primarily as a current awareness tool, allowing them to be notified of new articles and papers and to find others from partial information.

Acknowledgements

The authors wish to acknowledge the contribution to the development of *zetoc* by their colleagues at the British Library (Stephen Andrews and Andrew Braid) and at MIMAS (Alison Murphy, Ashley Sanders, Andrew Weeks and Vicky Wiseman). The initial development of the *zetoc* service was funded by the British Library, who owns and supplies the Electronic Table of Contents data. The *zetoc* enhancement project is funded by the British Library and by the Joint Information Systems Committee (JISC) for UK higher and further education, as part of 'Join-Up' within the Distributed National Electronic Resource (DNER) development programme.

References

Apps, A. and MacIntyre, R. (2001) *zetoc*: a Dublin-core based current-awareness service, *Proceedings of the International Conference on Dublin Core and Metadata Applications 2001* (DC2001 – **www.nii.ac.jp/dc2001/**), National Institute of Informatics, Tokyo, Japan, 22–26 October 2001.

Atkins, H. et al. (2000) Reference linking with DOIs, *D-Lib Magazine*, **6** (2), (February), available at **www.dlib.org/dlib/february00/02risher.html**

25

A VISUAL TOOLKIT FOR INFORMATION RETRIEVAL

Antony Corfield, Matthew Dovey, Richard Mawby and Colin Tatham

Overview

JAFER (Java Access For Electronic Resources) is a two-year project funded by the UK's JISC (Joint Information Systems Committee), under the DNER (Distributed National Electronic Resource) development programme. This project began on the 4 January 2001 and is currently funded until 31 December 2002.

Within the current designs of the DNER, information retrieval will be achieved by using the Z39.50 protocol:

> Z39.50 is a computer-to-computer communications protocol designed to support searching and retrieval of information – full-text documents, bibliographic data, images and multimedia – in a distributed network environment. Based on client/server architecture and operating over the internet, the Z39.50 protocol is supporting an increasing number of applications. (Moen (n.d.)

However, the JISC notes that 'Z39.50 is of considerable vintage . . . and a heavy weight solution which is unattractive to some developers' (Joint Information Systems Committee, 1999). Z39.50 implementations are hampered by the lack of powerful, easy to use, Z39.50-based tools for building clients and servers, and hence the need for a high degree of development time.

Building on the extensive Z39.50 experience of the Oxford University Libraries Automation Service (in the MALIBU Project, part of the Electronic Libraries Programme (eLib)), the JAFER toolkit project's goal is to address the problem highlighted by JISC above and to produce a lightweight Z39.50 toolkit for creating internet-based services which provide access to teaching and learning packages.

JAFER components provide an easy-to-use visual toolkit enabling users to build portals and information sources without having to deal with the intricate technical aspects of the protocols involved, and in doing so simplifying the use of the Z39.50 protocol. JAFER is open source and written in the Java programming language, creating a versatile and scalable toolkit, aimed at an audience of librarians, academics and information providers. The users will find that the infrastructure will allow them to achieve their objectives more effectively, without having to deal with complex technical details.

The JAFER toolkit has two basic components:

1 A ZClient implementation, developed as a JavaBean component, which provides a visual configuration of Bean properties. The ZClient Bean uses the latest XML technology, allowing information to be handled in a way that is easy to read, process and generate. This combination of XML and Java provides portable code and portable data, encouraging users to design portals which can pull data dynamically from Z39.50 information sources such as libraries, museum and archive catalogues, with the same ease currently offered by other web development tools.

2 A server component with additional functionalities such as gateway and proxy software to allow Z39.50 access to non-Z39.50 services. For instance, information sources and databases using protocols such as ODBC (Open Database Connectivity) can be configured using visual tools to publish data to the DNER using Z39.50.

JAFER is also working with the Z39.50 community to develop an implementers' agreement for operating Z39.50 over XML and SOAP (Simple Object Access Protocol) rather than the current BER (Basic Encoding Rules) implementations. This involves the development of gateways between Z39.50 over XML and Z39.50 over BER and looking at how to incorporate this version of Z39.50 in the forthcoming next generation of development tools.

ZClient

The JAFER ZClient has been developed as a JavaBean, a re-usable persistent component which allows *visual* configuration of Bean properties. The Bean is designed to run within a lightweight web server or servlet container, so users can develop Java server pages (JSPs) and run servlets. (JSP technology is an extension of the servlet technology created to support authoring of HTML and XML pages. Servlets provide a component-based, platform-independent method for building web-based applications, without the performance limitations of other programming languages.) This provides a fast and simple way of developing portals for access to Z39.50 information sources. Developers also have access to the ZClient public methods or API (Application Programming Interface) enabling implementations of further Z39.50 applications.

Architecture

The ZClient consists of two basic components: a JavaBean ZSession Manager and a ZSession component that implements basic Z39.50 functions, including search and present (see Figure 25.1). The latter currently employs version 1.4 of ZedJava (Crossnet Systems, 2001), which provides a BER Java package generated from an ASN.1 to Java compiler. A simple interface between the two components gives a pluggable ability so that other BER implementations can be substituted with ease.

XML Query builds queries which encompass the expressive power of the Z39.50 standard for Boolean search queries (Z39.50 query 'type-101'). It is based on the 'search' mechanism being developed by the GILS (Global Information Locator Service, 2001), which defines a generic information search and retrieval interface, represented in XML, and suited to implementation over the internet.

Search attributes defined by the Bath Profile, for example, can be specified as a default search profile so that the user simply specifies the search terms (see Figure 25.2).

Records from ZSession search and present are passed as simple DataObjects to the ZClient Bean where they are cached. The data can be accessed in a 'raw' form (e.g. as MARC, GRS1 records) or as an XML DOM document representing the entire tagged record. The Document Object Model (DOM) 'provides a standard set of objects for representing HTML and XML documents, a standard

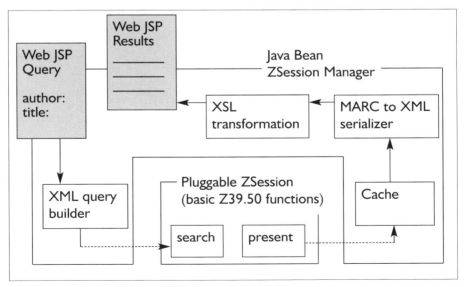

Fig. 25.1 *General view of ZClient architecture*

```
<?xml version="1.0" encoding="UTF-8" standalone="no"?>
<query>
    <boolean>
        <and>
            <constraintModel>
                <constraint>
                    <semantic>4</semantic>                    title
                    <relation>3</relation>                    equals
                    <position>3</position>                    any position in field
                    <structure>2</structure>                  word
                    <truncation>100</truncation>                    do not truncate
                    <completeness>1</completeness>            incomplete
                </constraint>
                <model>Macbeth</model>                        SEARCH TERM
            </constraintModel>
            <constraintModel>
                <constraint>
                    <semantic>1003</semantic>                     author
                    <relation>3</relation>
                    <position>3</position>
                    <structure>2</structure>
                    <truncation>100</truncation>
                    <completeness>1</completeness>
                </constraint>
                <model>Shakespeare</model>                   SEARCH TERM
            </constraintModel>
        </and>
    </boolean>
</query>
```

Fig. 25.2   *XML query based on GILS search mechanism*

model of how these objects can be combined, and a standard interface for accessing and manipulating them' (World Wide Web Consortium, 1998).

For example, MARC 21 field 260 holds publishing information contained in several sub-fields (see Figure 25.3). The MARC to XML Serializer generates XML for this field which conforms to the Open Archives Initiative (OAI) schema for MARC to XML. This schema 'has been successfully applied for MARC 21 records. It is likely to also work for older versions of USMARC and CANMARC. Application of this Schema for other MARC formats has not been tested and may require some adjustments' (Open Archives Initiative, 2001).

```
MARC 21 Field 260:     260##$aNew York, N.Y. : $bElsevier, $c1984.


<?xml version="1.0" encoding="UTF-8" standalone="no"?>

<MARCRecord dbName="MAIN*BIBMAST">

....


<varfield id="260" i1="" i2="">
    <subfield label="a">New York, N.Y. : </subfield-a>
    <subfield label="b"> Elsevier,</subfield-b>
    <subfield label="c">1984</subfield-c>
</ varfield >
```

Fig. 25.3   *'Raw' XML generated by Serializer from MARC 21 field 260*

A set of standard XSLT transformations (see below) are provided as XSL style sheets which transform the 'raw' XML containing all the fields for a particular record. The benefit of such transformations is that data is made more accessible and in a form that can be tailored to the user's needs, so that search results can be displayed with ease.

The W3C has described XSLT in the following way:

> XSLT is designed for use as part of XSL, which is a stylesheet language for XML. In addition to XSLT, XSL includes an XML vocabulary for specifying formatting. XSL specifies the styling of an XML document by using XSLT to describe how the document is transformed into another XML document that uses the formatting vocabulary. (World Wide Web Consortium, 2000)

Using the previous example, an appropriate transformation would produce the following XML from the MARC record (see Figure 25.4).

```
<?xml version="1.0" encoding="UTF-8" standalone="no"?>

<MARCRecord dbName="MAIN*BIBMAST">

....


<publisher>New York, N.Y. : Elsevier, 1984</publisher>
```

Fig. 25.4   *Transformed XML*

Visual configuration

Visual configuration of the ZClient Bean is achieved through the use of builder tools used by developers, or by the standalone user interface.

Typically, a JavaBean is a re-usable software component which can be *visually* manipulated in builder tools such as JBuilder. The ZClient conforms to the JavaBean specification (Sun Microsystems, 2001a), which provides support for Bean introspection, properties and persistence. Properties are the public attributes of a Bean that affect its appearance or behaviour whilst persistence allows JavaBean which have been customized to have their state saved and restored.

The Beans Development Kit (BDK) is intended to support the development of JavaBean components and to act as a standard reference base for both Bean developers and tool vendors. The BDK provides a reference Bean container – the 'BeanBox'. Developers or users familiar with BeanBox or builder tools can set the ZClient properties by dropping the Bean into a design window and editing the corresponding property sheet (see Figure 25.5). The properties are discovered and displayed indirectly through introspection via a supporting Bean-info class, which identifies defined property editors in org.jafer.propertyeditor package (e.g. RecordFormatEditor and SearchProfileEditor). Bean properties are typically saved and restored by an application builder's save and load menu commands or the BeanBox Serialize Component command.

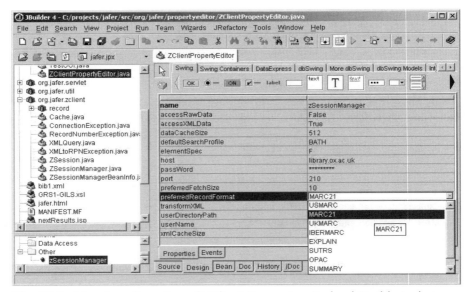

Fig. 25.5 *Visual configuration of ZClient Bean using Borland JBuilder's design window*

ZClient support for persistence through Java object serialization is provided by implementing the java.io.Serializable interface. The standard classes used for persistence are ObjectOutputStream and ObjectInputStream (java.io.package), which read and write primitive data types and graphs of Java objects in a binary form by using a file for the stream.

However, the Long-Term Persistence (LTP) (Java Community Process, 2001) added in Beta version 1.4 of Java 2 SDK (Sun Microsystems, 2001b) provides an API which supports a general mechanism for serializing JavaBeans to and from XML. The LTP uses instances of the XMLEncoder class to write out files representing JavaBean components using an XML schema. This method of persistence has the advantage of being portable and structurally compact whilst providing a textual representation of the JavaBean and all its properties. The latest version of the ZClient Bean will support LTP using XML in the near future.

A simple alternative method for visual configuration aimed at general users implements a graphical user interface (GUI) using JFC AWT and Swing components (Sun Microsystems, 2001c). The ZClientPropertyEditor presents several categories via a tabbed pane through which users can edit the Bean properties (see Figure 25.6). For example, selecting the Data panel allows the user to set the preferred format for retrieving records, XML transformation and the corresponding XSL file (see Figure 25.7). Again, support is provided for persistence

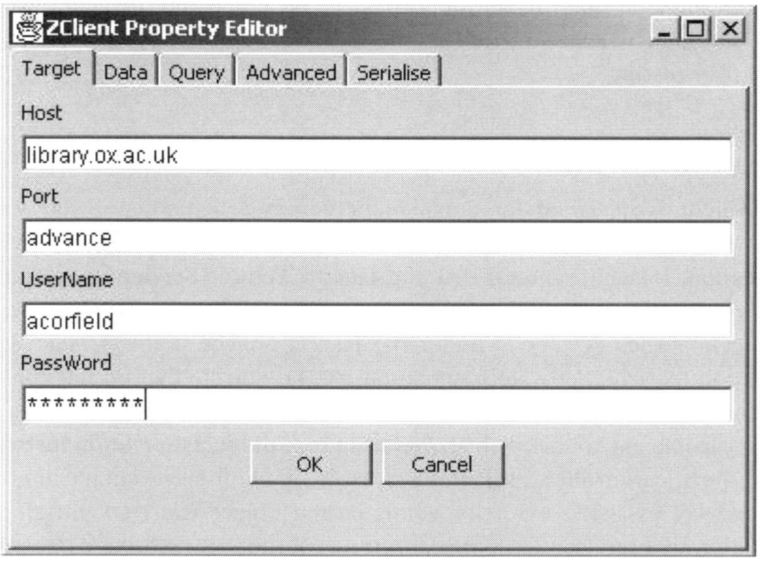

Fig. 25.6 *Visual configuration of ZClient Bean using Swing GUI*

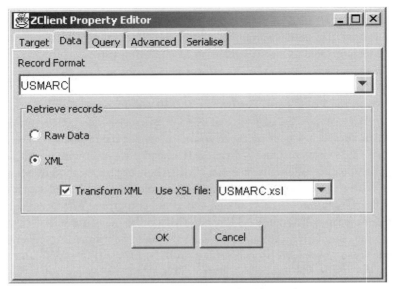

Fig. 25.7   *Setting properties for record retrieval using ZClient GUI*

through serialization, so that the Bean properties may be saved or restored.

It is anticipated that further properties will be added and the general look and feel of the GUI will be updated as the ZClient Bean evolves and responds to further user testing.

XML configuration

The ZClient is designed for deployment within a lightweight web server or servlet container (e.g. Tomcat) and as such takes advantage of the Servlet API specification. It may be noted that the Jakarta Tomcat Servlet Container is the official open-source reference implementation for the Java Servlet and JavaServer Pages technologies developed under the Jakarta project at the Apache Software Foundation (Apache Software Foundation, 2001). Servers that do not conform to this standard can utilize add-on engines which transform a web server into a servlet and JSP capable environment (**http://java.sun.com/products/servlet/industry.html**).

The specification allows JSP and Servlets to read initialization parameters in a standard way by using a servlet configuration object (ServletConfig) to pass information to a servlet during initialization. Methods for setting parameters are server-specific, but typically this is done through supplying an XML file as with Tomcat (see Figure 25.8).

```
<init-param>
 <param-name>target</param-name>
 <param-value>library.ox.ac.uk</param-value>
</init-param>
<init-param>
 <param-name>dataBase</param-name>
 <param-value>advance</param-value>
</init-param>
<init-param>
 <param-name>port</param-name>
 <param-value>210</param-value>
</init-param>
```

Fig. 25.8   *Initialization parameters supplied by Tomcat web.xml file for setting ZClient Bean properties*

It is envisaged that implementation of LTP serialization to XML in future versions of the ZClient Bean will include support for automatic creation of XML initialization files, thus allowing administrators the option of using the visual configuration methods described above.

Uses

The client bean has been designed with a number of uses in mind. As described later, the bean is used in the server component of JAFER when building Z39.50 proxies or Z39.50 distributed search servers. However the bean is also used in a number of other applications.

The first is a simple servlet aimed at linking services – for example, to link from an online reading list or a bibliographic reference service such as FirstSearch or WebSpirs to a record in a local library system indicating the location of the item. OCLC FirstSearch (**www.oclc.org/firstsearch/**) and SilverPlatter WebSpirs (**www.silverplatter.com/iss.html**) are both commercial abstracting services whereby users can search for journal articles by author, title, subject and various other search terms. Typically they return a description of the article concerned as well as the details of the journal in which the article occurs. The JAFER servlet allows the user to go from such a description to the local holding information. An earlier version of this servlet (called ZGet) has been in use for this purpose by Oxford since 1999. The JAFER version, as well as offering additional functionality, has been redesigned with far more flexible configuration to allow deployment at other sites. The servlet performs a simple connect, search and retrieve for the item record via Z39.50 and displays the result as Z39.50. Configuration is via a specified XSLT for generating the html page displayed to the end-user, and via an XML file mapping the URL of the servlet to the Z39.50 query. XML mapping is supplied for a simple URL based on the Z39.50 bib-1 attributes as well as for supporting OpenUR-formatted URLs. OpenURL is an emerging standard which makes it easier for bibliographic reference services to send referrals to local servers for retrieving local holdings information (**www.sfxit.com/OpenURL/**).

The second application is a reading-list generator. This is a Z39.50 client which allows the user to build a 'shopping basket' of items from various Z39.50 sources and then generate an html web page by selecting from a collection of design templates (specified using XSLT). The web page includes clickable hyperlinks to the original records using the servlet described above.

The main use of the Bean, however, will be in creating JSP pages for far richer web applications. Currently developers of information and educational websites can use JSP to create dynamic web pages, and the Bean will allow them to pull information dynamically from Z39.50 information sources. The Bean is currently being used in the web gateways for the BookHAD (**www.linst.ac.uk/rslp/ bookhad/**) and Music Libraries Online (**www.musiconline.ac.uk**) projects, which are creating virtual subject-based catalogues (on Art History & Design and Music respectively) by cross-searching specialist subject catalogues.

The following is a very simple JSP page using the Bean to undertake an author/title search and return the results as a HTML table (see Figure 25.9). This shows how the Bean has been designed so that it offers a fairly natural API.

The project is currently investigating the creation of plug-ins for various HTML/JSP visual development environments to make the process of generating such JSP pages easier.

The project is also looking at other platforms as well as Java-based web servers. For example, the Microsoft platform uses ActiveX objects in much the same way that Java uses JavaBeans, and has a web-scripting architecture called ASP which performs a very similar function to JSP. The Java ActiveX to JavaBean [19] will be used in order to target developers on these platforms. They will also lead to the development of plugins for applications such as Microsoft FrontPage and Microsoft Office.

On a more pure research note, the Bean is being used via JSP and servlets to assist with the ongoing investigation by the Z39.50 community into SOAP and XML-based versions of Z39.50 by building a bridging proxy between these new protocol developments and traditional Z39.50 (see **http://java.sun.com/products/ plugin/1.3/activex.faq.html**).

```
<!DOCTYPE html public "-//W3C//DTD HTML 4.0 Final//EN">
<jsp:useBean id="bean" scope="session" class="org.jafer.zclient.ZSessionManager" />
<html>
  <head>
    <title>JAFER search results</title>
  </head>
  <%
    bean.setHost("olis.ox.ac.uk");
    bean.setPort(210);
    bean.setDataBases(new String[]{"ADVANCE"});
    bean.init();

    org.jafer.zclient.XMLQuery query = bean.newQuery();

    int nResults;
    String title = request.getParameter("title").trim();
    String author = request.getParameter("author").trim();

    nResults = query.submit(query.and(title, "use title", author, "use author"));

    out.print("<p>Your search has generated " + nResults + " results</p>");
  %>
    <table  border="1" cellpadding="5" cellspacing="0" width = "700">
  <%
    for(int n = 1; n <= thisPage; n++) {
      bean.setRecordCursor(n);
      out.print("<tr><td>" + n + "</td>");
      out.print("<td>" + bean.getCurrentRecord().get("title")[0].getValue() + </td>");
      out.print("<td>" + bean.getCurrentRecord().get("author")[0].getValue() +"</td>");
      out.print("</tr>");
    }
  %></table>
  </body>
</html>
```

Fig. 25.9 *Simple JSP page using the Bean to do an author/title search*

ZServer

The JAFER server component (ZServer) can be used in a variety of ways to provide different functionality, the simplest case being where a user needs to provide a Z39.50 interface to an existing non-Z39.50 database (see Figure 25.10).

The Z39.50 interface can be accessed by existing Z39.50 Origins or from a web browser via a Z39.50 client, which may or may not be running alongside the server.

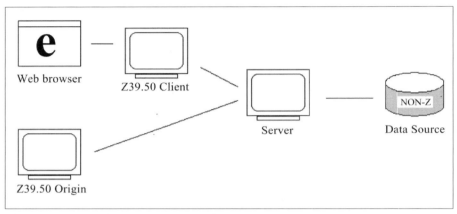

Fig. 25.10   *Providing a Z39.50 interface*

This basic format can be expanded to incorporate distributed searches, or to create multilevel 'clumps' – servers performing distributed searches, which are themselves targets of a higher-level distributed search (see Figure 25.11).

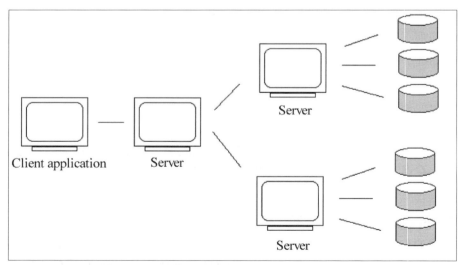

Fig. 25.11   *Multilevel distributed searching*

Architecture and uses

In keeping with the JAFER toolkit's component architecture, the ZServer component itself is made up of components which can be used in different configurations according to the function required. It is intended that the internal configuration of the components can be modified easily via a GUI to allow local customization (see below).

The possible applications for ZServer include providing a new service, or adding additional features to an existing Z39.50 service as discussed below.

Z39.50 interface to a non-Z39.50 data source

In the simplest case, mentioned above, a single handler component is plugged into the ZServer component (see Figure 25.12). The handler component makes use of the JDBC/ODBC bridge, using a JDBC driver matching the underlying database in use. The server listens for incoming Z39.50 search requests, typically on port 210. These are then translated into the query format supported by the database's DBMS (e.g. SQL) and executed on the database. (Third-party tools may be incorporated to produce the SQL to XML bindings.) An XML version of each of the records returned by the database is constructed, which is then transformed using XSLT, resulting in an XML representation of the chosen record format. This is then used to create the binary record format for transmission. For example, if a MARC record format is required, the transform applied could follow the OAI schema (Open Archives Initiative, 2001), and the final output would be a binary MARC format (Figure 25.13 overleaf).

Z39.50 Origin or client   Server and handler   Data source

Fig. 25.12 *Z39.50 interface to a non-Z39-50 data source*

It is also possible to use ZServer in this arrangement to translate incoming requests into other protocol formats, allowing, for example, Z39.50 access to DASL and RDF-Query gateways.

Distributed searching across multiple Z39.50 data sources

The client and server components of the JAFER toolkit can be used in combination

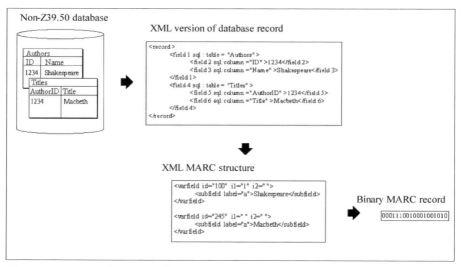

Fig. 25.13   *Transformation flow*

to provide co-ordinated searches across a number of distributed Z39.50-compliant data sources (see Figure 25.14). Multiple instances of the low-level component of the client (ZSession) are each configured to send requests to a specific Z39.50 data source. The resulting responses from each client are passed on to a single instance of the high-level client component (ZSessionsManager), which handles collating all of the results and manages a data cache. The interface between ZServer and ZSessionsManager is provided by a Z39.50 handler component, which in this case functions more as a 'shim' for translating the requests and responses, and for data transfer.

Distributed searching across a mixture of data sources

There are two possible solutions using the JAFER toolkit. The first uses a mixed set of handlers, each matching one of the data sources to be searched. The second, preferred solution (see Figure 25.15), is to use the Z39.50 handler and client components as described in the preceding example to handle the Z39.50 sources, and then provide additional server and handler components for each of the non-Z39.50 sources, accessed as further Z39.50 sources. (The additional servers would need to be listening on different port numbers from the principal server.)

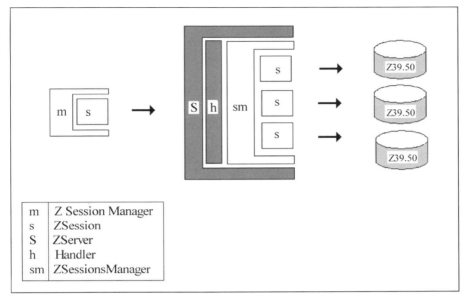

Fig. 25.14 *Distributed searching across multiple Z39.50 data sources*

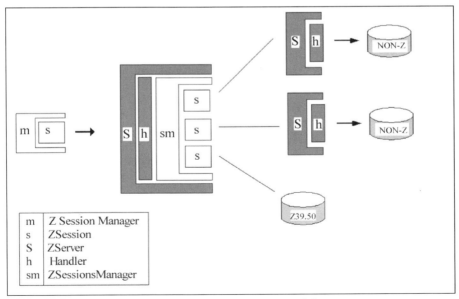

Fig. 25.15 *Distributed searching across a mixture of data sources*

Proxy server functions

There are various applications where the JAFER server component can be used as a proxy server:

1 *Authentication/IP validation.* In a situation where access to a resource is normally limited to users providing a user name and password, but where it is also desirable to allow access to users from a certain domain, a proxy server could be configured to check whether a user's IP address is within the domain and, if it is, provide a connection by supplying a user name and password. This eliminates, amongst other things, the need for distributing user names and passwords to all possible users.
2 *Query adaptation.* There may be applications where incoming queries to a server need to be modified before being passed on to the database. This could be achieved by passing the queries through a proxy server for modification (and possibly making the choice of whether or not to apply the modification being based on the identification of the origin of the request).
3 *Profile conformance.* A proxy server could be used to present a server front-end that conforms to a standard profile, or to ensure that results being returned by a server conform to a profile, such as the Bath Profile.
4 *Filtering.* A search facility being provided by a subject-based portal, for example, may be required to retrieve only relevant records, or records of a certain type. This could be achieved by adding additional terms to each query submitted via the proxy server, to produce filtered results.
5 *Record conversion.* Enabling conversion from one record format to another (e.g. USMARC to UKMARC) with local modification possible via the GUI interface.

ZServer visual configuration

The server component can be configured and monitored using a configuration GUI, which allows control of multiple servers. Modification of the mapping being used between non-Z39.50 databases and the Z39.50 protocol is also possible.

Server configuration

The main screen (see Figure 25.16) is used to add a new Z39.50 server, which then appears in a list with any other servers which have already been added. A server selected from the list can be started and stopped using the buttons provided, and configured or monitored using the input boxes on the tabbed panels on the right-hand side:

- IP Address binding (for multi-homed servers)
- IP Port binding
- backend data source selection (e.g. JDBC or Z39.50)
- IP Address restrictions (for validation, if applicable)
- authentication module (e.g. anonymous, flat file of username/passwords, ATHENS).

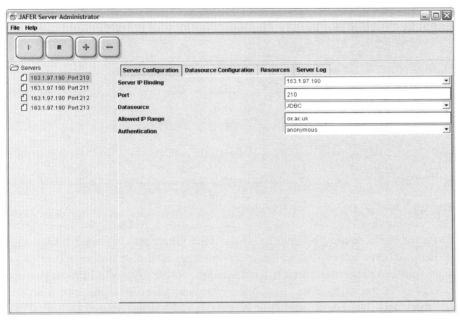

Fig. 25.16   *Configuration GUI – main screen*

Data source configuration

The panel displayed here (see Figure 25.17 overleaf) matches the data source that was selected in the previous panel, and allows configuration of the handler component. For a JDBC data source, the configuration options are as follows:

1   *Attribute configuration.* The underlying database tables are displayed in the right-hand window in a tree structure (with an indication of any table relationships). Use attributes are listed in the left-hand window. The mapping between the tables and the use attributes can be modified by dragging and dropping the database column names onto the appropriate use attribute.

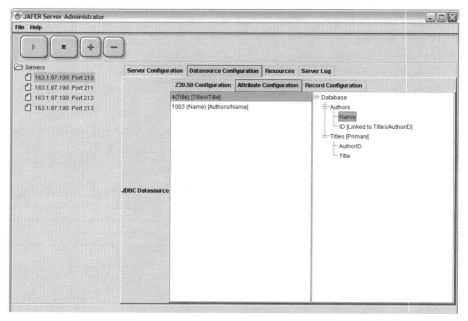

Fig. 25.17 *Data source configuration*

2 *Record configuration.* The underlying database tables are displayed in the right-hand window again, and a tree representation of the record structure to be output is displayed in the left-hand window. (Different record formats can be chosen by selecting a tab from the right-hand side.) Mapping between the tables and the record fields can be modified by dragging and dropping the database column names onto the record structure.

3 *Resources.* A visual display is included to enable monitoring of CPU and memory usage.

4 *Server log.* A visual display showing details of connected clients and current requests being processed, and a text log (see Figure 25.18).

Conclusion

Z39.50 is an extensive and powerful protocol, providing complex distributed searching abilities and retrieval of structured data from databases hosted on any platform. The design of the JAFER toolkit allows users to take advantage of Z39.50's capability more easily – being written in Java means that the software is platform-independent, and the JavaBean architecture allows components to be incorporated into other software under development. Furthermore, the JAFER software can easily be configured by non-technical users via the GUI interface, or

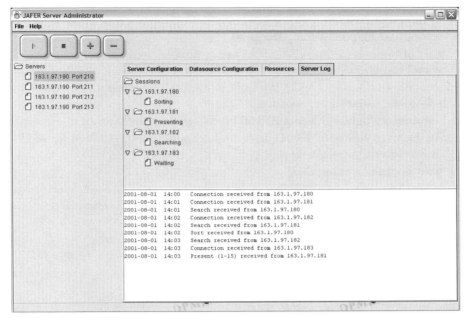

Fig. 25.18   *Server log*

by more advanced users via the XML configuration files and JavaBean properties. Making the JAFER code available as Open Source will encourage ongoing development and maintenance of the software in the future.

References

Apache Software Foundation (2001) *Tomcat: a free, open-source implementation of JavaServer Pages and Java Servlet technologies developed under the Jakarta project at the Apache Software Foundation*, available at
http://jakarta.apache.org/tomcat/index.html

Crossnet Systems (2001) *ZedJava: Z39.50 Java software development kit version 1.4 (compiled with the JDK1.1.3 Java compiler)*, from Crossnet Systems Limited and DSTC Pty Ltd, available at
www.crxnet.com/zjava.html

Global Information Locator Service (2001) *Search: a mechanism for search interoperability*, available at
www.gils.net/search.html#ogc_ccql

Java Community Process (2001) *Java Specification Requests JSR 057 Long-Term Persistence for JavaBeans specification*, available at
http://jcp.org/jsr/detail/057.jsp

Joint Information Systems Committee (1999) *JISC Circular 5/99*, available at
www.jisc.ac.uk/pub99/dner_desc.html

Library of Congress (2001) *ZNG 'Z39.50 next generation'*, available at
www.loc.gov/z3950

Moen, W. (n.d.) *The ANSI/NISO Z39.50 Protocol: information retrieval in the information infrastructure*, available at
www.cni.org/pub/NISO/docs/Z39.50-brochure/50.brochure.toc.html

Open Archives Initiative (2001) *Open Archives Initiative (OAI) schema for MARC metadata format*, available at
www.openarchives.org/OAI/

Sun Microsystems Inc. (2001a) *The JavaBeans 1.01 specification developed by Sun defines a set of standard component software APIs for the Java platform as present in JDK 1.1*, available at
http://java.sun.com/products/javabeans/docs/spec.html

Sun Microsystems Inc. (2001b) *Java 2 SDK, Standard Edition, v 1.4.0 Beta (SDK)*, available at
http://java.sun.com/j2se/1.4/

Sun Microsystems Inc. (2001c) *Java foundation classes*, available at
http://java.sun.com/products/jfc/

World Wide Web Consortium (1998) *REC-DOM-Level-1-19981001, Document Object Model (DOM) Level 1 Specification*, Version 1.0, available at
www.w3.org/TR/REC-DOM-Level-1/

World Wide Web Consortium (2000) *Extensible Stylesheet Language (XSL) Version 1.0 W3C Candidate Recommendation 21 November 2000*, available at
www.w3.org/TR/2000/CR-xsl-20001121/xslspec.html

INDEX

Attracting, Educating and Serving Remote Users through the Web
A how-to-do-it manual for librarians

EDITED BY DONNELYN CURTIS; COMPANION WEBSITE FOR UK AND EUROPEAN USERS PREPARED BY IAN WINSHIP

In an increasingly internet-centred world, the expectations of library users are gradually changing beyond recognition. Today's information seekers expect their information quest to be easy and convenient, and preferably made accessible at home or at work. Developments in the technology of document delivery have led to a situation where remote users now make up an ever-increasing proportion of library customers.

However, it is not unusual for library professionals to feel frustrated in their efforts to provide a good information service to remote users. Although remote access services can be extremely effective, they are often underutilized and misunderstood.

In this timely handbook, ten accomplished professionals in the field provide step-by-step guidance through the development and management of innovative, effective and popular remote library services. Written in a practical, hands-on style and supported by a wealth of examples, the text outlines key methods of attracting and educating remote users, identifying and understanding their needs, and supporting and evaluating their use of remote resources. Chapters include:

- Reaching out: the library's new role
- Getting to know remote users
- Presenting the virtual library
- Providing electronic reference services
- Maximizing current awareness and document delivery services
- Providing library instruction for remote users
- Integrating library resources into online instruction
- Supporting the remote user of licensed resources
- Fundraising and public relations in the electronic environment.

A companion website for UK and European users has been prepared by Ian Winship, and will be continually available to purchasers of this title at **www.facetpublishing.co.uk/curtis**.

This book is a dynamic resource that will be invaluable for the information professional in any sector striving to better serve this fast growing segment of users, to create a co-ordinated suite of useful and user-friendly electronic resources, and to build financial and political support for a library of the future.

2002; 278pp; paperback; 1-85604-461-0; £34.95

Planning for Integrated Systems and Technologies

A how-to-do-it manual for librarians

Second edition

JOHN M. COHN, ANNE L. KELSEY AND KEITH MICHAEL FIELS; REVISED AND ADAPTED FOR THE UK AND EUROPE BY DAVID SALTER

The information professional is increasingly faced with large-scale and challenging projects for planning and integrating library systems and technologies. Today's integrated system must automate traditional library functions and also be capable of connecting with remote databases and the internet. Such projects can appear daunting, and expert advice is needed to demystify the complexities of the tasks involved.

This handbook is a basic, comprehensive guide for information services planning to introduce a new or replacement integrated system. Emphasis is placed throughout on the crucial contribution that careful and systematic strategic planning makes to successful systems implementation. This fully updated edition includes new chapters on developing a strategic approach to regularly assessing and evaluating your technology plan; accessing electronic resources, databases, and e-books using your system; and incorporating digitized collections into your website. Other topics covered include:

- developing a basic technology plan
- planning for system migrations
- assessing needs and setting priorities
- writing and updating your strategic technology plan
- a model two-day process for developing a basic strategic plan
- selecting and implementing integrated library systems
- planning in-house collection databases
- maintaining the bibliographic database
- applying MARC and other standards
- working with consultants.

Completely adapted for the non-US market by a UK library systems consultant, the text is fully supported throughout by sample forms and charts and by a full range of sources and readings.

This practical, hands-on manual is essential reading for all those responsible for planning and carrying out automated systems projects in smaller and medium-sized libraries and information services in any sector. It will also be of great value to students on library and information science courses

2002; 224pp; paperback; 1-85604-431-9; £27.50

Co-operation in Action

Collaborative initiatives in the world of information

STELLA PILLING AND STEPHANIE KENNA, EDITORS

There is a growing awareness within the library and information sector that organizations need to co-operate in order to make the most of their services and resources. Collaboration is becoming increasingly important in areas such as collection development, access, preservation and records management, and it has a crucial role to play in support of lifelong learning and in underpinning the move towards increased social inclusion and economic regeneration.

This collection, contributed by foremost professionals in the filed, examines the initiatives currently in place in the UK and worldwide and considers the significance that co-operative activity has for the future success of library and information services. Each contributor writes with a broad international approach and the issue of e-resources in the field of co-operation permeates each chapter. Contents include:

- the view from the British Library – the national library perspective
- mapping the British co-operative landscape
- the view from Resource
- the regional perspective
- co-operation in academia
- co-operation in preservation
- e-co-operation
- joined-up funding: promoting and facilitating collaborative work
- the international dimension.

The text is fully supported by a glossary and a list of further information accessible on the web.

Focused on the needs of information professionals and policy makers in libraries, museums and archives around the world, this is an essential guide to co-operation and partnership within and between these sectors.

Foreword by Tessa Blackstone, Minister of State for the Arts.

Contributors: Stuart Brewer; Julie Carpenter; Graham P. Cornish; Vivien Griffiths; Derek Law; Neville Mackay; Ronald Milne; Nick Moore; Bernard Naylor; Helen Shenton.

2002; 192pp; hardback; 1-85604-424-6; £39.95

Public Internet Access in Libraries and Information Services

PAUL STURGES

Public access to the internet is arguably the most important current development in library and information services. It presents a series of highly demanding issues for information professionals in all sectors. Public concerns about harmful internet content and inappropriate use, particularly by children, continue to be debated. All this is against a background of ongoing debate about how new technology affects legal and human rights areas such as copyright and other intellectual property;confidentiality, privacy, data protection and official secrecy; freedom of information; and harassment, obscenity and defamation.

This book is a much-needed guide for information professionals requiring a fuller understanding of these areas of law and ethics, and provides essential guidance on access policy and management. Whilst working on the basic principle that freedom of expression and freedom of access to information are simultaneously human rights and fundamentals of librarianship, it also takes into account the ethical and legal ambiguity of internet provision and uset. A step-by-step guide to developing an internet access policy is offered, including guidance on controversial aspects such as surveillance and monitoring of use, and software filtering and blocking. Helpful appendices provide access to a range of current codes of conduct, guidance documents, internal policy documents and public policy documents, together with Council of Europe Guidelines originally drafted by the author.

The major areas covered are:

- public access to information on the internet
- the internet problem
- the ethics of internet access management
- the law and the internet
- managing internet access
- making a policy for public internet access.

Illustrated with a broad range of international case studies and scenarios, this is an invaluable guide to internet access management for practising information professionals across all sectors. It will also be essential reading for students on library and information studies courses offering modules covering internet access and broader legal and ethical issues.

2002; 240pp; hardback; 1-85604-425-4; £34.95